Praise for DEAR SUGAR

"These pieces are nothing short of dynamite, the kind of remarkable, revelatory storytelling that makes young people want to become writers in the first place. Over here at the *Salon* offices, we're reading the columns with boxes of tissue and raised fists of solidarity, shaking our heads with awe and amusement." —Sarah Hepola, *Salon*

"Sugar doesn't coddle her readers—she believes them, and hears the stories inside the story they think they want to tell. She manages astonishing levels of empathy without dissolving into sentiment, and sees problems before the reader can. Sugar doesn't promise to make anyone feel good, only that she understands a question well enough to answer it." —Sasha Frere-Jones, *The New Yorker* critic

"Powerful and soulful, *Tiny Beautiful Things* is destined to become a classic of the form, the sort of book readers will carry around in purses and backpacks during difficult times as a token or talisman because of the radiant wisdom and depth within." —Aimee Bender, author of *The Particular Sadness of Lemon Cake*

"Sugar is turning the advice column on its head." —Jessica Francis Kane, author of *The Report*

"Sugar's columns are easily the most beautiful thing I've read all year. They should be taught in schools and put on little slips of paper and dropped from airplanes, for all to read." —Meakin Armstrong, *Guernica* editor

"Dear Sugar will save your soul. I belong to the Church of Sugar." —Samantha Dunn, author of *Failing Paris*

"Charming, idiosyncratic, luminous, profane. . . . [Sugar] is remaking a genre that has existed, in more or less the same form, since well before Nathanael West's *Miss Lonelyhearts* first put a face on the figure in 1933. . . . Her version of tough love ranges from hip-older-sister-loving to governess-stern. Sugar shines out amid the sea of fakeness." —Ruth Franklin, *The New Republic*

Cheryl Strayed

TINY BEAUTIFUL THINGS

Cheryl Strayed is the author of *Wild: From Lost to Found on the Pacific Crest Trail* and the novel *Torch*. Her stories and essays have been published in *The New York Times Magazine*, *The Washington Post Magazine*, *Vogue, Allure, The Rumpus, The Missouri Review, The Sun, The Best American Essays,* and elsewhere. She lives in Portland, Oregon.

Cheryl Strayed is available for select readings
and lectures. To inquire about a possible appearance,
please contact the Random House Speakers Bureau at
rhspeakers@randomhouse.com.

ALSO BY CHERYL STRAYED

Wild: From Lost to Found on the Pacific Crest Trail

Torch

TINY
BEAUTIFUL
THINGS

Advice on Love and Life from Dear Sugar

Cheryl Strayed

Vintage Books
A Division of Random House, Inc. · New York

A VINTAGE BOOKS ORIGINAL, JULY 2012

Much of the material in this work was originally published in the
Dear Sugar column on TheRumpus.net.

Library of Congress Cataloging-in-Publication Data
Strayed, Cheryl, 1968–
Tiny beautiful things : advice on love and life from Dear Sugar / Cheryl
Strayed.
p. cm. —(A Vintage Books original)
ISBN 978-0-307-94933-2 (pbk.)
1. Conduct of life—Miscellanea. I. Title.
BJ1589.S84 2012
070.4'44—dc23
2012007154

Book design by Claudia Martinez
Cover design by John Gall

www.vintagebooks.com

Printed in the United States of America
20   19   18   17   16

For Stephen Elliott and Isaac Fitzgerald

And for all the people who wrote to me

CONTENTS

Part III
CARRY THE WATER YOURSELF

Part IV
YOU DON'T HAVE TO BE BROKEN FOR ME

Part V
PUT IT IN A BOX AND WAIT

TINY BEAUTIFUL THINGS

I Was Sugar Once: Lessons in Radical Empathy

Long ago, before there was a Sugar, there was Stephen Elliott. He had this idea for a website, which sounds pretty awful, I admit, except that his idea was really to build an online community around literature, called *The Rumpus.* Being a writer himself, and therefore impoverished, Stephen prevailed upon his likewise impoverished writer friends to help.

And we, his friends, all said yes, because we love Stephen and because (if I may speak for the group) we were all desperate for a noble-seeming distraction. My contribution was an advice column, which I suggested we call Dear Sugar Butt, after the endearment Stephen and I had taken to using in our email correspondence. I will not belabor the goofy homoeroticism that would lead to such an endearment. It will be enough to note that Dear Sugar Butt was shortened, mercifully, to Dear Sugar.

Handing yourself a job as an advice columnist is a pretty arrogant thing to do, which is par for my particular course. But I justified it by supposing that I could create a different sort of advice column, both irreverent and brutally honest. The design flaw was that I conceived of Sugar as a persona, a woman with a troubled past and a slightly reckless tongue.

And while there were moments when she felt real to me, when I could feel myself locking into the pain of my correspondents, more often I faked it, making do with wit where my heart failed me. After a year of dashing off columns, I quit.

And that might have been the end of Sugar had I not, around this time, come across a nonfiction piece by Cheryl Strayed. I knew Cheryl as the author of a gorgeous and wrenching novel called *Torch*. But reading this essay, a searing recollection of infidelity and mourning, filled me with a tingling hunch. I wrote to ask if she wanted to take over as Sugar.

It was an insane request. Like me, Cheryl had two small kids at home, a mountain of debt, and no regular academic gig. The last thing she needed was an online advice column for which she would be paid nothing. Of course, I did have an ace in the hole: Cheryl had written the one and only fan letter I'd received as Sugar.

* * *

The column that launched Sugar as a phenomenon was written in response to what would have been, for anyone else, a throwaway letter. *Dear Sugar,* wrote a presumably young man. *WTF, WTF, WTF? I'm asking this question as it applies to everything every day.* Cheryl's reply began as follows:

Dear WTF,

My father's father made me jack him off when I was three and four and five. I wasn't any good at it. My hands were too small and I couldn't get the rhythm right and I didn't understand what I was doing. I only knew I didn't want to do it. Knew that it made me feel miserable and anxious in a way so sickeningly particular that I can feel that same particular sickness rising this very minute in my throat.

It was an absolutely unprecedented moment. Advice columnists, after all, adhere to an unspoken code: focus on the letter writer, dispense the necessary bromides, make it all seem bearable. Disclosing your own sexual assault is not part of the code.

But Cheryl wasn't just trying to shock some callow kid into greater compassion. She was announcing the nature of her mission as Sugar. Inexplicable sorrows await all of us. That was her essential point. Life isn't some narcissistic game you play online. It all matters—every sin, every regret, every affliction. As proof, she offered an account of her own struggle to reckon with a cruelty she'd absorbed before she was old enough even to understand it. *Ask better questions, sweet pea,* she concluded, with great gentleness. *The fuck is your life. Answer it.*

Like a lot of folks, I read the piece with tears in my eyes—which is how one reads Sugar. This wasn't some pro forma kibitzer, sifting through a stack of modern anxieties. She was a real human being laying herself bare, fearlessly, that we might come to understand the nature of our own predicaments.

* * *

I happen to believe that America is dying of loneliness, that we, as a people, have bought into the false dream of conve-

nience, and turned away from a deep engagement with our
internal lives—those fountains of inconvenient feeling—and
toward the frantic enticements of what our friends in the
Greed Business call the Free Market.

We're hurtling through time and space and information
faster and faster, seeking that network connection. But at
the same time we're falling away from our families and our
neighbors and ourselves. We ego-surf and update our status
and brush up on which celebrities are ruining themselves,
and how. But the cure won't stick.

And this, I think, is why Sugar has become so important
to so many people. Because she's offering something almost
unheard of in our culture: radical empathy. People come to
her in real pain and she ministers to them, by telling stories about her own life, the particular ways in which she's
felt thwarted and lost, and how she got found again. She is
able to transmute the raw material of the self-help aisle into
genuine literature.

I think here of the response she offered a man wrecked
by his son's death, who asked her how he might become
human again. "The strange and painful truth is that I'm a
better person because I lost my mom young," she wrote.
"When you say you experience my writing as sacred what
you are touching is the divine place within me that is
my mother. Sugar is the temple I built in my obliterated
place."

In this sense, *Tiny Beautiful Things* can be read as a kind
of ad hoc memoir. But it's a memoir with an agenda. With
great patience, and eloquence, she assures her readers that
within the chaos of our shame and disappointment and

rage there is meaning, and within that meaning is the possibility of rescue.

* * *

It is striking that Sugar was born on the Internet, that shadow world to which people apply with a need to escape from their true selves, to remake their identities on the cheap, to shine their buttons in public. The Internet can be many things, of course. Too often it's a cesspool of distraction, a place where we indulge in the modern sport of snark and schadenfreude, building the case for our own bigotries, where we mock and thereby dismiss the suffering of others.

But the lurking dream of all us online lurkers is that we might someday confess to our own suffering, that we might find someone who will *listen* to us, who will not turn away in the face of our ugliest revelations. That someone is Sugar.

There's nothing you can tell Sugar that doesn't strike her as beautiful and human. Which is why men and women write to her about intimacies they can't share with anyone else, unspeakable urges, insoluble grief. She understands that attention is the first and final act of love, and that the ultimate dwindling resource in the human arrangement isn't cheap oil or potable water or even common sense, but mercy.

With each of her pieces—I hesitate to use the word "columns," which seems to cheapen what she does—she performs the same miraculous act: she absorbs our stories. She lets them inhabit her, and thinks about the stories they evoke from her own life. She also recognizes that there's another, truer story beneath the one we generally offer the world, the stuff we can't or won't see, the evasions and delusions, the places where we're simply stuck. Sugar may be tender, but she doesn't sugarcoat. In this sense, she offers what we wish every mother would: enough compassion to make us feel safe within our broken need, and enough wisdom to hold on to hope.

I ask you, brave people: who else is doing this work today? Not the fame merchants of Hollywood, with their explosions and shiny tits, not the for-profit demagogues of the Fourth Estate, and not the politicians who murder morals on behalf of the corporate sponsors and call it policy.

Sugar does this work. It's what makes her an artist.

* * *

Cheryl Strayed was an artist long before she became Sugar. Those of you fortunate enough to have read Cheryl's novel, *Torch*, or her memoir, *Wild*, already know this.

It's been tricky for Cheryl to negotiate the business of leading two lives: one as an anonymous columnist with a huge cult following, and the other as writer and mother and wife trying to make ends meet. Critics and Internet snipes will have a good time fulminating on this Cheryl/Sugar dichotomy. But the name on the byline is never what matters to readers. What matters to them are the words on the page.

Tiny Beautiful Things will endure as a piece of literary art, as will Cheryl's other books, because they do the essential work of literary art: they make us more human than we were before. We need books, and Cheryl's books in particular, because we are all, in the private kingdom of our hearts, desperate for the company of a wise, true friend. Someone who isn't embarrassed by our emotions, or her own, who recognizes that life is short and that all we have to offer, in the end, is love.

Radical empathy isn't the fashion of the day. Late-model capitalism works overtime to keep us focused on the product, not the people. That's why we need Sugar so badly right now. You'll see what I mean when you turn the page.

Run toward the darkness, sweet peas, and shine.

—*Steve Almond*

PART ONE

IT WAS ALWAYS ONLY US

What is this book?

It's a selection of Dear Sugar columns. Many were originally published on TheRumpus.net. Others appear here for the first time. The letters in this book were emailed to Sugar via an anonymous form on *The Rumpus* or mailed directly to Sugar's email address. Most people who sent me letters didn't know I was Cheryl Strayed and likewise most of the letter writers were entirely anonymous to me. This book is a collection of intimate exchanges between strangers.

Did you change the letters before publishing them?

In some cases I lightly edited the letters for length and/or clarity, but most appear exactly as they were written by people who felt moved to write to me.

What sorts of letters do you answer?

All sorts. Some are about romance and love, others are about grief and loss, and others still about money or family troubles. My criteria for selecting letters to answer in the Dear Sugar column are highly subjective: I'll answer anything, so long as it interests or challenges or touches me.

What sort of advice do you give?

The best I can think of.

LIKE AN IRON BELL

Dear Sugar,

My twenty-year marriage fell apart. Whose fault? Mine? My wife's? Society's? I don't know. We were too immature to get married back in the eighties, and we both worked hard to avoid dealing with the unhappiness that was hanging over us.

But that's in the past. I've had a few relationships in the three years since the split. One casual, one serious, and one current. There was no issue with the casual one: I was up-front about not wanting to settle down so soon. The second one started out casual, and I actually broke it off when she got serious, but I couldn't stay away and promised to consider long-term plans with her. I also told her I loved her after a year of avoiding that word, the definition of which I don't really understand. I balked when it came time to piss or get off the pot and I lost both a lover and a friend in her.

Now I've again met a woman with whom I click very nicely. We have been dating and being intimate for about four months. She's going through a bitter divorce and wasn't looking for a commitment. That sounded perfect, but in reality neither of us was interested in dating more than one person, so here we are in an exclusive relationship.

She sounds like she's falling in love with me, though she won't say the word. I am avoiding that word as well, but clearly we're both thinking it. I'm afraid of saying it out loud, as my experience shows that word "love" comes loaded with promises and commitments that are highly fragile and easily broken.

My question to you is, when is it right to take that big step and say I love you? And what is this "love" thing all about?

Best,
Johnny

Dear Johnny,

The last word my mother ever said to me was "love." She was so sick and weak and out of her head she couldn't muster the "I" or the "you," but it didn't matter. That puny word has the power to stand on its own.

I wasn't with my mom when she died. No one was. She died alone in a hospital room, and for so many years it felt like three-quarters of my insides were frozen solid because of that. I ran it over and over in my mind, the series of events and choices that kept me from being beside my mom in her last hours, but thinking about it didn't do a thing. Thinking about it was a long dive into a bucket of shit that didn't have a bottom.

I would never be with my mother when she died. She would never be alive again. The last thing that happened between us would always be the last thing. There would be the way I bent to kiss her and the way she said, "Please, no," when I got close because she couldn't any longer bear the physical pain of people touching her. There would be the way that I explained I'd return in the morning and the way she just barely nodded in response. There would be the way I got my coat and said, "I love you," and the way she was silent until I was almost out the door and she called, "*love*." And there would be the way that she was still lying in that bed when I returned the next morning, but dead.

My mother's last word to me clanks inside me like an iron bell that someone beats at dinnertime: *love, love, love, love, love*.

I suppose you think this has nothing to do with your question, Johnny, but it has everything to do with my answer. It has everything to do with *every* answer I have ever given to anyone. It's Sugar's genesis story. And it's the thing my mind kept swirling back to over these five weeks since you wrote to me and said you didn't know the definition of "love."

It is not so incomprehensible as you pretend, sweet pea. Love is the feeling we have for those we care deeply about and hold in high regard. It can be light as the hug we give a friend or heavy as the sacrifices we make for our children. It can be romantic, platonic, familial, fleeting, everlasting, conditional, unconditional, imbued with sorrow, stoked by sex, sullied by abuse, amplified by kindness, twisted by betrayal, deepened by time, darkened by difficulty, leavened by generosity, nourished by humor, and "loaded with promises and commitments" that we may or may not want or keep. The best thing you can possibly do with your life is to tackle the motherfucking shit out of love. And, Johnny, on this front, I think you have some work to do.

But before we get to that, I want to say this, darling: *I sort of love you.*

I love the way you wrote to me with your searching, scared, knuckleheaded, nonchalant, withholding dudelio heart on full display. I love that you compelled me to write "dudelio," even though—on top of the fact that "dudelio" isn't a word—I am morally opposed to the entire dude and dude-related lexicon. I love how for five long weeks hardly a day has passed that I haven't thought: *But what about Johnny? What will I tell Johnny?* I love that one recent evening when I was lying in bed with Mr. Sugar and he was reading *The New Yorker* and I was reading *Brain, Child,* I had to stop and put my magazine on my chest because I was thinking about you and what you asked me and so then Mr. Sugar put his magazine on his chest and asked what I was thinking about and I told him and we had a conversation about your troubles and then we turned off the lights and he fell asleep and I lay there wide awake with my eyes closed writing my answer to you in my head for so long that I realized I wasn't going to fall asleep, so I got up and walked through the house and got a glass of water and sat at the kitchen table in the dark and looked out the window at the wet street and my cat came and jumped up on the table and sat there beside me and after a while I turned to her and said, "What will I tell Johnny?" and she purred.

I always knew what I would tell you. Not knowing wasn't exactly the problem. What I was mulling over is how I'd get at the layers of things your letter implies to me: the questions you didn't ask that stand so brightly behind the questions you did.

You aren't afraid of love. You're afraid of all the junk you've yoked to love. And you've convinced yourself that withholding one tiny word from the woman you think you love will shield you from that junk. But it won't. We are obligated to the people we care about and who we allow to care about us, whether we say we love them or not. Our main obligation is to be forthright—to elucidate the nature of our affection when such elucidation would be meaningful or clarifying.

And in your case, it will be. You asked me when is the right time to tell your lover that you love her and the answer is when you think you love her. That's also the right time to tell her what your love for her means to you. If you continue using avoidance as the main tactic in your romantic relationships with women, you're going to stunt not only your happiness, but your life.

I encourage you to do more than throw up your hands in your examination of "whose fault" it was that your twenty-year marriage fell apart. It was no one's fault, darling, but it's still all on you. It would behoove you to reflect upon what went right in that relationship and what went wrong; to contemplate how you might carry forth the former in your current and/or future relationships and quash the latter.

There's a saying about drug addicts that they stop maturing emotionally at the age they started using, and I've known enough addicts to believe this to be true enough. I think the same thing can happen in longtime monogamy. Perhaps some of your limited interpretations about what it means to say the word "love" are left over from what you thought it meant all those years ago, when you first committed yourself to your ex-wife. That was the past, as you say, but I suspect that a piece of yourself is still frozen there.

A proclamation of love is not inherently "loaded with promises and commitments that are highly fragile and easily broken." The terms you agree to in any given relationship are connected to, but not defined by, whether you've said "I love you" or not. "I love you" can mean *I think you're groovy and beautiful and I'm going to do everything in my power to be your partner for the rest of my life.* It can mean *I think you're groovy and beautiful but I'm in transition right now, so let's go easy on the promises and take it as it comes.* It can mean *I think you're groovy and beautiful but I'm not interested in a commitment with you, now or probably ever, no matter how groovy or beautiful you continue to be.*

The point is, Johnny, *you get to say.* You get to define the terms of your life. You get to negotiate and articulate the complexities and contradictions of your feelings for this woman. You get to describe the particular kind of oh-shit-I-didn't-mean-to-fall-in-love-but-I-sorta-did love you appear to have for her. Together, the two of you get to come to grips with what it means to have an exclusive, nicely clicking, noncommitted commitment in the midst of her bitter divorce and in the not-too-distant wake of your decades-long marriage.

Do it. Doing so will free your relationship from the tense tangle that withholding weaves. Do you realize that your refusal to utter the word "love" to your lover has created a force field all its own? Withholding distorts reality. It makes the people who do the withholding ugly and small-hearted. It makes the people from whom things are withheld crazy and desperate and incapable of knowing what they actually feel.

So release yourself from that. Don't be strategic or coy. Strategic and coy are for jackasses. Be brave. Be authentic. Practice saying the word "love" to the people you love so when it matters the most to say it, you will.

We're all going to die, Johnny. Hit the iron bell like it's dinnertime.

Yours,
Sugar

HOW YOU GET UNSTUCK

Dear Sugar,

About eighteen months ago, I got pregnant. In a move that surprised both my boyfriend and me, we decided we wanted to keep the baby. Though the pregnancy was unplanned, we were excited to become parents. The child was very much loved and wanted. When I was six and a half months pregnant, I miscarried. Since then, I've struggled to get out of bed.

Not a day has gone by when I haven't thought about who that child would have been. It was a girl. She had a name. Every day I wake up and think, "My daughter would be six months old," or "My daughter would maybe have started crawling today." Sometimes, all I can think is the word "daughter" over and over and over.

Of course, it seems that everyone around me is having a baby and everywhere I go all I see are babies, so I have to force myself to be happy for them and swallow how empty I feel. The truth is, I don't feel much of anything anymore and yet everything hurts. Most of the people in my life expect me to be over my sorrow by now. As one person pointed out, "It was only a miscarriage." So I also feel guilty about being so stuck, grieving for a child that never was when I should just walk it off or something.

I don't talk very much about it. I pretend it never happened. I go to work and hang out and smile and act like everything is fine. My boyfriend has been fantastic and supportive, though I don't think he understands how badly I'm doing. He wants us to get married and try for another child. He thinks this should cheer me up. It doesn't. It makes me want to punch him in the head for not feeling the way I do.

Then there is the reason I lost the baby. In the hospital, my doctor said he wasn't surprised I lost the baby because my pregnancy was high risk because I was overweight. It was not an easy thing to hear that the miscarriage was my fault. Part of me thinks the doctor was a real asshole, but another part of me thinks, "Maybe he was right." It kills me to think that this was my fault, that I brought the miscarriage on myself. I can't even breathe sometimes, I feel so guilty. When I got out of the hospital, I got a personal trainer and went on a diet and started losing weight but I'm totally out of control now. Sometimes, I don't eat for days, and then sometimes I eat everything in sight and throw it all up. I spend hours at the gym, walking on the treadmill until I can't lift my legs.

My friends and family think I'm doing just fine, Sugar, but nothing could be further from the truth. All I can think about is how I fucked up. Everything feels like it is more than I can handle. The rational part of me understands that if I don't pull myself out of this, I'll do serious damage to myself. I know this, and yet I just don't care.

I want to know how to care again. I want to know how to not feel so guilty, how to not feel like I killed my baby.

My daughter, she had a name. She was loved. I feel like the only one who cares. Then I feel like shit for mourning "just a miscarriage" after nearly a year. I'm stuck.

Best,
Stuck

Dear Stuck,

I'm so sorry that your baby girl died. So terribly sorry. I can feel your suffering vibrating right through my computer screen. This is to be expected. It is as it should be. Though we live in a time and place and culture that tries to tell us otherwise, suffering is what happens when truly horrible things happen to us.

Don't listen to those people who suggest you should be "over" your daughter's death by now. The people who squawk the loudest about such things have almost never had to get over anything. Or at least not anything that was genuinely, mind-fuckingly, soul-crushingly life altering. Some of those people believe they're being helpful by minimizing your pain. Others are scared of the intensity of your loss and so they use their words to push your grief away. Many of those people love you and are worthy of your love, but they are not the people who will be helpful to you when it comes to healing the pain of your daughter's death.

They live on Planet Earth. You live on Planet My Baby Died.

It seems to me that you feel like you're all alone there. You aren't. There are women reading this right now who have tears in their eyes. There are women who have spent their days chanting *daughter, daughter* or *son, son* silently to themselves. Women who have been privately tormented about the things they did or didn't do that they fear caused the deaths of their babies. You need to find those women. They're your tribe.

I know because I've lived on a few planets that aren't Planet Earth myself.

The healing power of even the most microscopic exchange with someone who knows in a flash precisely what you're talking about because she experienced that thing too cannot be overestimated. Call your local hospitals and birth centers and inquire about support groups for people who've lost babies at or before or shortly after birth. Read Elizabeth McCracken's memoir *An Exact Replica of a Figment of My Imagination.* Find online communities where you can have conversations with people during which you don't have to pretend a thing.

And stop pretending with your sweet boyfriend too. Tell him you'd like to punch him in the head and explain to him precisely why. Ask him what he has to say about the death of your daughter and do your very best to listen to his experience without comparing it to your own. I think you should see a therapist—both alone and with your boyfriend—and I strongly encourage you to call and make an appointment today. A therapist will help you air and examine the complex grief you're holding so tightly inside of you, and he or she will also help you manage your (probably situational) depression.

This is how you get unstuck, Stuck. You reach. Not so you can walk away from the daughter you loved, but so you can live the life that is yours—the one that includes the sad loss of your daughter, but is not arrested by it. The one that eventually leads you to a place in which you not only grieve her, but also feel lucky to have had the privilege of loving her. That place of true healing is a fierce place. It's a giant place. It's a place of monstrous beauty and endless dark and glimmering light. And you have to work really, really, really hard to get there, but you can do it. You're a woman who can travel that far. I know it. Your ability to get there is evident to me in every word of your bright shining grief star of a letter.

To be Sugar is at times a haunting thing. It's fun and it's funny; it's intriguing and interesting, but every now and then one of the questions I get seeps its way into my mind in the same way characters or scenes or situations in the other sorts of writing I do seep into my mind and I am haunted by it. I can't let it go. I answer the question, but there is something else and I know it and I can't finish my reply until I figure out what it is. I can feel it there the way the princess can feel the pea under her twenty mattresses and twenty featherbeds. Until it's removed, I simply cannot rest. This is the case when it comes to your question, my dear. And so while it's true that you should find your tribe and talk to your boyfriend and make an appointment with a therapist, there is something truer that I have to tell you and it is this.

Several years ago I worked with barely teenage girls in a middle school. Most of them were poor white kids in seventh and eighth grade. Not one of them had a decent father. Their dads were in prison or unknown to them or roving the streets of our city strung out on drugs or fucking them. Their moms were young used and abused drug-and-alcohol addled women who were often abusive themselves. The twenty-some girls who were assigned to meet with me as a group and also individually were deemed "at highest risk" by the faculty at the school.

My job title was *youth advocate*. My approach was unconditional positive regard. My mission was to help the girl youth succeed in spite of the unspeakably harrowing crap stew they'd been simmering in all of their lives. Succeeding in this context meant getting neither pregnant nor locked up before graduating high school. It meant eventually holding down a job at Taco Bell or Walmart. It was only that! It was such a small thing and yet it was enormous. It was like trying to push an eighteen-wheeler with your pinkie finger.

I was not technically qualified to be a youth advocate. I'd never worked with youth or counseled anyone. I had degrees in neither education nor psychology. I'd been a waitress who wrote stories every chance I got for most of the preceding years. But for some reason, I wanted this job and so I talked my way into it.

I wasn't meant to let the girls know I was trying to help them succeed. I was meant to silently, secretly, covertly empower them by taking them to do things they'd never done at places they'd never been. I took them to a rock-climbing gym and to the ballet and to a poetry reading at an independent bookstore. The theory was that if they liked to pull the weight of their blossoming girl bodies up a faux boulder with little pebble-esque plastic hand- and footholds then perhaps they would not get knocked up. If they glommed on to the beauty of art witnessed live—made before their very eyes—they would not become meth addicts and steal someone's wallet and go to jail at the age of fifteen.

Instead, they'd grow up and get a job at Walmart. That was the hope, the goal, the reason I was being paid a salary. And while we did those empowering things, I was meant to talk to them about sex and drugs and boys and mothers and relationships and healthy homework habits and the importance of self-esteem and answer every question they had with honesty and affirm every story they told with unconditional positive regard.

I was scared of them at first. Intimidated. They were thirteen and I was twenty-eight. Almost all of them had one of three names: Crystal, Brittany, or Desiré. They were distant and scoffing, self-conscious and surly. They were varnished in layers upon layers of girl lotions and potions and hair products that all smelled faintly like strawberry gum. They hated everything and everything was boring and stupid and either totally cool or totally gay, and I had to forbid them to use the word "gay" in that context and explain to them why they shouldn't say the word "gay" to mean stupid, and they thought I was a total fag for thinking that by "gay" they actually meant *gay* and then I had to tell them not to say "fag" and we laughed and after a while I passed around journals I'd purchased for them.

"Do we get to keep these? Do we get to keep these?" they clamored in a great, desperate joyous girl chorus.

"Yes," I said. "Open them."

I asked them each to write down three true things about themselves and one lie, and then we read them out loud, going around in the circle, guessing which one was the lie, and by the time we were about halfway around the room they all loved me intensely.

Not me. But who I was. Not who I was, but how I held them: with unconditional positive regard.

I had never been the recipient of so much desire. If I had a flower clip in my hair, they wanted to remove the flower clip and put it in their own hair. If I had a pen, they asked if I would give it to them. If I had a sandwich, they wondered if they could have a bite. If I had a purse, they wanted to see what was inside. And most of all they wanted to tell me everything. Everything. Every last thing about their lives. And they did.

Ghastly, horrible, shocking, sad, merciless things. Things that would compel me to squint my eyes as I listened, as if by squinting I could protect myself by hearing it less distinctly. Things that would make me close the door of my office after they left and cry my heart out. Endless stories of abuse and betrayal and absence and devastation and the sort of sorrow that spirals so tightly into an impossible clusterfuck of eternal despair that it doesn't even look like a spiral anymore.

One of the girls was truly beautiful. She resembled a young Elizabeth Taylor without the curvy hips. Flawlessly luminescent skin. Water-blue eyes. Long shimmering black hair. A D-cup rack and the rest of her model-thin. She'd just turned thirteen when I met her. She'd already fucked five guys and blown ten. She'd lost her virginity at eleven to her mother's ex-boyfriend, who was now in jail for stealing a TV. Her current lover was thirty-two. He picked her up most days on the edge of the school parking lot. I convinced her to let me take her to Planned Parenthood so she could get a Depo-Provera shot, but when we got there, she did not get the shot. She refused to let the female doctor give her a pelvic exam and the doctor would not give her the shot without one. She cried and cried and cried. She cried with such sharp fear and pain that it was like someone had walked into the room and pressed a hot iron against her gorgeous ass. I said a million consoling, inspiring, empowering things. The female doctor spoke in comforting yet commanding tones. But that girl who had fucked five guys and blown ten by the time she turned thirteen would not recline for three minutes on the examining table in a well-lit room in the company of two women with good intentions.

One girl wore an enormous hooded sweatshirt that went down to her knees with the hood pulled up over her head no matter the temperature. Across her face hung a dense curtain of punk-rock-colored hair. It looked like she had two backs of her head and no face. To get around, she tilted her head discreetly in various ways and peeked out the bottom of her hair curtain. She refused to speak for weeks. She was the last person who asked if she could have my pen. Getting to know her was like trying to ingratiate oneself with a feral cat. Nearly impossible. One step forward and a thousand steps back. But when I did—when I tamed her, when she parted her hair and I saw her pale and fragile and acne-covered face—she told me that she slept most nights in a falling-down wooden shed near the alley behind the apartment building where she lived with her mom. She did this because she couldn't take staying inside, where her mother ranted and raved, alcoholic and mentally ill and off her meds and occasionally physically violent. She pulled the sleeves of her hoodie up and showed me the slashes on her arms where she'd repeatedly cut herself with a razor blade because it felt so good.

One girl told me that when her mom's boyfriend got mad he dragged her into the backyard and turned on the hose and held her face up to the ice-cold running water until she almost drowned and then he locked her outside for two hours. It was November. Forty-some degrees. It wasn't the first time he'd done this. Or the last.

I told the girls that these sorts of things were not okay. That they were unacceptable. Illegal. That I would call someone and that someone would intervene and this would stop. I called the police. I called the state's child protection services. I called them every day and no one did one thing. Not one person. Not one thing. Ever. No matter how many times that man almost drowned that little girl with a garden hose in the back-yard or how many times the thirty-two-year-old picked up the thirteen-year-old with the great rack in the school parking lot or how many times the hooded girl with no face slept in the falling-down woodshed in the alley while her mother raged.

I had not lived a sheltered life. I'd had my share of hardships and sorrows. I thought I knew how the world worked, but this I could not believe. I thought that if it was known that bad things were happening to children, those bad things would be stopped. But that is not the sort of society we live in, I realized. There is no such society.

One day when I called child protective services I asked the woman who answered the phone to explain to me exactly why no one was protecting the children and she told me that there was no funding for teenagers who were not in imminent danger because the state was broke and so the thing the child protective services did was make priorities. They intervened quickly with kids under the age of twelve, but for those over twelve they wrote reports when people called and put the reports in a file and put the child's name on a long list of children who someone would someday perhaps check up on when there was time and money, if there ever was time and money. The good thing about teens, she told me confidentially, was that if it got bad enough at home they usually ran away and there was more funding for runaways.

I hung up the phone feeling like my sternum had cracked open. Before I could even take a breath, in walked the girl whose mother's boyfriend repeatedly almost drowned her with the garden hose in the backyard. She sat down in the chair near my desk where all the girls sat narrating their horrible stories and she told me another horrible story and I told her something different this time.

I told her it was not okay, that it was unacceptable, that it was illegal and that I would call and report this latest horrible thing. But I did not tell her it would stop. I did not promise that anyone would intervene. I told her it would likely go on and she'd have to survive it. That she'd have to find a way within herself to not only escape the shit, but to transcend it, and if she wasn't able to do that, then her whole life would be shit, forever and ever and ever. I told her that escaping the shit would be hard, but that if she wanted to not make her mother's life her destiny, she had to be the one to make it happen. She had to do more than hold on. She had to *reach*. She had to want it more than she'd ever wanted anything. She had to grab like a drowning girl for every good thing that came her way and she had to swim like fuck away from every bad thing. She had to count the years and let them roll by, to grow up and then run as far as she could in the direction of her best and happiest dreams across the bridge that was built by her own desire to heal.

She seemed to listen, in that desultory and dismissive way that teens do. I said it to every girl who came into my office and sat in the horrible-story chair. It became my gospel. It became the thing I said most because it was the thing that was most true.

It is also the most true for you, Stuck, and for anyone who has ever had anything truly horrible happen to them.

You will never stop loving your daughter. You will never forget her. You will always know her name. But she will always be dead. Nobody can intervene and make that right and nobody will. Nobody can take it back with silence or push it away with words. Nobody will protect you from your suffering. You can't cry it away or eat it away or starve it away or walk it away or punch it away or even therapy it away. It's just there, and you have to survive it. You have to endure it. You have to live through it and love it and move on and be better for it and run as far as you can in the direction of your best and happiest dreams across the bridge that was built by your own desire to heal. Therapists and friends and other people who live on Planet My Baby Died can help you along the way, but the healing—the genuine healing, the actual real deal down-on-your-knees-in-the-mud change—is entirely and absolutely up to you.

That job at the middle school was the best job I ever had, but I only stayed for a year. It was a heavy gig and I was a writer and so I left it for less emotionally taxing forms of employment so I could write. One day six years after I quit, I ate lunch at a Taco Bell not far from the school where I'd worked with the girls. Just as I was gathering my things to leave, a woman in a Taco Bell uniform approached and said my name. It was the faceless girl who'd lived in the falling-down shed. Her hair was pulled back into a ponytail now. She was grown up. She was twenty and I was thirty-five.

"Is that you?" I exclaimed and we embraced.

We talked about how she was soon to be promoted to assistant manager at the Taco Bell, about which of the girls from our group she was still in touch with and what they were doing, about how I'd taken her rock climbing and to the ballet and to a poetry reading at an independent bookstore and how she hadn't done any of those things again.

"I never forgot you, even after all these years," she told me.

"I'm so proud of you," I said, squeezing her shoulder.

"I made it," she said. "Didn't I?"

"You did," I said. "You absolutely did."

I never forgot her either. Her name was Desiré.

Yours,
Sugar

THAT ECSTATIC PARADE

Dear Sugar,

I'm a twenty-one-year-old guy. I'm in college right now. Though I work full-time to pay for some of my bills, I'm still dependent on my parents for room and board. I also use their car. I have no problem with living with my parents—at least I wouldn't if I wasn't gay. My parents are fundamentalist Christians. They believe that being a homosexual is a "sin" that someone struggles with similar to alcoholism or drug addiction and that gays should repent and see Jesus.

My parents know I'm gay but they don't acknowledge it. They believe I've repented and found Jesus. When I was seventeen, my mom threatened to kick me out of the house because she didn't want "my diseased behavior under her roof." In order for me to stay at my parents' house I had to go to Christian counseling to undo my gay-ness. I went, but it did absolutely nothing for me. It only confused me more. I don't hate my parents, but I strongly dislike them for their treatment of me. They think I'm straight, but they don't trust me. My mom constantly checks on me, often barging into my room seemingly in hopes of catching me doing something. If I go out, I have to tell my parents exactly who I'm with or I won't be able to use their car. They refuse to leave the Internet connected if I'm at home alone, and they hide the modem when they go to bed because they are afraid that I'll look at "sinful" material that will pull me back into the "gay lifestyle."

Though I act straight around my parents and sister, I am out to friends and co-workers and also to my brother (who accepts me unconditionally). It's a huge strain to live a double life. I've had two gay relationships. My parents know my current boy-friend is gay and they treat him like he's going to reinfect me with his gay-ness.

I would move out, but I can't find any available rooms within my budget. One option that has arisen recently is that a good friend asked if I wanted to move to the Pacific Northwest with her—I live on the East Coast—and I'm seriously considering it. The thing is, I don't want to run away from my problems and I really like the guy I'm in a relationship with, but right now I feel like I'm stuck in a situation that is hopeless. I feel suffocated by the expectations of those on both sides of my double life. One side would damn me to hell if they found out I was gay. The other side wants me to cut myself off from my family.

Is there any advice you could offer that could help?

Suffocated

Dear Suffocated,

Yes. There is something I can offer that will help. I can tell you to get yourself out of that house. You mustn't live with people who wish to annihilate you. Even if you love them. Even if they are your mom and dad. You're an adult now. Figure out how to pay the rent. Your psychological well-being is more important than free access to a car.

It's miserable that your parents are ill-informed bigots. I'm sorry they've made you suffer so, sweet pea. There is nothing correct about their ideas regarding homosexuality (or alcoholism or drug addiction, for that matter). We are all entitled to our opinions and religious beliefs, but we are not entitled to make shit up and then use the shit we made up to oppress other people. This is what your parents are doing to you. And by choosing to pretend you're straight in order to placate them, you're also doing it to yourself.

You must stop. Stopping is not running away from your problems. It's solving them. In your question you write that you feel "suffocated by the expectations of those on both sides," but there are not two sides. There is only one and you're it. The real you. The authentic you. The gay you.

Be him.

Even if you aren't ready to come out to your parents yet, I implore you to remove yourself from their company. Pack up your things and go. To the Pacific Northwest, across town, to your wacky cousin's basement in Tuscaloosa, it doesn't matter. Just stop living with the people who sent you to reeducation camp because they equate your (normal, healthy) sexuality with a disease.

This doesn't mean you have to break all ties with them. There is a middle path, but it goes in only one direction: toward the light. Your light. The one that goes *blink, blink, blink* inside your chest when you know what you're doing is right. Listen to it. Trust it. Let it make you stronger than you are.

Your lunatic parents are going to figure out you're gay whether you tell them or not. In fact, they know already. They aren't banishing you from the Internet so you won't watch Scooby Doo, doll. I encourage you to leave your parents' home not so you can make some giant *I'm gay!* pronouncement to them, but so you can live your life with dignity among people who accept you while you sort out your relationship with them from an emotionally safe distance. Sooner or later—whether they learn it from you or discern it on their own—your folks are going to have to grapple with the reality that you are a homo beyond (their) God's reach. It seems that the best-case scenario when this happens is that you will lose their approval. The worst-case scenario is that they will disown you. Perhaps permanently. Which would mean that their love for you hinges entirely on:

> Nothing. Because you are their beloved son   √ **NO**
> and their primary obligation to you as your
> parents is to nurture you and foster your
> growth, even if you turn out to be someone
> they didn't precisely imagine.

> Your agreement to refrain from touching   √ **YES**
> other men's man parts.

Wow. *Really?* Isn't that so sad and crazy? I know I'm being a bit glib about it, but only because if I look at it stone cold serious it smashes my heart into smithereens. More importantly, I'm trying to make a point: love based on conditions such as those set forth by your parents is ugly, skimpy, diseased love. Yes, diseased. And it's a kind of love that will kill you if you let it.

So don't. There is a world of people out here who will love you for who you are. A whole, vibrant, fucked-up, happy, conflicted, joyous, and depressed mass of people who will say, *You're gay? So the fuck what?* We want you to be among us.

That's the message of the It Gets Better Project. Hold on, it says, and stick it out, because guess what? *It gets better.*

And true as that is and moved as I've been by many of the videos made by gay, lesbian, bi, and trans people telling their stories, I think there's an important piece missing in that message. All those people in the wonderful videos? It didn't just get better for them. They *made* it better. Each and every one of those people rose at a moment in their lives—one that is very much like this moment in your life, Suffocated—and at that moment they chose to tell the truth about themselves instead of staying "safe" inside the lie. They realized that, in fact, the lie wasn't safe. That it threatened their existence more profoundly than the truth did.

That's when it started to get better for those folks. When they had the courage to say, *This is who I am even if you'll crucify me for it.*

Some of those people lost jobs because they said that. Some lost family and friends. Some even lost their lives. But in saying that, they gained themselves. It's a sentence that lives in each one of us, I believe—the one in which we assert that we will be who it is we are, regardless—but sadly it has to live especially strong in you, Suffocated. I hope you'll find it within you. Not just the sentence, but also all the beauty and nerve that has gotten you this far, so that when you say it, you'll say it loud and true.

Have you ever been to a LGBT Pride parade? Every year I take the baby Sugars to the one in our city and every year I cry while watching it. There are the drag queens riding in Corvettes. There are the queer cops and firefighters all spiffed out in their uniforms. There are the lesbians on bicycles pulling their kids on tag-alongs and trailers. There are the gay samba dancers in thongs and feathers. There are the drummers and politicians and the odd people who are really into retro automobiles. There are choirs and brass bands and battalions of people riding horses. There are real estate agents and clowns, schoolteachers and Republicans. And they all go marching by us while my kids laugh and I weep.

My kids never understand why I'm crying. The parade seems like a party to them, and when I try to explain that the party is an explosion of love that has its roots in hate, I only confuse them more, so together we just stand on the sidelines, laughing and crying, watching that ecstatic parade.

I think I cry because it always strikes me as sacred, all those people going by. People who decided simply to live their truth, even when doing so wasn't simple. Each and every one of them had the courage to say, *This is who I am even if you'll crucify me for it.*

Just like Jesus did.

Yours,
Sugar

A MOTORCYCLE WITH NO ONE ON IT

Dear Sugar,

I'm crushing in middle age. That's pretty much it. I'm middle-aged, married, and crushing on a friend. And it's full-blown, just like in high school, sweaty palms, distracted, giddy, the whole shebang. So far it has gone no further than flirting and I really, really know better. My question isn't what should I do (I'm pretty clear I should behave), but what should I do with all this delightful but distressing energy?

Crushed

Dear Crushed,

Steer clear of the object of your crush and use that "delightful but distressing energy" to reinvest in what matters most to you—your marriage, it seems. Do something extra sweet for your spouse this week. Have sex tonight and make it hella hot and good. Go for a long walk or a lingering dinner together and lovingly discuss how you're going to keep your love as well as your romance strong. You're clear you don't want to act on your crush, so trust that clarity and be grateful that you have it. My inbox is jammed with emails from people who are not so clear. They're tortured by indecision and guilt and lust.

They love X but want to fuck Z. It is the plight of almost every
monogamous person at one time or another. We all love X but
want to fuck Z.

Z is so gleaming, so crystalline, so unlikely to bitch at you
for neglecting to take out the recycling. Nobody has to haggle
with Z. Z doesn't wear a watch. Z is like a motorcycle with no
one on it. Beautiful. Going nowhere.

Yours,
Sugar

THE RECKONING

Dear Sugar,

I am the lucky mama of one darling baby and oh, how I treasure every moment! Unfortunately—or fortunately, depending on how you look at it—the baby's daddy does not follow suit on treasuring every moment.

Baby's daddy lives in another state. He left while I was still pregnant and did not attend our child's birth. Though he proclaims via emails every six or so weeks to care for his child, he does not pay child support, nor has he seen his baby since mere weeks after birth (our baby is now over one). He has never even called to find out how his child is doing.

My question is this: Am I obligated to send pictures and keep him updated about his child since he sends somewhat pitiful emails every couple of months about himself? I am heavily leaning toward no updates, but I would gladly take into consideration the opinion of a lovely sweet pea, such as yourself, Sugar.

I want to do what is best for my little bundle, even if what I want to do is kick the baby's daddy in the groin with steel-toed boots, screaming, "What the HELL is the matter with you, you narcissistic crazy!"

Whew. That felt good to say. Let the healing begin!

Joy & love, dearest Sugar,
Oh Mama

Dear Oh Mama,

Do you own a pair of steel-toed boots? I do. And I'm happy to loan them to you so that you can properly kick the ass of that fool. Your rage is justified. Your angry astonishment over your baby daddy's failure to be a true father to your beautiful baby makes all the sense in the world.

But you know what? It doesn't matter one fig.

At least not in the face of what's at stake for your child if you choose to let your perfectly reasonable fury guide the decisions you make when it comes to the way you conduct yourself on the subject of his or her father. That this man is your child's father is one of the most essential facts of his or her life. It remains a fact no matter what happens—whether the man with whom you've reproduced ever has a relationship with your child or not. One day, years from now, your son or daughter will have to account for his or her father (and for you, as well). There will be a reckoning. There is always a reckoning. For every one of us. Accounting for what happened in our childhoods and why and who our parents are and how they succeeded and failed us is the work we all do when we do the work of becoming whole, grown-up people. That reckoning is especially fraught when a parent has failed a child and so I advise you to (a) do everything in your power to thwart a fail between your child and his or her father, and (b) keep yourself from failing, should the father of your child persist in doing so.

It's apparent that you're struggling with the rage and disappointment you rightly feel toward your baby's father. I don't fault you for this and no one would. But what's your fault and what isn't is beside the point. The point—as you state in your letter—is what's best for your child. You asked if you were obligated to send pictures and updates in response to the intermittent emails the father of your child sends you, and my answer is yes. Not because you're obligated to the man—you owe him nothing—but because you're obligated to your child. Given the fact that Baby Daddy sounds like only a pathetic fuck (rather than an abusive one), the best thing you can do for your sweet baby is nurture a father-child bond, especially this early in your child's life.

As you've so depressingly detailed, it hasn't begun well. Baby Daddy has thus far failed on every front. This is not your responsibility, but it is your problem. Your efforts in the direction of inclusion, communication, acceptance, and forgiveness could lead to a positive relationship between your child and his or her father that profoundly affects the course of his or her life. Or not. We can't know yet. But it's a big enough deal that I strongly encourage you to try.

I don't say this with a light heart. It would be much more fun to kick this guy with your steel-toed boots. I would be happy to help you do that. I understand how outrageously unjust it is that you should be expected to respond to this "narcissistic crazy" with grace and integrity. But every now and then each of us must do so, honey bun, and this is your time. This is when it counts. Because, of course, you aren't doing this for you—you're doing this for your child. I know you know this already. I can tell that you're a great mom. Your good mom-ness shimmers right through your letter. And now—appallingly!—I implore you to see what you can do to help the man who knocked you up to likewise shimmer.

Our kids deserve that, don't they? To be loved shimmeringly? Yes, they do. So let's get to it.

The first thing I advise you to do is compel Baby Daddy to

pay child support. This can be done through peaceful legal negotiation or you can sue his ass. Either way, I encourage you to do it through formal channels, rather than personal agreement, so that you have recourse should Baby Daddy fail to pay. By requiring this man to contribute financially, you're not only protecting your child, but also communicating two important facts: that you expect something from Baby Daddy and that he owes something to his child. If he's any sort of decent fellow, he'll hand over the dough without too much protest. If he's a good guy going through a rough patch, he'll thank you later. I encourage you to hire an attorney immediately.

The second thing I advise you to do is compose an email addressed to your child's father that (a) compassionately acknowledges his absence in his child's life, (b) asks directly about making arrangements for a visit, and (c) provides an update on your child's personality and development. Attach a couple of pictures. Tell a few stories. When I say "compassionately acknowledges," I mean: does a little dance around the fact that Baby Daddy's not stepped up as a father so far. I mean: gives him some room to change. I mean: does not imply that you might team up with an advice columnist to kick his teeth out with some very serious steel-toed boots. I mean: be your best, most gigantic self. Which sometimes, for a tiny bit, means faking it. As in: *Hello, Baby Daddy! I hope you're well. Baby is getting so big and more beautiful and amazing every day. Even though our relationship is a thing of the past, it's important to me that Baby has a relationship with his/her daddy and, based on what you have written to me in your emails, I know it's important to you too. I want to set a date for a visit.*

The third thing I advise you to do is arrange for child care for a few hours on a regular basis so you can go out with your coolest friends and rage with them about all the hurt and anger and befuddlement you have over the fact that a man you once slept with—*the man who is biologically half of your precious child!*—is a complete jackass. This may seem extraneous, but it isn't. It's a vital piece of the survival puzzle. You must find a place to put your negative feelings about the father of your child. If you don't, they will rule you. Very likely what has gone down between you and Baby Daddy has only begun. Even if it goes well, I wouldn't be surprised if there were many times over the coming years that you'd like to throttle him. If you don't find a place to put those feelings, you may not be able to keep yourself from putting them on your child.

And that's a terrible place to put them.

A couple of years ago, I read the findings of a study on the effects of divorced and separated parents talking negatively about their exes in the presence of their children. I tried to locate it when I was writing this column so I could cite it properly and quote it directly, but I had no luck. That's fine because what I remember about the study most vividly is really just one thing: that it's devastating for a child to hear one parent speak ill of the other. In fact, so much so that the researchers found it was less psychologically damaging if a parent said directly to the child *You are a worthless piece of shit* than it was for a parent to say *Your mother/father is a worthless piece of shit*. I don't remember if they had any theories about why that was so, but it made sense to me. I think we all have something sturdier inside of us that rears up when we're being attacked that we simply can't call upon when someone we love is being attacked, especially if that someone is our parent, half of us— the primal other—and the person doing the attacking is the other half, the other primal other.

I know of what I speak. My own father was a destructive force in my life. If you made a map of my life and traced everything back—all the moves and decisions and transitions and events—my mother mustering the courage to divorce my father when I was six was probably the single best thing that ever happened to me.

My father got my mom pregnant when they were both nineteen. They weren't very much in love, but abortion was illegal and my mom wasn't willing to go away to a home for wayward girls and give her baby to someone else, so she married my father in a quickie wedding. Over the next nine years they had three children—my two siblings and me—and some very hard things happened. I have so many horrible stories about the years with my dad, who was often violent and mean. But those aren't the stories you need to hear.

What you need to hear is how much, as a child, I loved him. My father. My dad. My daddy. The love I had for him was tremendous, irrefutable, bigger than my terror and sorrow. I could not keep myself from loving my dad. It was simply there. To not love him had never occurred to me, no matter how ugly it got. I hated what he did to my mom and my siblings and me. I wept and shrieked and hid and got age-inappropriate headaches and peed my bed way beyond the age that's normal. But he was my father and so when my mom finally left him, I begged her to go back. I mean, I *begged* her in a way I have never begged anyone for anything in all of my life. I sobbed my six-year-old girl brains out because I knew that if it was really over, if my mother really left my father, I would no longer have a dad.

And you know what? I was right. After my parents divorced, I no longer had a dad.

I've seen him three times since then—short visits during which sad and creepy things happened. But mostly there was nothing. No dad. There was only the great fatherless alone for years of my childhood, during which I lived in cheap apartment buildings occupied by other children of single mothers, most of whom also had little to do with their fathers. A couple of times a year an envelope would arrive addressed in my father's hand to me and my siblings. It would be waiting for us in the mailbox when we returned from school, our mother at work. My brother and sister and I would rip those letters open with a glee so entire that a surge of something runs through my body still, as I type these words.

A letter! From our dad! Aletterfromourdad!Fromourdadfrom ourdadfromourdad!

But of course we should have known better. We knew better, but we couldn't bear to let ourselves know. The envelope had our names on it, but the letter inside was never for us. It was always something else and always the same thing: a nasty and vulgar diatribe directed at our mom. How she was a whore and welfare mooch. How he should've made her get that illegal abortion years ago. How she was a horrible mom. How he would come and get me and my siblings when she least expected it and then she'd be sorry. Then she'd pay. Then she'd never see her children again. How would she like that?

The thought of my father kidnapping me terrified me more than anything. It was with me always, the prospect of being snatched. I readied myself, playing out intricate fantasies about how my siblings and I would escape, how I'd get us all back to our mother at any cost. We'd walk across the country barefoot if we had to. We'd follow rivers and hide in ditches. We'd steal apples from trees and clothes from clotheslines.

But our father never took us. He never had any intention of doing so, I realized one day when I was twenty-seven. *He never wanted me!* I thought with such clarity and surprise and grief that I instantly broke into sobs.

Will the father of your baby ever father his child, Oh Mama? We don't know. That letter hasn't been ripped open yet. Anything could be inside. People change. People make dreadful mistakes and then repair them. Men who are distant when their children are babies sometimes turn into wonderful dads. Others continue to be only more of the same. Whatever happens, you will do right by your child by keeping whatever you feel about his or her father separate from the choices you make and the actions you take in regard to his or her relationship with his or her dad. Your behavior and words will deeply impact your child's life—both how he or she feels about his or her father and also how he or she feels about him or herself.

My mother never spoke an ill word about my father to my siblings and me. She had every right to hate him, to turn us against him, but she didn't. It wasn't that she lied to us about him. We spoke often and honestly about the hard things we'd witnessed and suffered at his hands. But she didn't demonize him. She cast him as human: complicated, flawed, and capable of redemption. Which means, in spite of everything, she made it possible for me to love my father, this absent man who was half of me. When I was a child and asked her what had made her fall in love with my dad, she thought of things to tell me, even if she couldn't rightly remember them anymore. When I was a teenager and we argued about her refusal to condemn my father, she told me that she was grateful for him because without him she wouldn't have had my siblings and me. When I was just barely becoming a woman and my mother knew she was going to die, she stroked my hair and told me it was okay if I wanted to reach out to my father again, that I should always be open to the possibility of forgiveness and reconciliation and change, and that doing so was not a betrayal of her, but rather evidence of the woman she'd raised me to be.

It isn't fair that she had to be so kind to such an unkind man. I hope she raged about him to her coolest friends. As a single mother—and by that I mean truly a mother alone like you, Oh Mama, one who does not share custody or co-parent—she had to be her best self more often than it's reasonable for any human to be. And you know what's so never-endingly beautiful to me? *She was.* She was imperfect. She made mistakes. But she was her best self more often than it's reasonable for any human to be.

And that is the gift of my life.

Long after she was dead, it was her words and conduct that formed the bridge I teetered across to heal the wounds my father had made. That's the gift you have to give your child, regardless of how your baby's father decides to conduct himself, regardless if he ever steps up and becomes the father to your son or daughter he should be. It's what most of us have to give a few times over the course of our lives: to love with a mindfully clear sense of purpose, even when it feels outrageous to do so. Even when you'd rather put on your steel-toed boots and scream.

Give it. You won't regret it. It will come out in the reckoning.

Yours,
Sugar

THERE'S A BUNDLE ON YOUR HEAD

Dear Sugar,

I'm in my early twenties. I've been in a serious relationship with the same guy for six years—on and off (the "off" portion taking place when I was younger). I have been very distracted and have been second-guessing the relationship for a while now, but I can't come to grips with losing this person that seems to be right for me permanently—and of course I don't want to break his heart. Then again, I don't want to settle and have regrets later in life. I feel like we want different things out of life and we have different interests, but I just can't decide. I have talked to him about my feelings, but to no avail. We went on a little "break," but breaks never work.

My biggest fear is being alone and never finding anyone that measures up. It doesn't help that my closest friends are settling down with their boyfriends and are talking about marriage. Please help, Sugar!

Sincerely,
Scared & Confused

Dear Scared & Confused,

I lived in London when I was twenty. I was technically home-less and desperately broke, but I didn't have the papers an

American needs to get a job in London, so I spent most of my time walking the streets searching for coins that people had dropped. One day, a man in a business suit approached and asked me if I wanted an under-the-table job three days a week at a major accounting firm that has since collapsed due to corruption.

"Sure," I said.

And this is how I became *coffee girl one two three.*

Coffee girl was my actual job title. The *one two three* was tacked on to communicate the fact that I was responsible for providing fresh and hot coffee and tea to all the accountants and secretaries who worked on the first three floors of the building. It was a harder job than you might think. "Coffee girl," men would call as I passed them with my tray, often snapping their fingers to draw my attention their way. I wore a black skirt over white tights and a black vest over a white shirt and I was almost always out of breath. Banned from the elevator, I had to race up and down steps in a stairwell that ran along the back of the building to get from one floor to the next.

That stairwell was my sanctuary, the only place where nobody snapped their fingers and called me coffee girl. During my breaks I walked down to the first floor and went outside and sat on a patch of concrete that edged the building that housed the major accounting firm that has since collapsed due to corruption. One day while I was sitting there, an old woman came along and asked me where in America I was from and I told her and she said that years before she'd visited the place in America where I'm from and we had a nice conversation, and each day after that she came along during the time when I was sitting on the patch of concrete and we talked.

She wasn't the only person who came to talk to me. I was in love with someone at the time. In fact, I was married to that someone. And I was in way over my head. At night after I made love to this man I would lie beside him and cry because I knew that I loved him and that I couldn't bear to stay with him because I wasn't ready to love only one person yet and I knew that if I left him I would die of a broken heart and I would kill him of a broken heart too and it would be over for me when it came to love because there would never be another person who I'd love as much as I loved him or who loved me as much as he loved me or who was as sweet and sexy and cool and compassionate and good through and through. So I stayed. We looked for coins on the streets of London together. And sometimes he would come and visit me at the major accounting firm that has since collapsed due to corruption while I was on my breaks.

One day he came while the old woman was there. My husband and the old woman had never come at the same time, but I had told him about her—detailing the conversations I'd had with her—and I had told her about him too. "Is this your husband?" the old woman exclaimed with jubilant recognition when he walked up, and she shook his hand with both of her hands and they chatted for a few minutes and then she left. The man I loved was silent for a good while, giving the old woman time to walk away, and then he looked at me and said with some astonishment, "She has a bundle on her head."

"She has a bundle on her head?" I said.

"She has a bundle on her head," he said back.

And then we laughed and laughed and laughed so hard it might to this day still be the time I laughed the hardest. He was right. *He was right!* That old woman, all that time, all through the conversations we'd had as I sat on the concrete patch, had had an enormous bundle on her head. She appeared perfectly normal in every way but this one: she wore an impossible three-foot tower of ratty old rags and ripped-up blankets and towels on top of her head, held there by a complicated system of ropes tied beneath her chin and fastened to loops on the shoulders of her raincoat. It was a bizarre sight, but in all my conversations with my husband about the old woman, I'd never mentioned it.

She has a bundle on her head! we shrieked to each other through our laughter on the patch of concrete that day, but before long I wasn't laughing anymore. I was crying. I cried and cried and cried as hard as I'd laughed. I cried so hard I didn't go back to work. My job as *coffee girl one two three* ended right then and there.

"Why are you crying?" asked my husband as he held me.

"Because I'm hungry," I said, but it wasn't true. It was true that I was hungry—during that time we never had enough money or enough food—but it wasn't the reason I was crying. I was crying because there was a bundle on the old woman's head and I hadn't been able to say that there was and because I knew that that was somehow connected to the fact that I didn't want to stay with a man I loved anymore but I couldn't bring myself to acknowledge what was so very obvious and so very true.

That was such a long time ago, Scared & Confused, but it all came back when I read your letter. It made me think that perhaps that moment delivered me here to say this to you: You have a bundle on your head, sweet pea. And though that bundle may be impossible for you to see right now, it's entirely visible to me. You aren't torn. You're only just afraid. You no longer wish to be in a relationship with your lover even though he's a great guy. Fear of being alone is not a good reason to stay. Leaving this man you've been with for six years won't be easy, but you'll be okay and so will he. The end of your relationship with him will likely also mark the end of an era of your life. In moving into this next era there are going to be things you lose and things you gain.

Trust yourself. It's Sugar's golden rule. Trusting yourself means living out what you already know to be true.

Yours,
Sugar

WRITE LIKE A MOTHERFUCKER

Dear Sugar,

I write like a girl. I write about my lady life experiences, and that usually comes out as unfiltered emotion, unrequited love, and eventual discussion of my vagina as metaphor. And that's when I can write, which doesn't happen to be true anymore.

Right now, I am a pathetic and confused young woman of twenty-six, a writer who can't write. I am up late asking you a question, really questioning myself. I've sat here, at my desk, for hours, mentally immobile. I look up people I used to love and wonder why they never loved me. I lie facedown on my bed and feel scared. I get up, go to the computer, feel worse.

David Foster Wallace called himself a failed writer at twenty-eight. Several months ago, when depression hooked its teeth into me, I complained to my then-boyfriend about how I'll never be as good as Wallace; he screamed at me on Guerrero Street in San Francisco, "STOP IT. HE KILLED HIMSELF, ELISSA. I HOPE TO GOD YOU ARE NEVER LIKE HIM."

I understand women like me are hurting and dealing with self-trivialization, contempt for other, more successful people, misplaced compassion, addiction, and depression, whether they are writers or not. Think of the canon of women writers: a unifying theme is that so many of their careers ended in suicide. I often explain to my mother that to be a writer/a woman/a woman writer means to suffer mercilessly and eventually collapse in a heap of "I could have been better than this." She pleads with me: Can't it be different?

Can it? I want to jump out the window for what I've boiled down to is one reason: I can't write a book. But it's not that I want to die so much as have an entirely different life. I start to think that I should choose another profession—as Lorrie Moore suggests, "movie star/astronaut, a movie star/missionary, a movie star/kindergarten teacher." I want to throw off everything I've accumulated and begin as someone new, someone better.

I don't have a bad life. I didn't have a painful childhood. I know I'm not the first depressed writer. "Depressed writer"—because the latter is less accurate, the former is more acute. I've been clinically diagnosed with major depressive disorder and have an off-and-on relationship with prescription medication, which I confide so it doesn't seem I throw around the term "depression."

That said, I'm high-functioning—a high-functioning head case, one who jokes enough that most people don't know the truth. The truth: I am sick with panic that I cannot—will not—override my limitations, insecurities, jealousies, and ineptitude, to write well, with intelligence and heart and lengthiness. And I fear that even if I do manage to write, that the stories I write—about my vagina, etc.—will be disregarded and mocked.

How do I reach the page when I can't lift my face off the bed? How does one go on, Sugar, when you realize you might not have it in you? How does a woman get up and become the writer she wishes she'd be?

Sincerely,
Elissa Bassist

Dear Elissa Bassist,

When I was twenty-eight I had a chalkboard in my living room. It was one of those two-sided wooden A-frames that stand on their own and fold flat. On one side of the chalkboard I wrote, *"The first product of self-knowledge is humility,"* Flannery O'Connor, and on the other side I wrote, *"She sat and thought of only one thing, of her mother holding and holding onto their hands,"* Eudora Welty.

The quote by Eudora Welty is from her novel *The Optimist's Daughter*, which won the Pulitzer Prize for Fiction in 1972. It was a book I read again and again, and that line about the woman who sat thinking of only one thing was at the heart of the reason why. I sat like that too. Thinking of only one thing. One thing that was actually two things pressed together, like the back-to-back quotes on my chalkboard: how much I missed my mother and how the only way I could bear to live without her was to write a book. *My* book. The one that I'd known was in me since way before I knew people like me could have books inside of them. The one I felt pulsing in my chest like a second heart, formless and unimaginable until my mother died, and there it was, the plot revealed, the story I couldn't live without telling.

That I hadn't written the book by the time I was twenty-eight was a sad shock to me. Of myself, I'd expected greater things. I was a bit like you then, Elissa Bassist. Without a book, but not entirely without literary acclaim. I'd won a few grants and awards, published a couple of stories and essays. These minor successes stoked the grandiose ideas I had about what I would achieve and by what age I would achieve it. I read voraciously. I practically memorized the work of writers I loved. I recorded my life copiously and artfully in my journals. I wrote stories in feverish, intermittent bursts, believing they'd miraculously form a novel without my having to suffer too much over it.

But I was wrong. The second heart inside me beat ever stronger, but nothing miraculously became a book. As my thirtieth birthday approached, I realized that if I truly wanted to write the story I had to tell, I would have to gather everything within me to make it happen. I would have to sit and think of only one thing longer and harder than I thought possible. I would have to suffer. By which I mean *work*.

At the time, I believed that I'd wasted my twenties by not having come out of them with a finished book, and I bitterly lambasted myself for that. I thought a lot of the same things about myself that you do, Elissa Bassist. That I was lazy and lame. That even though I had the story in me, I didn't have it in me to see it to fruition, to actually get it out of my body and onto the page, to write, as you say, with "intelligence and heart and lengthiness." But I'd finally reached a point where the prospect of not writing a book was more awful than the one of writing a book that sucked. And so at last, I got to serious work on the book.

When I was done writing it, I understood that things happened just as they were meant to. That I couldn't have written my book before I did. I simply wasn't capable of doing so, either as a writer or a person. To get to the point I had to get to to write my first book, I had to do everything I did in my twenties. I had to write a lot of sentences that never turned into anything and stories that never miraculously formed a novel. I had to read voraciously and compose exhaustive entries in my journals. I had to waste time and grieve my mother and come to terms with my childhood and have stupid and sweet and scandalous sexual relationships and grow up. In short, I had to gain the self-knowledge that Flannery O'Connor mentions in that quote I wrote on my chalkboard. And once I got there I had to make a hard stop at self-knowledge's first product: humility.

Do you know what that is, sweat pea? To be humble? The word comes from the Latin words *humilis* and *humus.* To be *down low.* To be *of the earth.* To be *on the ground.* That's where I went when I wrote the last word of my first book. Straight onto the cool tile floor to weep. I sobbed and I wailed and I laughed through my tears. I didn't get up for half an hour. I was too happy and grateful to stand. I had turned thirty-five a few weeks before. I was two months pregnant with my first child. I didn't know if people would think my book was good or bad or horrible or beautiful and I didn't care. I only knew I no longer had two hearts beating in my chest. I'd pulled one out with my own bare hands. I'd suffered. I'd given it everything I had.

I'd finally been able to give it because I'd let go of all the grandiose ideas I'd once had about myself and my writing—*so talented! so young!* I'd stopped being grandiose. I'd lowered myself to the notion that the absolute only thing that mattered was getting that extra beating heart out of my chest. Which meant I had to write my book. My very possibly mediocre book. My very possibly never-going-to-be-published book. My absolutely nowhere-in-league-with-the-writers-I'd-admired-so-much-that-I-practically-memorized-their-sentences book. It was only then, when I humbly surrendered, that I was able to do the work I needed to do.

I hope you'll think hard about that, honey bun. If you had

a two-sided chalkboard in your living room I'd write *humility* on one side and *surrender* on the other for you. That's what I think you need to find and do to get yourself out of the funk you're in. The most fascinating thing to me about your letter is that buried beneath all the anxiety and sorrow and fear and self-loathing, there's arrogance at its core. It presumes you *should* be successful at twenty-six, when really it takes most writers so much longer to get there. It laments that you'll never be as good as David Foster Wallace—a genius, a master of the craft—while at the same time describing how little you write. You loathe yourself, and yet you're consumed by the grandiose ideas you have about your own importance. You're up too high and down too low. Neither is the place where we get any work done.

We get the work done on the ground level. And the kindest thing I can do for you is to tell you to get your ass on the floor. I know it's hard to write, darling. But it's harder not to. The only way you'll find out if you "have it in you" is to get to work and see if you do. The only way to override your "limitations, insecurities, jealousies, and ineptitude" is to produce. You have limitations. You are in some ways inept. This is true of every writer, and it's especially true of writers who are twenty-six. You will feel insecure and jealous. How much power you give those feelings is entirely up to you.

That you struggle with major depressive disorder certainly adds a layer to your difficulties. I've not focused on it in my answer because I believe—and it seems you believe—that it's only a layer. It goes without saying that your life is more important than your writing and that you should consult your doctor about how your depression may contribute to the despair you're feeling about your work. I'm not a doctor, so I cannot advise you about that. But I can tell you that you're not alone in your insecurities and fears; they're typical of writers, even those who don't have depression. Artists of all sorts reading this will understand your struggles. Including me.

Another layer of your anxiety seems rooted in your concern that as a woman your writing, which features "unfiltered emotion, unrequited love," and discussion of your "vagina as metaphor" will be taken less seriously than that of men. Yes, it probably will. Our culture has made significant progress when it comes to sexism and racism and homophobia, but we're not all the way there. It's still true that literary works by women, gays, and writers of color are often framed as specific rather than universal, small rather than big, personal or particular rather than socially significant. There are things you can do to shed light on and challenge those biases and bullshit moves.

But the best possible thing you can do is get your ass down onto the floor. Write so blazingly good that you can't be framed. Nobody is going to ask you to write about your vagina, hon. Nobody is going to give you a thing. You have to give it to yourself. You have to tell us what you have to say.

That's what women writers throughout time have done and it's what we'll continue to do. It's not true that to be "a woman writer means to suffer mercilessly and eventually collapse in a heap of 'I could have been better than *this*,'" nor is it true that a "unifying theme is that so many of their careers ended in suicide," and I strongly encourage you to let go of these beliefs. They are inaccurate and melodramatic and they do not serve you. People of all professions suffer and kill themselves. In spite of various mythologies regarding artists and how psychologically fragile we are, the fact is that occupation is not a top predictor for suicide. Yes, we can rattle off a list of women

writers who've killed themselves and yes, we may conjecture
that their status as women in the societies in which they lived
contributed to the depressive and desperate state that caused
them to do so. But it isn't the unifying theme.

You know what is?

How many women wrote beautiful novels and stories and
poems and essays and plays and scripts and songs in spite of
all the crap they endured. How many of them didn't collapse
in a heap of "I could have been better than *this*" and instead
went right ahead and became better than anyone would have
predicted or allowed them to be. The unifying theme is resil-
ience and faith. The unifying theme is being a warrior and a
motherfucker. It is not fragility. It's strength. It's nerve. And
"if your Nerve, deny you—," as Emily Dickinson wrote, "go
above your Nerve." Writing is hard for every last one of us—
straight white men included. Coal mining is harder. Do you
think miners stand around all day talking about how hard it is
to mine for coal? They do not. They simply *dig*.

You need to do the same, dear sweet arrogant beautiful
crazy talented tortured rising star glowbug. That you're so
bound up about writing tells me that writing is what you're
here to do. And when people are here to do that, they almost
always tell us something we need to hear. I want to know what
you have inside you. I want to see the contours of your second
beating heart.

So write, Elissa Bassist. Not like a girl. Not like a boy. Write
like a motherfucker.

Yours,
Sugar

A NEW, MORE FRACTURED LIGHT

Dear Sugar,

My parents recently decided to get a divorce. To be more accurate, my father left my mother for a younger woman. A cliché story, except when it happened to my family I was shattered, as if it was the first time it had ever happened. I'm an adult. I've always been close with my father. I looked up to him as a role model. To find out he'd been seeing someone else without telling my mom and that he'd been lying to all of us about it was very painful. Suddenly I can't trust this man I've always counted on and loved.

  I'm trying to be understanding. I imagine my father struggled and this wasn't easy for him. I'm also angry and hurt that he's moved on so quickly and that he lied to us. I want our old relationship back and at the same time, I feel I can't have it back because of the way I feel now. There's also the reality that he's with someone new and that he's approaching his role of being my dad differently. How do I reconnect with him in a genuine way?

Signed,
Dealing with Divorce

Dear Dealing with Divorce,

There's nothing good about one's father leaving one's mother for anyone, but especially for a younger woman, and especially after a period of having lied about it. I'm sorry for your pain.

I think you reconnect with your dad in a genuine way by being genuine. To be genuine means to be actual, to be true, to be sincere and honest. You need to tell your father how you feel about his actions and choices. You need to share your hurt and anger with him, as well as your desire to rebuild the relationship that was damaged by his dishonesty. You also need to do your best to listen to what he has to say.

I can't know this for certain, but I'll guess your father didn't want to hurt you. He probably didn't want to hurt your mother either, though it sounds as if he very much did. Good people do all sorts of idiotic stuff when it comes to sex and love. Though your father's deceit feels like a personal betrayal, what happened is between him and your mom. He couldn't reveal his affair to you until he was ready to reveal it to your mother. He wasn't trying to lie to you. It's only that you got tangled up in his lies. You had an up-close view of an intimacy that ultimately did not include you. You mustn't interpret this betrayal as if it did. Just because your father proved to be undeserving of your mother's trust doesn't mean he's unworthy of yours.

I know it sounds as if I'm defending your father's actions, but please let me assure you I'm not. I understand entirely why you feel the way you do. I'd be furious and hurt too. But transformation often demands that we separate our emotional responses from our rational minds. Your rational mind knows that men leave their wives for younger women all the time. Your emotional response is you can't believe your father did.

Your rational mind knows that it's hard for even strong, ethical people to sustain a long-term monogamy. Your emotional response is you're shocked your own parents failed to do so. I think it would help you to lean rather hard into the rational right now. Not to deny your grief, but rather to put into perspective what seems to be most true: your father didn't manage to be a good husband to your mother in the end, but that doesn't mean he won't manage to be a good father to you.

I encourage you to give him the opportunity. I don't think you should let him off the hook, but you should not keep him on it either. Find a way to weave your father's failing into the tapestry of your lifelong bond. Bravely explore what his new relationship means to him and ask where you fit into it.

It's going to be difficult, but that's no surprise. The story of human intimacy is one of constantly allowing ourselves to see those we love most deeply in a new, more fractured light. Look hard. Risk that.

Yours,
Sugar

DUDES IN THE WOODS

Dear Sugar,

Three of my best college buddies and I go away for an annual guys' weekend at a cabin in the woods. We're all in our mid-thirties and we've been doing these get-togethers for close to a decade. It's our way of staying in touch, since we've all got busy lives and some of us reside in different cities. Though at times I'll go months without talking to them, I consider these guys my closest friends. We've seen each other through several relationships, two weddings, one divorce, one of us coming out as gay, one of us realizing he's an alcoholic and getting sober, one of us becoming a father, dysfunctional family issues, the death of another one of our close college friends, professional successes and failures, and—you get the picture.

On our most recent get-together a couple of months ago, I overheard my friends discussing me. Before this incident occurred, the four of us had been on the subject of my love life. My longtime girlfriend and I broke up last year for reasons I won't go into here, but I did go into with my friends back when she and I decided to end things. Not long before my weekend with the guys, she and I got back together and I told them my ex and I were making a go of it again. They didn't say much in response, but I wouldn't have expected them to.

Later that day I stepped out for a walk, but soon realized I'd forgotten my hat, so I returned to the cabin to get it. The moment I opened the door I could hear my friends in the kitchen discussing me. I wasn't trying to eavesdrop, but I couldn't keep myself from listening, since they were talking about my girlfriend and me. I wouldn't say they were trashing me, but they did make critical remarks about the way I "justify" my relationship and other things about my personality that were unflattering. About five minutes into this, I opened the door and shut it hard so they would know I was there and they stopped talking.

I tried to pretend I hadn't heard what they'd said, but soon I told them what had happened. They were extremely embarrassed. Each of them apologized, assured me they meant nothing by what they said, and claimed they were only concerned that I'd gotten back together with my girlfriend, who they don't think is good for me. I played it off like it was cool and acted like I wanted to let bygones be bygones, but it's been two months and I'm still bothered by what happened. I feel betrayed. It's none of their business who I choose to date for one thing, and for another I'm pissed they were running me down like that.

I recognize that I'm possibly taking this too hard. I'll admit that I have talked about each of them with the others over the years. I've made statements I wouldn't want the person in question to hear, even secondhand. The rational part of me understands that these sorts of discussions among friends are to be expected. It sounds weak to admit this, but I'm hurt. Part of me wants to tell them to go fuck themselves when it comes to the weekend at the cabin next year.

What do you think? Should I forgive and forget or find a new batch of buddies?

Odd Man Out

Dear Odd Man Out,

What a disaster. How dreadful it must have been to hear your
friends saying negative things about you. How mortified they
must have felt when they learned you'd been listening. You
have every reason to be upset and hurt.

And yet . . . *and yet*—you knew there was going to be an
"and yet," didn't you?—in the scheme of things this is quite
small, quite ordinary. I'm positive you should not toss these
friends aside for a new batch of them. Besides—those new
friends? They'd only talk about you behind your back too.

But I'm getting ahead of myself.

Perhaps the first step in getting over this is to acknowledge
that what happened was indeed deeply unfortunate. By hearing what you were not meant to hear, you punctured a social
code that's in place to protect your feelings. You heard your
friends express opinions about you that they are too polite
to tell you and they expressed them in blunt language they
would not have used had they known you were listening. You
witnessed a discussion that was being had about you that was
unbound by concern for your feelings. No wonder you feel so
stung. Anyone would.

That your friends have those opinions, however, does not
mean that they don't love you or value you as a friend or otherwise think you are one of the best people they know. That
may be difficult to believe at this moment, when your feelings
are so raw, but it's true.

We talk about our friends behind their backs. We do. Ask
any social scientist who has studied human communication
behaviors. Even you admitted to doing this. Our friends are
witness to our attributes and flaws, our bad habits and good

qualities, our contradictions and our contrivances. That they need to occasionally discuss the negative aspects of our lives and personalities in terms less than admiring is to be expected. Like anything, there are healthy and constructive ways to do this, and unhealthy and destructive ways.

A healthy way is rooted in respect and love. In this case, we make critical assessments and uncomplimentary observations entirely within the context of our affection and concern for the individual in question. Sometimes we talk behind a friend's back in order to grapple with our doubts about or disapproval of the choices he or she has made. Sometimes we do it because our friends possess qualities that confound, confuse, or annoy the shit out of us, though we love them anyway. Sometimes we discuss our friends with others because we had a weird or rude or dumb interaction with one of them and we simply need to blow off steam. The baseline of these discussions is a grounded knowledge that we love and care for the friend—regardless of the things that irk, confuse, or disappoint us about him or her. The negative thoughts we express about this friend are outweighed by the many positive thoughts we have.

An unhealthy way to talk about a friend behind his or her back is rooted in cruelty and ill will. There is a lack of generosity and a cutting glee; one takes pleasure in ripping the so-called friend to shreds. Though we may pretend otherwise, we don't truly want good things for him or her. We are judgmental and petty. We will not protect that friend, but are instead willing to betray him or her if the situation serves us. On the other hand, we are happy to use this "friendship" to our advantage, should the opportunity arise. Our affection is one of convenience rather than heart.

So. There's a good way and a bad way to gossip, but either

way it pretty much sucks to overhear it if you happen to be the subject of the conversation. There is no question that given what happened, Odd Man Out, you and your friends are going to have to repair a bit of damage. I believe that with some time, you can do that.

I have no doubt that your friends were discussing you from a place of love and concern—the healthy place. My hunch is that your friends were unconsciously attempting to strengthen their bond with you rather than rend it when they were discussing you that day at the cabin. After all, when this "incident" occurred, you'd just informed them that you'd reunited with a woman they all apparently believe—fairly or not—is a negative force in your life. If they didn't care about you, they wouldn't have bothered to discuss this turn of events. Because they do care about you, they began speaking about it the moment they believed you were out of earshot. Collectively, they hashed out their feelings—in preparation, perhaps, to share a watered-down version of them with you.

This is because they love you.

You heard things you should not have heard. They said things they would not have said if they'd known of your presence. But it doesn't mean they betrayed you. It means only that you all got caught in an embarrassing situation that I'll guess every last one of us can imagine being on both sides of.

I suggest that you talk to your friends again about what happened, only this time you do it more forthrightly. No doubt, your hurt feelings are lingering in part because you so quickly attempted to brush them aside. Let this dudes-in-the-woods debacle bring you closer to your friends rather than force you apart. Use this awkward experience as an opportunity to clear the air on the subject of your girlfriend and whatever it is your dearest friends think you're justifying about your relationship with her. Tell them how hurt you were to hear what they said. Tell them why you think they are wrong. Tell them why you love your girlfriend and why they should be open to loving her too. Then ask them why they said what they did about you and her and do your best to listen.

Your choice of romantic partners is none of their business, it's true, but the reason they have an opinion about it is because they want you to have a good life. They know you. They have listened to what you've told them about your relationship with this woman and they've made their own observations. I'm not suggesting that you dump your girlfriend because your friends don't like her, but rather that you hear what they have to say. Perhaps they have a negative opinion of her because when you broke up with her and shared the story of that breakup with your friends, you cast her in an inaccurately unflattering light. Perhaps they simply don't know what they're talking about and you need to set them straight. Perhaps they see something you cannot see right now, blinded as you may be by desire for this relationship to work.

We can't know. Time will tell. But I encourage you to swallow your pride and hear your friends out, to look at the image of yourself they're reflecting back to you. It might be useful. It might piss you off. It might help you get over the tender feelings you have about what happened at the cabin. The complicated thing about friends is that sometimes they are totally wrong about us and sometimes they are totally right and it's almost always only in retrospect that we know which is which.

I have this dear friend I'll call Beth. She fell in love fast and hard with a guy I'll call Tom. Over the course of a year or two Tom took Beth on a ride of highs and lows. There was love, deception, abandonment, lies, passion, promises, and a whole bunch of absolute bullshit. She was up. She was down. She was standing on my front stoop shaking and crying or calling me to say how amazing Tom was. When I'd been witness to this relationship long enough that I'd formed my own opinion about it, I began sharing my concerns with Beth. I was gentle at first, but before long I could not keep myself from telling her exactly what I thought in the most blunt terms: this man was a player and by not ridding herself of him entirely she was only bringing pain upon herself.

It took another several months and false starts and betrayals before she believed I was right. By then she'd wished she'd listened to what I'd said way back when, but the thing is, I didn't blame her. I wouldn't have listened either. Who does what a friend tells her to do? I can't say I ever have, even when later I fully recognized that I should have.

Several months later Beth began dating another guy. I'll call him Dave. About a month into their relationship she called me up and told me they were engaged.

"To be married?" I stuttered, trying to conceal my disapproval and fear that this Dave person was going to be another disaster, another Tom.

"Yes! I know it's fast, but we're in love and we're getting married," she said. She was sure. He was great. She was so happy. She knew this was right.

I spent a half hour asking her one question after another in a tone of voice that I hoped sounded upbeat, but when I hung up I didn't feel upbeat. I felt worried. I immediately emailed another of Beth's close friends—a woman with whom I'm only acquainted. I asked her what she thought about this crazy business of Beth getting married to this guy she'd only been dating for a month. We went back and forth, discussing Beth. We shared with each other her tendencies when it came to men, our observations of her strengths and her weaknesses, the things we hoped for her and also feared. We knew her. We loved her. We wanted her to be happy, but we were talking shamelessly about her behind her back.

Months later, after Beth married Dave, after I realized Dave really did make Beth happy and that he was good not just to her, but for her, I told her what I'd done. I told her how I'd emailed her friend because I'd been distressed about how quickly she and Dave had committed to each other. I could see the tension cross her face as I informed her that two of her best friends had been discussing her. I could understand why it made her feel defensive and uncomfortable. Who were we to weigh in on the subject of who she married and how fast? I understood that completely.

But I also understood who it was we were. We were two of her best friends. We were the people who listened to her tell all those awful and glorious stories about Tom and we would be the people who would be there for her regardless of how things turned out with Dave. We would be her friends no matter what. Because we loved her. If she needed us, we would go to her anytime. We would stand by her. She knew this, and I knew the same about her. I knew she'd always tell me the truth, even if it hurt, and I also knew that she'd take care not to hurt me. I knew over the course of our friendship she too might have opinions or concerns about me that she'd opt to discuss with someone else in words that would be best for me not to hear. And I knew that was okay, that it was a perfectly natural part of sustaining a true friendship over many years, that it wasn't a betrayal, but a blessing.

That's what you have in these men, Odd Man Out. True friends. Real blessings. Forgive them. Feel lucky you have them. Move along.

Yours,
Sugar

ICKY THOUGHTS TURN ME ON

Dear Sugar,

I'm a straight woman, soon to be thirty-four. Icky thoughts turn me on—thoughts about father-daughter incest or men "taking" me aggressively and my being submissive in bed. I've always tried to push these thoughts away because they're out of line with who I am and also because they're repulsive and embarrassing, but I usually can't help myself and my mind wanders there anyway. They are, essentially, the way I get myself off.

I'm a strong, independent, "normal," feminist-minded woman who is of course against rape and incest and male domination, so I feel more than terrible that I have these thoughts and yet I can't seem to stop them. I've had three serious boyfriends over the years and a few shorter-term dating partners/lovers, and recently I've started seeing a man I like a lot. With some of these men I've had a tiny bit of sexual power play, but I've never revealed the full extent of my desires and fantasies to anyone. I think one reason I feel so ashamed is that my father was mildly sexually abusive to me early on in my life (i.e., "light fondling" off and on for about a year). He died in a car accident when I was eight, so it didn't go on very long, thank God, but I worry that my sick thoughts go back to him and what he did, especially because "daddy/daughter" fantasies play rather prominently in my mind—which makes me want to puke.

I'm writing to ask what you would do if you were me, Sugar. Should I give way to my sick thoughts or should I fight them off?

I know people do lots of kinky things, but I have zero interest in getting involved with an S&M community—that stuff is way too heavy for my taste anyway. I'm not into any sort of power imbalance outside the bedroom and I'm not a masochist in the slightest. I don't want a dungeon or a whip or to be anyone's slave. I just yearn to be lovingly but firmly dominated in bed (in ways that are almost exclusively psychological/conversational and nothing beyond tenderly firm when it comes to the physical aspects). I feel like I either need to purge these fantasies for good or fully embrace them so that I have a more fulfilled sex life. What would you do? How would you do it? Do you think I could ever risk sharing this with a man or would he think I was a sicko and run away?

Aching to Submit

Dear Aching to Submit,

Did you ever play that game as a kid where you'd go into a dark bathroom and stare at your shadowy reflection in the mirror and repeat *Mary Worth, Mary Worth, Mary Worth* thirteen times? The legend in my neck of the woods had it that by the time you spoke that last *Mary Worth* the mirror would crack and drip with blood and quite possibly Mary Worth herself would appear.

I remembered that game when I read your heartbreaking letter, Aching to Submit. I know it's corny, but I'd like you to play your own version of the Mary Worth game with me. Step into the bathroom and gaze at your reflection in the mirror and repeat this sentence to yourself thirteen times, but let's leave on the lights:

Icky thoughts turn me on.
Icky thoughts turn me on.
Icky thoughts turn me on.
Icky thoughts turn me on.
Icky thoughts turn me on.
Icky thoughts turn me on.
Icky thoughts turn me on.
Icky thoughts turn me on.
Icky thoughts turn me on.
Icky thoughts turn me on.
Icky thoughts turn me on.
Icky thoughts turn me on.
Icky thoughts turn me on.

Did the mirror crack and drip with blood? Did any scary faces appear? Did you run shrieking from the room? I hope your answer is no. I hope you stood right there and met your own gaze. Every agonizing bit of self-loathing in your letter and every conundrum you pose will be soothed and solved by your ability to do so, sweet pea.

Of course you're not a sicko because icky thoughts turn you on! You aren't even weird. Do you know how many women have these same fantasies? Invite your best girlfriends over and do a little *I'll tell you mine if you tell me yours.* Pick up any book that has the words "women" and "erotic" in the subtitle and thumb your way through a veritable *feast* of spankings and bossy brutes, big daddies and naughty little girls. You can be a "strong, independent, 'normal,' feminist-minded woman" and still want this crazy shit in bed. In fact, being a "strong, independent, 'normal,' feminist-minded woman" only increases your chance of getting what you want from sex.

So let's talk about how you can do that, my submissive little plum.

It's clear to me that you have some healing to do in regards to your father. He sexually abused you and then he died. That's big, hard stuff. A good psychotherapist will help you make sense of your loss, your violation, and the love you likely still have for your dad. He or she will also help you explore how your history is connected to your current sexual desires.

My guess is that it *is* connected—at least murkily—as uncomfortable as that makes you feel. But that doesn't mean you wanted your father to fuck you or that you would like to be raped or bullied by men. It means, perhaps, that you lost something or were wounded in a place that your sexual longings are maybe—and only maybe!—attempting to recover and repair. It's impossible to know, but I encourage you to seek as much insight into your own shadow world as you can. Not so you'll rid yourself of your "sick thoughts," but so you can finally embrace your sexuality and have some fun.

And fun it is. The deal with sexual fantasy is that it's *pretend*. And when a fantasy is acted out, it's done so between and among *consenting adults*. There's a world of difference between being raped and asking someone to rip your clothes off and fuck you. You are the agent of power in your sex life, even if what you want is to relinquish your power and agency while you're having sex. You can take that power back at any moment.

Which means, of course, that you always had it.

Rape victims don't. Incest victims don't. Victims of domineering bullies don't. You're missing this key point when you lambaste yourself for having the desires that you do, when you reject the reality that *icky thoughts turn you on.* The ickiest part of each of these acts is that someone is being hurt because he/she is being forced to do what he/she does not want to do.

You want the opposite. You want someone to do what you *want* him to do. And once you understand this distinction, you'll stop feeling so horrible about your desires and you'll start asking the men in your life to help you fulfill them. It will be good, hot, beautiful fun.

It will also be a little bit scary, the way it always is when we're brave enough to touch the rawest, realest truths. When we have the guts to look directly into the mirror and say *Mary Worth* thirteen times without pause and see—thrillingly, terrifyingly—that it was never her we had to fear.

It was always only us.

Yours,
Sugar

REACH

Dear Sugar,

I was raised in the very conservative Christian "Deep South," where I've discovered that my life has been sheltered from the views and lifestyles in other areas of the country. Our town has a population of about 6,000. The whole county has less than 30,000. I know that people are pretty much the same everywhere, but in the South people tend to keep things out of the public eye.

I am a professional in a real-estate-related field and I own my own business. I've been married for twenty-plus years and have four children. The first half of my marriage was what I considered utopia, but we've grown apart over the last ten years or so. Now it seems that we simply cohabitate peacefully, similar to siblings. Neither of us is happy, but we stay together for the kids.

Several years ago, I was involved in an accident that damaged my spine. I was told by a neurosurgeon that operating wouldn't help, and he referred me to a pain management clinic. Now I am hopelessly addicted to the pain meds. In my youth, I experimented with drinking and drugs. Much of that was spurred on by the suicide of an older sibling. I never had a problem as far as addiction, though. Now, I take a month's supply of some very strong pain meds in about seven to ten days, then I crash and have to beg or borrow from others to make it to the next appointment. I know that these drugs will end up turning my liver into a rock if I don't accidentally overdose first. I know that I have a serious problem.

When the economy went bad, so did business, and we ended up losing our health insurance. I no longer have employees, so if I don't work every day, we don't eat. Rehab is realistically impossible. I can't depend on my wife for support and don't have any other family anywhere close. I feel totally alone except for my children. I tried everything I could think of, from prayer to "cold turkey." I simply don't have the discipline to follow through. I've come to depend on the drugs mentally as much or more than physically. I depend on the drugs to help me deal with the lack of work and income as well as dealing with a loveless marriage. Couple that with the loss of my dear mother a year and a half ago, and soon thereafter one of my best friends to cancer. Now I have begun to have problems with depression and suicidal thoughts that I'm sure are related to the meds as much as the economy or anything else. The choices I see are:

1. Continue like I have been, knowing that there is a good chance that it will kill me.

2. Find a way to go to rehab and lose the house and business (my wife doesn't work).

3. Go to AA/NA meetings in this small town. This would almost surely ruin what's left of my business.

I hope you can see some other options because I just don't see any of the ones I've listed working out. Please be honest, blunt, and give me a new perspective on my multifaceted problem.

Thank you,
Ruler of a Fallen Empire

Dear Ruler of a Fallen Empire,

I'm terribly sorry for your misfortune. You listed the three
options you believe you have, but really they all say the same
thing: that you believe you're fucked before you begin. I understand why you feel this way. Your convergence of physical pain,
drug addiction, financial woe, no health insurance, and an
unhappy marriage is truly daunting. But you don't have the
luxury of despair. You can find a way to overcome these difficulties, and you must. There aren't three options. There is only
one. As Rilke says, "You must change your life."

You have the capacity to do that, Ruler. It seems impossible
now, but you aren't thinking clearly. The drugs and desperation and depression have muddled your head. If there is only
one thought that you hold in your mind right now, please let
it be that one. It was that thought that got me out of my own
drug/money/love disaster several years ago. Someone I trusted
told me what to do when I couldn't think right for myself and
listening to him saved my life.

You say that you don't have the "discipline to follow
through" when it comes to kicking your addiction, but you do.
It's that you can't do it alone. You need to reach out for help.
Here's what I think you should do:

1. Talk to a medical doctor at your pain management
    clinic and tell him or her that you've become addicted
    to your pain medication and also that you're depressed
    and broke. Tell the whole story. Don't conceal anything.
    You aren't alone. You have nothing to be ashamed of.
    I know your first instinct is to lie to your doctor, lest
    he or she cut off your drug supply, but don't trust that

instinct. That's the instinct that will ruin your life and possibly kill you. Trust the man inside you who you really are, and if you can't do that, trust me. Your doctor can help you safely taper off the drug to which you've become addicted, prescribe an alternative, nonaddictive drug, refer you to drug addiction treatment programs and/or psychological counseling, or all of the above.

2. Perhaps your doctor knows of a drug treatment program available to you at no cost, but if this isn't an option, I implore you to attend a Narcotics Anonymous (NA) meeting (or an Alcoholics Anonymous [AA] meeting, if that's what's available in your town). Of course you're afraid of being judged and condemned. Some people will judge and condemn you, but most won't. Our minds are small, but our hearts are big. Just about every one of us has fucked up at one point or another. You're in a pickle. You did things you didn't hope to do. You have not always been your best self. This means that you're like the rest of us. I've never been in a humiliating situation when I wasn't shocked by all the "normal" people who were also in the very same humiliating position. Humans are beautifully imperfect and complex. We're horny, ass-saving, ego-driven drug fiends, among other, more noble things. I think you'll be comforted when you go to the AA/NA meeting and see how many have problems similar to yours—including people you assumed would not. Those people will help you heal yourself, darling. They'll support you as you face this addiction. And they'll do it for free. I know a lot of people who

have transformed their lives thanks to those meetings. Not one of them thought they were the "AA/NA type" before they went. They knew that they were smarter or more sophisticated or less religious or more skeptical or less strung out or more independent than all those other hopeless freaks who went to AA or NA. They were all wrong. You worry that your business will be ruined if word gets around that you're attending meetings. I think people are more generous than you're imagining—yes, even in the "very conservative, Christian 'Deep South.'" But, Ruler, even if you're right, what's the alternative? Your addiction and depression will only deepen if you continue on this path. Would you rather have your business go down because you refused to make a change in your life or because you live among a community of punishing jerks who condemned you for seeking help?

3.   Talk to your wife and tell her about your addiction and your depression. This might be the first item on the list or the last—I can't gauge from your letter. Will your wife be an important advocate for you as you make the initial reach for help or will she be more supportive if you tell her after you've made a few positive changes on your own? Either way, I imagine she'll feel betrayed to learn that you've been concealing your addiction from her, and eventually relieved that she knows the truth. You say your marriage is "loveless" and perhaps you're correct that your relationship has come to its natural .end, but I'd like you to consider the notion that you aren't the best judge of that right now. You're a psychologically distressed drug addict with four kids, no

health insurance, uncertain business prospects, and a pile of bills. I wouldn't expect your marriage to be thriving. I doubt you've been an excellent partner in recent years, and it doesn't sound like your wife has either. But that the two of you have managed—after your ten happy years together—to roll on for another ten "peaceably," in spite of the enormous stress you're under, is an accomplishment that you mustn't fail to recognize. It may indicate that the love you once shared isn't dead. Perhaps you can rebuild your marriage. Perhaps you can't. Either way, I encourage you to see.

4. Make a financial plan, even if that plan is an anatomy of a disaster. You cite money as the reason you can't go into rehab, or even to AA/NA meetings, but surely you know that the financial repercussions will be far worse if you continue on your present course. Everything is at stake, Ruler. Your children. Your career. Your marriage. Your home. Your life. If you need to spend some money to cure yourself, so be it. The only way out of a hole is to climb out. After you consult with your doctor and see what options are available to you, and after you have a heart-to-heart with your wife about your situation, sit down with her and have a discussion about money in which everything is on the table. Perhaps you qualify for public assistance. Perhaps your wife can get a job, either temporarily or permanently. Perhaps you can get a loan from a friend or family member. Perhaps things won't seem so dire once you make the first steps in the direction of healing, and you'll be able to maintain your job while you recover. I know you feel panicked about your financial standing

because you have four children to support, but every choice you're currently making is hurting your cause. The only way for you to support your family financially is to get yourself together.

I lived in Brooklyn for several months when I was twenty-four. I shared an apartment with the man who was then my husband in a building that was mostly empty. Below us there was a bodega; above us a couple who got into raging fights in the middle of the night. The rest of the building—though full of apartments—was unoccupied for reasons that were never clear to me. I spent my days alone writing in the apartment while my husband worked his job as an assistant to a rich friend. In the evenings I worked as a waitress.

"Did you hear something strange?" my husband asked me one night when I got home from work.

"Hear something?" I asked.

"Behind the walls," he said. "I heard something earlier and I wondered if you heard it too, while you were alone today."

"I didn't hear anything," I said.

But the next day I did. Something behind the walls, and then from the ceiling. Something close, then distant, then close again, then gone. I didn't know what it was. It sounded awful. Like a baby who was extremely discreet. Its keen had the weight of a feather, the velocity of a dried leaf falling from a tree. It could have been nothing. It could have been me. It was the exact expression of the sound my insides were making every time I thought of my life and how I needed to change it and how impossible that seemed.

"I heard something," I told my husband that night.

He went to the wall and touched it. There was nothing

there. It was silent. "I think we're imagining things," he said, and I agreed.

But the sound kept coming and going, all through December, impossible to define or reach. Christmas came and we were all alone. My husband had received a bonus from his friend and we spent some of it on tickets to the opera in way-back seats. It was Mozart's *The Magic Flute.*

"I keep hearing it," I said to my husband on the subway home. "The sound behind the walls."

"Yeah," he said. "Me too."

On New Year's Day we woke at seven to a yowling. We jumped out of bed. The sound was the same one we'd been hearing for three weeks, but it wasn't discreet anymore. It was coming very clearly from the ceiling of our closet. My husband immediately got a hammer and started pounding away at the plaster with the claw end, chipping it in great chalky chunks that fell over our clothes. Within ten minutes, he'd clawed almost the entire closet ceiling away. We didn't care that we were ruining the place. We knew only that we had to get to the source of that sound, which had stopped during the pounding. Once there was no more closet ceiling to claw away, we went silent and stared up into the mysterious black innards of the building.

At first it seemed there was nothing—that the horrible sound-maker had again gone away, or perhaps we really had imagined it—but a moment later two emaciated kittens appeared, coming to peer down at us from the jagged edge of the hole. They were the strangest things I've ever seen. So skeletal they should have been dead, visibly shaking with fear, caked in soot and spiderwebs and globs of black grease, their eyes enormous and blazing.

"Meow," one of them said.

"Meow," wailed the other.

My husband and I held up our palms and the kittens walked into them immediately. They were so light it was like holding air with the smallest possible thing in it. They were like two sparrows in our hands.

I've tried to write about this experience several times over the years. It was an odd thing that happened to me during a sad and uncertain era of my life that I hoped would tell readers something deep about my ex-husband and me. About how in love we were and also how lost. About how we were like those kittens who'd been trapped and starving for weeks. Or maybe not about the kittens at all. Maybe the meaning was in how we heard the sound, but did nothing about it until it was so loud we had no choice.

I never found a way to write about it until I wrote this letter to you, Ruler, when I realized it was a story you needed to hear. Not how the kittens suffered during those weeks they were wandering inside the dark building with no way out—though surely there's something there too—but how they saved themselves. How frightened those kittens were, and yet how they persisted. How when two strangers offered up their palms, they stepped in.

Yours,
Sugar

PART TWO

WHATEVER MYSTERIOUS STARLIGHT THAT GUIDED YOU THIS FAR

Are the letters you publish really sent in by anonymous people? Most are so well written that it seems you or The Rumpus *writers must be creating them.*

The letters published in my column and in this book were sent to me by people who sought my advice. In most cases the name and/or email address of the letter writer is not visible to me. I do not write the letters, nor does anyone at *The Rumpus*. Because I have thousands of letters from which to choose, well-written letters probably have a higher chance of being plucked from the proverbial pile simply because they're more concise and complex. I agree with you that the letters are lovely. I have even more in my inbox.

Do you ever hear from the letter writers after they read the answers you gave them? I'd be interested in knowing what they have to say.

I've heard from about half of them. Each has responded warmly, even when my advice brought up difficult emotions. I imagine it's very intense to have your letter published and answered. I feel honored they trusted me to ponder their lives.

You seem so emotionally healthy, but from your column I can tell you've had your own struggles in the past. Do you ever struggle anymore?

Of course.

Are you a therapist or have you gone through extensive psychotherapy?

I'm not a therapist, and I've only seen a therapist a handful of times in my life. Which means, in technical terms, I'm totally unqualified for this gig.

THE BABY BIRD

Dear Sugar,

WTF, WTF, WTF?
I'm asking this question as it applies to everything every day.

Best,
WTF

Dear WTF,

My father's father made me jack him off when I was three and four and five. I wasn't any good at it. My hands were too small and I couldn't get the rhythm right and I didn't understand what I was doing. I only knew I didn't want to do it. Knew that it made me feel miserable and anxious in a way so sickeningly particular that I can feel that same particular sickness rising this very minute in my throat. I hated having to rub my grandfather's cock, but there was nothing I could do. I *had* to do it. My grandfather babysat my sister and me a couple times a week in that era of my life, and most of the days that I was trapped in his house with him he would pull his already-getting-hard penis out of his pants and say *come here* and that was that.

I moved far away from him when I was nearly six and soon after that my parents split up and my father left my life and I never saw my grandfather again. He died of black lung disease when he was sixty-six and I was fifteen. When I learned he died, I wasn't sad. I wasn't happy either. He was no one to me and yet he was always there, the force of him and what he'd made me do moving through me like a dark river. For years, I didn't say a word about it to anyone. I hoped silence would make it disappear or turn it into nothing more than an ugly invention of my nasty little mind. But it didn't. It was there, this thing about which I'd wonder *What the fuck was up with that?*

There was nothing the fuck up with that and there never will be. I will die with there never being anything the fuck up with my grandfather making my hands do the things he made my hands do with his cock. But it took me years to figure that out. To hold the truth within me that some things are so sad and wrong and unanswerable that the question must simply stand alone like a spear in the mud.

So I railed against it, in search of the answer to what the fuck was up with my grandfather doing that to me. *What the fuck? What the fuck? What the fuck?*

But I could never shake it. That particular fuck would not be shook. Asking what the fuck only brought it around. Around and around it went, my grandfather's cock in my hands, the memory of it so vivid, so *palpable,* so very much a part of me. It came to me during sex and not during sex. It came to me in flashes and it came to me in dreams. It came to me one day when I found a baby bird, fallen from a tree.

I'd always heard that you're not supposed to pick up baby birds; that once you touch them their mama won't come back and get them, but it doesn't matter if that's true or not—this bird was a goner anyway. Its neck was broken, its head lolling treacherously to the side. I cradled it as delicately as I could in my palms, cooing to soothe it, but each time I cooed, it only struggled piteously to get away, terrified by my voice.

The bird's suffering would've been unbearable for me to witness at any time, but it was particularly unbearable at that moment in my life because my mother had just died. And because she was dead I was pretty much dead too. I was dead but alive. And I had a baby bird in my palms that was dead but alive as well. I knew there was only one humane thing to do, though it took me the better part of an hour to work up the courage to do it: I put the baby bird in a paper bag and smothered it with my hands.

Nothing that has died in my life has ever died easily, and this bird was no exception. This bird did not go down without a fight. I could feel it through the paper bag, pulsing against my hand and rearing up, simultaneously flaccid and ferocious beneath its translucent sheen of skin, precisely as my grandfather's cock had been.

There it was! There it was again. Right there in the paper bag. The ghost of that old man's cock would always be in my hands. But I understood what I was doing this time. I understood that I had to press against it harder than I could bear. It *had* to die. Pressing harder was murder. It was mercy.

That's what the fuck it was. The fuck was mine.

And the fuck is yours too, WTF. That question does not apply "to everything every day." If it does, you're wasting your life. If it does, you're a lazy coward, and you are not a lazy coward.

Ask better questions, sweet pea. The fuck is your life. Answer it.

Yours,
Sugar

GO! GO! GO!

Dear Sugar,

I've been playing music (guitar and bass) since I was eleven years old. I've been in the same band since I was twenty. I'm now twenty-six and still living in the same town, still playing the same gigs. I love my band. It's a part of who I am. And we've released an album that I'm proud of (self-produced, but the local kids love it). Still, I wonder what would happen if I left. I want to see other parts of the country. Move around. Explore before I have a family to take care of. But then again, my band is my family, and I feel I shouldn't abandon them. We're never going to make it big, and that's fine. But am I selfish if I decide to leave?

Thanks, Sugar,
Considering Going Solo

Dear CGS,

Go! Go! Go! You need it one more time, darling? GO.

Really. Truly. As soon as you can. Of this I am absolutely sure: Do not reach the era of child-rearing and real jobs with a guitar case full of crushing regret for all the things you wished you'd done in your youth. I know too many people who didn't do those things. They all end up mingy, addled, shrink-wrapped versions of the people they intended to be.

It's hard to go. It's scary and lonely and your bandmates will have a fit and half the time you'll be wondering why the hell you're in Cincinnati or Austin or North Dakota or Mongolia or wherever your melodious little finger-plucking heinie takes you. There will be boondoggles and discombobulated days, freaked-out nights and metaphorical flat tires.

But it will be soul-smashingly beautiful, Solo. It will open up your life.

Yours,
Sugar

THE BLACK ARC OF IT

Dear Sugar,

I'm a thirty-eight-year-old guy and engaged to be married. My fiancée is thirty-five. I don't need romantic advice. I'm writing to you about my fiancée's mother, who passed away from cancer several years before I met her, when my fiancée was twenty-three.

She and her mother were close. Her death was an awful blow to my fiancée at the time and it still hurts her deeply. It's not like she can't get out of bed or is struggling with depression. She has a great life. One of her friends calls her "joy on wheels" and that's accurate, but I know it isn't the whole story. Her mom's death is always lurking. It comes up on a regular basis. When she cries or talks about how much she misses her mom, I'm supportive, but I usually feel insufficient. I don't know what to say beyond lame things like "I'm sorry" and "I can imagine how you'd feel" (though I can't because my mom is still alive). She never had much of a relationship with her dad, who left the picture a long time ago, and she and her sister aren't very close, so I can't rely on someone in her family to be there for her. Sometimes I try to cheer her up or try to get her to forget about "the heavy stuff," but that usually backfires and only makes her feel worse.

I don't know how to handle this, Sugar. I feel lame in the face of her grief. I know you lost your mother too. What can you tell me? I want to be a better partner when it comes to handling grief.

Signed,
Bewildered

Dear Bewildered,

Several months after my mother died I found a glass jar of stones tucked in the far reaches of her bedroom closet. I was moving her things out of the house I'd thought of as home, but that no longer was. It was a devastating process—more brutal in its ruthless clarity than anything I've ever experienced or hope to again—but when I had that jar of rocks in my hands I felt a kind of elation I cannot describe in any other way except to say that in the cold clunk of its weight I felt ever so fleetingly as if I were holding my mother.

That jar of stones wasn't just any jar of stones. They were rocks my brother and sister and I had given to our mom. Stones we'd found as kids on beaches and trails and the grassy patches on the edges of parking lots and pressed into her hands, our mother's palms the receptacle for every last thing we thought worth saving.

I sat down on the bedroom floor and dumped them out, running my fingers over them as if they were the most sacred things on the earth. Most were smooth and black and smaller than a potato chip. *Worry stones* my mother had called them, the sort so pleasing against the palm she claimed they had the power to soothe the mind if you rubbed them right.

What do you do with the rocks you once gave to your dead mother? Where is their rightful place? To whom do they belong? To what are you obligated? Memory? Practicality?

Reason? Faith? Do you put them back in the jar and take them with you across the wild and unkempt sorrow of your twenties or do you simply carry them outside and dump them in the yard?

I couldn't know. Knowing was so far away. I could only touch the rocks, hoping to find my mother in them.

Not long before my mother died, a friend told me a story about a woman she knew, a resident at the group home for those with brain injuries where my friend worked. Several years before, the woman had been attacked as she walked home from a party. Her head hit the sidewalk so hard in the course of the assault that she'd never be the same again. She was incapable of living alone, incapable of so very much, and yet she remembered just enough of her former life as a painter and teacher that she was miserable in the group home and she desperately longed to return to her own house. She refused to accept the explanations given to her as to why she couldn't. She had come to fervently believe that in order to be released she had only to recite the correct combination of numbers to her captors, her caretakers.

93480219072, she'd say as they fed her and bathed her and helped her get ready for bed. *6552091783. 4106847508. 05298562347.* And on and on in a merciless spiral. But no matter what she said, she would never crack the code. There was no code. There was only the new fact of her life, changed irrevocably.

In the months after my mother died, I thought of this woman an inordinate amount and not only because I was distressed by her suffering. I thought of her because I understood her monumental desire and her groundless faith: I believed that I could crack a code too. That my own irrevocably changed life could be redeemed if only I could find the right combination of things. That in those objects my mother would be given back to me in some indefinable and figurative way that would make it okay for me to live the rest of my life without her.

And so I searched.

I didn't find it in the half-empty container of peppermint Tic Tacs that had been in the glove compartment of my mother's car on the day she died or in the fringed moccasins that still stank precisely of my mother's size six feet a whole year later. I didn't find it in her unfashionably large reading glasses or the gray porcelain horse that had sat on the shelf near her bed. I didn't find it in her pen from the bank with the real hundred-dollar bill shredded up inside or in the butter dish with the white marble ball in its top or in any one of the shirts she'd sewn for herself or for me.

And I didn't find it in those stones either, in spite of my hopes on that sad day. It wasn't anywhere, in anything, and it never would be.

"It will never be okay," a friend who lost her mom in her teens said to me a couple years ago. "It will never be okay that our mothers are dead."

At the time she said this to me she wasn't yet really my friend. We'd chatted passingly at parties, but this was the first time we were alone together. She was fiftysomething and I was forty. Our moms had been dead for ages. We were both writers with kids of our own now. We had good relationships and fulfilling careers. And yet the unadorned truth of what she'd said—*it will never be okay*—entirely unzipped me.

It will never be okay, and yet there we were, the two of us more than okay, both of us happier and luckier than anyone has a right to be. You could describe either one of us as "joy on

wheels," though there isn't one good thing that has happened
to either of us that we haven't experienced through the lens of
our grief. I'm not talking about weeping and wailing every day
(though sometimes we both did that). I'm talking about what
goes on inside, the words unspoken, the shaky quake at the
body's core. There was no mother at our college graduations.
There was no mother at our weddings. There was no mother
when we sold our first books. There was no mother when our
children were born. There was no mother, ever, at any turn for
either one of us in our entire adult lives and there never will be.

The same is true for your fiancée, Bewildered. She is your
joy on wheels whose every experience is informed and altered
by the fact that she lost the most essential, elemental, primal,
and central person in her life too soon. I know this without
knowing her. It will never be okay that she lost her mother.
And the kindest, most loving thing you can do for her is to bear
witness to that, to muster the strength, courage, and humility
it takes to accept the enormous reality of its *not okayness* and
be okay with it the same way she has to be. Get comfortable
being the man who says *Oh honey, I'm so sorry for your loss*
over and over again.

That's what the people who've consoled me the most deeply
in my sorrow have done. They've spoken those words or something like them every time I needed to hear it; they've plainly
acknowledged what is invisible to them, but so very real to
me. I know saying those clichéd and ordinary things makes
you feel squirmy and lame. I feel that way too when I say such
things to others who have lost someone they loved. We all do.
It feels lame because we like to think we can solve things. It
feels insufficient because there is nothing we can actually do
to change what's horribly true.

But compassion isn't about solutions. It's about giving all the love that you've got.

So give it. It's clear that you've done it already. Your kind letter is proof. But I encourage you to stop being bewildered. Have the guts to feel lame. Say that you're sorry for your lover's loss about three thousand times over the coming years. Ask about her mother sometimes without her prompting. Console her before she asks to be consoled. Honor her mother on your wedding day and in other ways as occasions arise. Your mother-in-law is dead, but she lives like a shadow mother in the woman you love. Make a place for her in your life too.

That's what Mr. Sugar has done for me. That's what some of my friends and even acquaintances have done. It doesn't make it okay, but it makes it better.

It's been more than twenty years since my mother died. So long I squint every time the thought comes to me. So long that I've finally convinced myself there isn't a code to crack. The search is over. The stones I once gave my mother have scattered, replaced by the stones my children give to me. I keep the best ones in my pockets. Sometimes there is one so perfect I carry it around for weeks, my hand finding it and finding it, soothing itself along the black arc of it.

Yours,
Sugar

HELL IS OTHER PEOPLE'S
BOYFRIENDS

Dear Sugar,

I'm a freshman in high school, and everyone knows how high school is—drama, drama, drama. And my best friend (let's say her name is Jill) is at the center of it.

See, Jill's dating this guy (let's call him Jack) who has a girlfriend who goes to another school. As Jill's best friend, I already don't like Jack. He doesn't want to break up with the girlfriend for Jill (he and his girlfriend have been together over a year), but, in my opinion, this situation is unacceptable. Jack seems like a nice guy, but there's that underlying scumbag quality that I just can't get past. It's obvious that Jack really likes Jill, but he just won't drop the girlfriend—or Jill.

I don't know which way I want it to go. On the one hand, I want Jill to be happy, so I want Jack to break up with the girlfriend. On the other hand, I want to punch Jack in the face and I think he would do the exact same thing to Jill that he's doing to his girlfriend. I've been thinking about having a "talk" with Jack, but I'm not sure if that would help the situation. Sugar: How do I make at least one of them see the light and realize that what they're doing is wrong?

Worried Friend

Dear Worried Friend,

Drama, drama, drama indeed! Oh, but this one's easy, sweet pea. And hard. But best to learn it now, since, as a freshman in high school, you're only at the very beginning of these sorts of hijinks. Jean-Paul Sartre famously said that "hell is other people," which is true enough, but truer still is *hell is other people's boyfriends* (or girlfriends, as the case may be).

I've been witness to those I care about cheating and being cheated on, lying and being lied to, emotionally abusing and being emotionally abused by their lovers. I've consoled and counseled. I've listened to long and tedious tales of spectacularly disastrous romantic woe that I predicted from the start because that same friend chose the same wrong person *yet a-fucking-gain*. But the sad news is that this is the way of the world, darling, and there isn't a ding dang damn thing you can do about it.

Have you read Shakespeare's *Romeo and Juliet* yet? People *die* because they want who they want. They do all kinds of crazy, stupid, sweet, tender, amazing, self-destructive things. You aren't going to make anyone "see the light and realize that what they're doing is wrong." You just aren't.

And you shouldn't even try. What's happening between Jack and Jill is between Jack and Jill. Jill knows that Jack is involved with someone else. She chooses to be in a romantic relationship with him anyway. Jack chooses to deceive a young woman he presumably cares for and string along another. These are not pretty things, but they are true things.

Don't get me wrong: I sympathize. I know I sound calm and collected, but the truth is I rather regularly come at least internally unglued over some buffoon or scoundrel that one or the other of my intimates has deemed to "love" (see: *hell is other people's boyfriends*). It's dreadful to watch a friend make choices that you fear will cause her pain. But this is where boundaries come in, my dear Worried Friend.

Do you know what boundaries are?

The best, sanest people on the planet do, and since I have no doubt that you will become one of those sorts of people, you might as well learn about them sooner rather than later. This little pickle with Jack and Jill and the young woman at the other school has given you just that opportunity. It's clear to me that the emotions that have arisen in your concern for Jill and your subsequent dislike of Jack have blurred your ability to understand appropriate boundaries. Your impulse to swoop in and set these lovebirds straight tells me that you're overestimating your power and influence, and you're also disrespecting Jill's right to romantic self-determination—which she absolutely has, no matter how maddening her decisions may be to you.

This isn't to say you should remain silent. Another thing that the best, sanest people on the planet do is they have the guts to tell the truth. You should tell Jill what you told me—that you want her to be happy, but because Jack is a two-timing tomcat you fear he will someday treat her the way he is treating his other, "real" girlfriend. Listen to what she says with an open heart and a critical mind. Love her even if she doesn't do what you hope she does once you point out the fact that her paramour is a scumbag. Wish her the best without getting yourself emotionally tangled up in a situation that has nothing to do with you. (Remember those boundaries? Her life is not yours. Yours is not hers. Et cetera.)

And then, Worried Friend, just let whatever happens between Jack and Jill happen. Laugh if they end up proving you wrong. Be there for Jill if you got it right. And in the meanwhile, cultivate an understanding of a bunch of the other things that the best, sanest people on the planet know: that life is long, that people both change and remain the same, that every last one of us will need to fuck up and be forgiven, that we're all just walking and walking and walking and trying to find our way, that all roads lead eventually to the mountaintop.

Yours,
Sugar

THWACK, THWACK, THWACK

Dear Sugar,

Two days ago my boss let me out of my shift early. I tried call-ing my boyfriend on the phone but he didn't answer. When I got home and opened the door to our apartment, I found him stand-ing in front of our full-length mirror in my panties. He slammed the door shut and locked it before I registered what I saw.

I was surprised, sure, but I was more surprised that when he opened the door back up, fully dressed (in his own clothes), he acted as though it never happened. We've always had an open and fun relationship, both sexually and emotionally, so I was thrown by this secretive behavior. I've always showed willingness and interest in experimentation. I can't understand why he'd keep this from me. Should I say something to him or, better yet, do something to show that I'm not turned off? Or do I continue to follow his lead and say nothing at all?

Yours,
Sharing Panties, but Not Fantasies

Dear SPBNF,

The first time Mr. Sugar spanked me we'd been lovers for a week. By then we'd fucked so hard, so often, so enthrallingly and excellently and shatteringly that the heat of what lived between us practically scorched the paint off the walls. I was jammed up against the bathroom sink and he was jammed up against me, both of us facing the mirror. I saw how his expression went serious and studied and a little bit hard the moment before that first *thwack*.

"You like that, baby?" he whispered into my hair, and I made a little moan of assent.

Thwack, thwack, thwack.

I didn't actually like it all that much, baby. But neither was I opposed to it. He was such a stellar man, such a stunningly adept lover, so unlike anyone I'd ever met and so profoundly much like the best, most secret parts of me that I was willing to put up with a mildly battered bum if that's what got him off. The thought of him being aroused by spanking me was more than enough to convince me to play along that first time, as we worked our way hotly down the sink's white porcelain pedestal to the dank underworld beneath, where we finally went still on the cream-colored vinyl floor among the grimy silver pipes, wondering exactly how we got there, so exquisitely spent that it didn't matter.

"Did you know your sink was made in Argentina?" I asked when I was able to speak.

"Argentina?" he replied.

By way of answer, I reached up and ran my finger over the tiny sticker on the bottom of his sink that said *Made in Argentina.*

"That was fun," he said. "Wasn't it?"

"It was," I said. "*Really* fun."

Thwack, thwack, thwack, we went, all through the next month. ("You like that, baby, don't you?"/"Yeah.") *Thwack.*

After a while, in spite of everything, I grew the slightest bit annoyed. His timing often threw me off my own little pleasure ride. His hand occasionally landed painfully on my tailbone instead of the fleshy bottom of my rump. "Can you please hit me lower?" I once snapped so sharply in the middle of the act that I ruined the mood and we had to stop.

"What turns you on about spanking me?" I finally asked him.

"It's sexy," he said with a nonchalant air.

"But what's sexy about it to you?" I pressed.

"That it turns you on so much," he answered.

"That it turns *me* on so much?" I replied.

"Yeah," he said, and his eyes met mine.

It didn't take anything more than that. The way our eyes locked, we both understood in a flash that we'd been acting out our own pornographic "The Gift of the Magi"—each of us making a sacrifice that nullified the gift of the other. I no more wanted to be spanked than I wanted to fuck a kangaroo. And vice versa. We were doing it because we thought that's what the other one wanted to do.

After we stopped laughing, we traced it back—how we'd come to this misunderstanding. Turns out, I'd made a comment on something like day three of our relationship that had to do with sex and control and submission and domination, tenderness and surrender and the social construct of gender and desire and incest and transgression and masculinity and power and a teenage fantasy I'd had that involved the Super Bowl and a bunch of men in business suits, and he took it to mean that I wanted to be punished like a naughty girl in a nunnery so he spanked the motherloving breath out of me for a month.

Isn't that the sweetest thing you ever *heard*?

"Actually," I said, "spanking doesn't do a thing for me."

"What *does*?" he asked.

And that is where we began nearly fifteen years ago. With his question, followed by my answer. With my question, followed by his. It was how we proceeded. Not on the heat so powerful that it might possibly scorch the paint off the walls, but with the sturdier, this-is-scary-but-let's-do-it-anyway nerve that it took to say what was true not just about ourselves, but about our *sexual selves*.

Which sometimes oddly, sometimes thrillingly, sometimes amusingly, sometimes darkly, sometimes depressingly turns out to not be terribly much like the sexual selves we'd choose if we got to choose them.

There is no question that your lover is embarrassed about the fact that he likes to wear women's panties. Who wouldn't be? What man would ask for such a thing? This isn't to say he can't cozy up to the idea—and I sincerely hope for his own sake that he will. But it's clear he isn't there yet. He's ashamed of it. Very likely he *loathes* it, and yet there it is and he can't deny it and so one day when he's got the place to himself he caves in and strips himself down and dresses himself up and without warning you appear—*you! His emotionally and experimentally open lover!*—and he slams the door in your face and pretends it never happened.

You know why? Because no matter how experimental he is, his life isn't an experiment. His life is like your life and my life and all the lives of all the people who are reading these words right now. It's a roiling stew of fear and need and desire and love and the hunger to be loved. And mostly, it's the latter.

You walked in on him at what he perceives as his most

unlovable moment. The pervert in the girly underpants. You saw his secret self before he told you his secret and that humiliates him beyond words.

There is no going back. You can't unwalk in on him. You have to address what you saw, but I don't think it's a good idea for you to "do something" to demonstrate that you're not turned off. You need to talk to him, honey bun. It's going to be scary and awkward, but you can do it. When I have something to say that's particularly hard to say, I often write it down first. If what happened to you happened to me, I'd write: "I want to talk to you about that day I came home from work early. I'm nervous about having this conversation, but I care about you, and our relationship is important enough to me that I'm willing to risk feeling uncomfortable. First and foremost, I want you to know that I don't judge you for what I saw—in fact, I'm intrigued. When I opened the door and saw you standing there in my underwear I was surprised because I thought you'd been open with me about your sexuality and desires, but I was far more surprised that you shut the door and didn't discuss it with me later. It's been bothering me because I want you to trust that you can be honest with me and also because I want to be intimate with you and I don't think we can do so with this silence about what happened that day between us. Will you talk to me about it?"

If he says no, your relationship is dead, though you may continue to fake it for a while.

If he says yes, that is the place from which you will proceed.

It's a real place, an underworld place, a place where we are all spent and crouched among the pipes, fingering the foreign and covert origins of our most primal desires. While you're down there with your guy, I suggest you share some things of your own. Give him a peek at whatever would make you slam the door shut if he walked in and caught you in front of the mirror.

That *Made in Argentina* sticker isn't under the bathroom sink anymore. We don't even live in the house with that bathroom sink. Before we moved out—years after we first became lovers—Mr. Sugar meticulously peeled the sticker off and with it he made me a card.

Made in Argentina it says on the front. Inside he wrote, "But it feels just like home."

Yours,
Sugar

THE WOMAN HANGING ON
THE END OF THE LINE

Dear Sugar,

I need your help with forgiveness. I am carrying a fierce anger in my body every day, and I can't seem to find my way out of it. Last year, I discovered that my husband and a young woman I hired were having a relationship. This woman who I'd invited into my life, who I'd helped with her career, who I'd invited into my family, responded by meeting secretly with my husband and writing him histrionic love letters pressuring him to leave me.

My whole view of the world has gone dim. People are capable of the most astonishing and selfish acts. I used to focus on pursuing real joy and delight in my life, and sharing that joy, too. But now it feels like that light has gone out forever. This woman has caused damage in my family that I never imagined possible. I know it harms me to say so, but I really, really hate her.

Recently I discovered that she is STILL writing my husband letters, some six months after he broke it off. I have a white ball of rage about it, a monster in my chest. I imagine terrible fates befalling her, and that consumes me every day. How do I find my way back to compassion and the joyful life I once had? Can I find even a little shred of peace?

Mourning and Raging

Dear Mourning and Raging,

How painful. I'm sorry this happened to you. There are few things more devastating than a betrayal such as the sort you describe. It's no wonder you have a mega-hot white monster ball raging inside of you. It's a reasonable response to a hurtful situation. And yet, as you know, you'll only destroy yourself if you continue to allow your rage to consume you. So let's talk about how you might find some peace.

Your letter implies that you and your husband have stayed together through this turmoil. You didn't ask for marital advice, so I'll refrain from giving it, but I'd be remiss if I didn't say that I think a huge chunk of your other-woman fury will be diffused once you and your husband repair the damage his affair has caused. What strikes me most about your letter is how little you say about him. Your rage appears to be directed solely toward the woman with whom he had an affair. You write that she has "caused damage in my family that I never imagined possible," but of course she couldn't have caused damage if your husband hadn't let her. They both violated your trust, but your husband committed the graver offense. He took a vow. She only took a job.

I don't point this out in order to dismiss her transgression, but rather to call your attention to a dynamic that's worth examining. To have a covert love affair with one member of the couple who employs you is bad form indeed, but why is your rage focused on her rather than him? Is it possible that you've subconsciously redirected your anger to the safer party, since hating her doesn't require you to dismantle your life, as hating him would? How did you express your anger toward your husband when you learned of the affair? How did you forgive him? Did your rage toward the other woman increase or decrease after you forgave your husband? Why? What does forgiveness in this context mean to you?

I encourage you to spend some time reflecting on these questions. Answering them may restore at least some sense of balance regarding your rage, and it will also require you to contemplate core issues that must be resolved before you'll be able to find "the joyful life" again. When bad things happen, often the only way back to wholeness is to take it all apart. You have the strength to do that, no matter how marriage-mucking and soul-shaking that will be. A terrible thing happened to you, but you mustn't let it define your life. Couples survive all kinds of shit, including shit like this. And individuals survive too, even when their marriages don't. There is a way forward.

You asked for help with forgiveness, but I don't think that's what you need to reach for just yet. You know how alcoholics who go to AA are always using that phrase "one day at a time"? They say that because to say "I will never drink again" is just too damn much. It's big and hard and bound to fail. This is how forgiveness feels for you at this moment, no doubt. It's the reason you can't do it. I suggest you forget about forgiveness for now and strive for acceptance instead.

Accept that the man you love was unfaithful to you. Accept that a woman you once held in regard treated you with disrespect. Accept that their actions hurt you deeply. Accept that this experience taught you something you didn't want to know. Accept that sorrow and strife are part of even a joyful life. Accept that it's going to take a long time for you to get that monster out of your chest. Accept that someday what pains you now will surely pain you less.

Just writing that to you makes me feel better, Mourning and Raging. Do you feel the shift? Acceptance has everything to do with simplicity, with sitting in the ordinary place, with bearing witness to the plain facts of our life, with not just starting at the essential, but ending up there. Your life has been profoundly shaken by these recent revelations. It's not your task to immediately forgive those who shook you. Your spoken desire to forgive the woman who betrayed you is in opposition to what you feel. Forgiveness forces an impossible internal face-off between you and a woman you hate.

Acceptance asks only that you embrace what's true.

Strange as it sounds, I don't think you've done that yet. I can hear it in the pitch of your letter. You're so outraged and surprised that this shitty thing happened to you that there's a piece of you that isn't yet convinced it did. You're looking for the explanation, the loophole, the bright twist in the dark tale that reverses its course. Anyone would be. It's the reason I've had to narrate my own stories of injustice about seven thousand times, as if by raging about it once more the story will change and by the end of it I won't still be the woman hanging on the end of the line.

But it won't change, for me or for you or for anyone who has ever been wronged, which is everyone. We are all at some point—and usually at many points over the course of a life—the woman hanging on the end of the line. Allow your acceptance of that to be a transformative experience. You do that by simply looking it square in the face and then moving on. You don't have to move fast or far. You can go just an inch. You can mark your progress breath by breath.

Literally. And it's there that I recommend you begin. Every time you think *I hate that fucking bitch*, I want you to neutralize that thought with a breath. Calm your mind. Breathe in deeply with intention, then breathe out. Do not think *I hate that fucking bitch* while you do it. Give yourself that. Blow that bitch right out of your chest. Then move on to something else.

I have breathed my way through so many people who I felt wronged by; through so many situations I couldn't change. Sometimes while doing this I have breathed in acceptance and breathed out love. Sometimes I've breathed in gratitude and out forgiveness. Sometimes I haven't been able to muster anything beyond the breath itself, my mind forced blank with nothing but the desire to be free of sorrow and rage.

It works. And the reason it works is the salve is being applied directly to the wound. It's not a coincidence that you describe your pain as being lodged in your chest. When you breathe with calm intention you're zapping the white rage monster precisely where it lives. You're cutting off its feeding tube and forcing a new thought into your head—one that nurtures rather than tortures you. It's essentially mental self-discipline. I'm not suggesting one deny negative emotions, but rather that you accept them and move through them by embracing the power we have to keep from wallowing in emotions that don't serve us well.

It's hard work. It's important work. I believe something like forgiveness is on the other side. You will get there, dear woman. Just try.

Yours,
Sugar

NO MYSTERY ABOUT SPERM

Dear Sugar,

I am a woman in my late thirties and still single. I never imagined this would be me at this age. I've had several relationships where I thought I had found "the one," only to have the rug pulled out from under me.

The most devastating of these ended about five years ago, at the age when most of my friends were getting married or having babies. My boyfriend of three years, with whom I lived, was divorced with a child. He abruptly decided to go back to his ex-wife just as we were looking to buy a house. This was after he had spent a fair amount of time in therapy at the beginning of our relationship to reach the conclusion that he was certain he wanted to build a life with me and have children with me. What a fool I was. When he left me, he assured me that it was only for his child, who was struggling, and that I was still his true love and he knew that once she was off to college, he would come back and we'd live happily ever after. She was eight. Apparently I was supposed to wait ten years, getting old while he finished up his other life.

I spent a couple of years wrecked and jaded over that relationship. I pulled myself together as best I could and dated a few people casually. Last year, I met someone I connected with. Unfortunately, he was even more jaded than I, and he didn't want to take a leap of faith with me. We split up a couple of months ago.

So now I find myself watching the end of my fertility looming. I always wanted to experience pregnancy and birth. I'm now considering becoming a single mom. I'm not even sure I know how to go about that, but I'm aware that time is running out, and even though I would prefer to raise a child with a partner, I don't have much faith in that happening anymore. Even if I met someone now, he'd pretty much have to want to have a baby right away, and that's not likely. Yet, I'm struggling with letting go of the idea that I will find love and have a baby with a partner. I'm paralyzed. It's hard to let that dream go. If I take this step, I am deciding definitively that I will not get married and have a child like I watched most of my friends do. (Did I mention the burning jealousy every time I see their happy family pictures on Facebook, the photos from the hospital where Mommy smiles with baby on chest, the congratulations I write, accompanied by a feeling like I've been sucker punched?)

How can I move forward and let go of that dream? Should I start calling sperm banks? I just can't believe that this is how my story ends.

Signed,

M

Dear M,

I'm of the opinion that there are some things one should never advise another to do: marry someone in particular, not marry someone in particular, pierce one's clitoris or cock, oil one's body and run around naked at a party wearing a homemade Alice B. Toklas mask, and have a baby.

And yet, I cannot help but say that it seems apparent to me that you should seriously consider having a baby. Not because I want you to, but because you want to.

Oh, the dream. The goddamned man + baby dream. Written by the High Commission on Heterosexual Love and Sexual Reproduction and practiced by couples across the land, the dream's a bitch if you're a maternally inclined straight female and not living it by the age of thirty-seven—a situation of a spermicidally toxic flavor. Of course you want to bring out your six-shooter every time you see another bloated mom hoisting up another pinched-faced spawn on Facebook. You want the dream too!

But, M, you didn't get it. Not yet. Not quite ever, perhaps. That doesn't mean all is lost. This is not "how your story ends." It's simply where it takes a turn you didn't expect.

I don't mean to downplay your sorrow. Your disappointment is justified; your paralysis understandable; your conundrum real. But please remember that the dream you have of finding a long-term romantic partner and having a baby is not just one dream. It's two. The partner dream and the baby dream are so intricately woven that you can be forgiven for thinking they're one. It's lovely if it *is* rolled up into one. It's more than lovely. It's convenient. It's conventional. It's economically advantageous. It's hella good when it's good.

But it isn't what you have. So let's see what you've got.

You have the strong desire to be a mother by biological means coupled with a deep regret that you aren't currently involved with a man with whom to reproduce. The only thing you need to make a biological baby of your own is sperm and luck. Getting sperm does not mean that you are "deciding definitively" that you "will not get married and have a child."

Life is long, darling. Who knows what's going to happen? You could meet your Big Love tomorrow. You could meet him in ten years. You could have a baby on your own now and another with him when you're forty-two. You don't know. The question about who you will love and when you will love him is out of your hands. It's a mystery that you can't solve.

There is, however, no mystery about sperm. There are vials to be had at banks for purchase. There are possibly friends or acquaintances willing to give you some for free. The time to answer your question about whether you want to try to conceive a baby on your own is upon you. The window of your reproductive viability will soon close. I agree with you that you've reached the point that it's reasonable to assume that your choice is between having a baby without a partner or having no biological baby at all. Which scenario makes you sadder? Which are you going to be happy you did when you're fifty? It's time to do the emotional and practical work you need to do so you can make a decision. The website of the organization Single Mothers by Choice is an excellent place to start.

I can't tell you what to do. No one can. But as the mother of two children, I can tell you what most moms will: that mothering is absurdly hard and profoundly sweet. Like the best thing you ever did. Like if you think you want to have a baby, you probably should. I say this in spite of the fact that children are giant endless suck machines. They don't give a whit if you need to sleep or eat or pee or get your work done or go out to a party naked and oiled up in a homemade Alice B. Toklas mask. They take everything. They will bring you to the furthest edge of your personality and abso-fucking-lutely to your knees.

They will also give you everything back. Not just all they

take, but many of the things you lost before they came along as well.

Every mother has a different story, though we tend to group them together. We like to think that partnered moms have it good and single moms have it rough, but the truth is that we're a diverse bunch. Some single mothers have lots of child-free time because their kids are regularly in the custody of their fathers. Some seldom get a break. Some partnered mothers split child-care duties with their spouses in egalitarian ways; others might as well be alone. Some mothers of both varieties have parents, siblings, and friends who play active roles in their children's lives in ways that significantly lighten the load. Others have to pay for every hour another person looks after their kids. Some mothers, single or partnered, can't afford to pay anyone for anything. Some can and do. Others can and won't. Some are aided financially by parents, or trust funds, or inheritances; others are entirely on their own. The reality is that, regardless of the circumstances, most moms are alternately blissed out by their love for their children and utterly overwhelmed by the spectacular amount of sacrifice they require.

What you must answer when you delve into this question about whether to have a baby alone, honey bun, is what the landscape will look like for you. Not what it looks like for "single mothers by choice," but how it will actually play out in your own life. How will you need to restructure or reconsider your life if you become a mother? What resources do you have, what resources will you need, and how will you get them?

Knowing what I know about having babies, three of the four big questions I'd have if I were considering parenting a child without a partner are surprisingly the same questions I asked myself when I—with my partner—pondered having a baby. They were

1. How the hell am I going to pay for this?

2. Who the hell is going to take care of the baby so I can work?

3. Will I ever have sex again?

So let's start with those.

You don't mention financial matters in your letter, but I presume you have to earn a living. Kids cost a fortune, especially if you have to pay someone to take care of them so you can work. My kids are now four and six. Preschool tuition over the past few years has nearly bankrupted Mr. Sugar and me. Literally. When our kids were babies we hired a part-time nanny and juggled child care between us the rest of the time—we both make our living as artists, so neither one of us has what's called a "real job." The nanny cost us $15 an hour. We hired her for twenty hours a week. When the nanny came, my husband and I would go into our shared office in the basement and ignore each other so we could each do our thing (at which point our children would invariably settle down for a long nap, strangely able to discern when we were paying someone else to look after them). Every hour that passed I'd think, "Did I make $15? Did I even make $7.50?"

Often enough, the answer was no. Which is a long way of saying that questions number 1 and number 2 are inextricably bound. More so than the man + baby High Commission on Heterosexual Love and Sexual Reproduction dream. Especially for you, since you'll be the sole breadwinner.

Many partners are great for watching the baby while you work or shower or make phone calls that go better if a small beast is not shrieking in the background. You won't have one—the partner, that is. You'll have only the small shrieking beast. What will you do? Do you have any support in the way of free child care? Do not believe all the sweet friends who say, "Oh, M! Have a baby! I'll totally help you with the baby! I'll be, like, the baby's *auntie!*" Those people have good intentions, but most of them are bons vivants who will not take your baby. Or they might take your baby once when it's spring and they get the urge to go to the zoo because they want to see the elephants. You need someone to take your baby every Monday and Wednesday and Friday from nine to three. One thing I've learned since becoming a mother is that most adults aren't willing to spend much time with other people's children unless there is some direct benefit to them—namely, money or the promise that you will someday return the favor and take their children.

There are, of course, exceptions. Some grandparents long to play a significant part in the lives of their grandchildren. Do you have an essentially sane, remotely physically fit, non-daytime-drinking, baby-loving parent or two who lives nearby? A sibling or friend who genuinely wants to commit to pitching in? If you don't have that sort of support, what will you do for child care and how will you structure it and how will you pay for it?

Next, we come to the question of whether your post-child life will be a dreary, sexless hell. There will probably not be too much action for a while. But worry not: this has little to do with your partner-less status. Mr. Sugar and I joke that the only reason we opted to have our second child was so we'd have sex at least one more time before we died. You'll be exhausted, hormonally altered, and perhaps vaginally or abdominally maimed by the baby, and thus not thinking about sex for a while, but eventually you'll come around and be interested in dating again. Some men won't be interested in dating you because you have a baby. Others will be fine with the baby and you'll date them and maybe one of them will turn out to be "the one."

Regardless of what happens with the men, you'll have a baby. An amazing little being who will blow your mind and expand your heart and make you think things you never thought and remember things you believed you forgot and heal things you imagined would never heal and forgive people you've begrudged for too long and understand things you didn't understand before you fell madly in love with a tiny tyrant who doesn't give a damn whether you need to pee. You will sing again if you stopped singing. You will dance again if you stopped dancing. You will crawl around on the floor and play chase and tickle and peek-a-boo. You'll make towers of teetering blocks and snakes and rabbits with clay.

It's an altogether cool thing.

And it will be lonely too, doing all that without a partner. How lonely, I can't say. You will hold your baby and cry sometimes in frustration, in rage, in despair, in exhaustion and inexplicable sorrow. You will watch your baby with joy and laugh at the wonder so pure and the beauty so unconcealed that it will make you ache. These are the times when it's really nice to have a partner, M. What will you do? How will you fill the place where the man you've been holding out for would have been?

That is your hard question for me—the one I didn't ask

myself when I decided to get pregnant and become a mother, though of course it was naïve for me to think I didn't have to. Not a single one of us knows what the future holds. The unexpected happens even when we've got everything mapped out. My friend A lost her husband in a car crash four days before her daughter was born. My friend B's husband died of cancer when their son wasn't yet two. My friend C's husband left her for another woman when their baby was six weeks old. My friend D's partner decided he wasn't all that into being a dad a few months after his child was born, moved across the country, and sees her once a year. I could go on. I could work my way all the way down the alphabet. Even if you get the dream, you don't know if it will stay true.

It works in reverse too. What you fear might not come to pass. You might decide to have your baby and find true love in the midst of that. You might search your soul and realize that you don't want a baby after all, not if it means going it without a man.

What's important is that you make the leap. Jump high and hard with intention and heart. Pay no mind to the vision the commission made up. It's up to you to make your life. Take what you have and stack it up like a tower of teetering blocks. Build your dream around that.

Yours,
Sugar

THE MAD SEX CONFESSOR

Dear Sugar,

My elderly father is coming to live with me in a few months. My mother passed away about three years ago. My father is going to be living with all of the rest of my siblings as well—he'll move from one place to the next every four or five months. He enjoys traveling, so we thought moving him around would make him feel more active and independent. I hesitate to say that I am my father's favorite since I do not particularly relish the idea of that, nor has he ever been a demonstrative or involved parent, but I will say that he depends on me slightly more than he depends on my other brothers and sisters. Recently that has become an emotional dependence as well.

Sugar, my father has begun confessing to me. At first these weird confessions were small and insignificant, and I chalked them up to the fact that he was feeling his own mortality and therefore taking stock of his life. But more recently his confessions have turned into a crimes and misdemeanors festival that's not fun for me at all. He's been telling me about the many women he cheated on my mother with, about how he isn't 100 percent certain that he hasn't fathered other children, and tawdry sexual details that spawn visuals I do not want to have. He told me that

*when my mom got pregnant with me she didn't want a fifth child
so she wanted to abort me, but feared someone might find out so
she canceled the appointment, but cut him off sex, which led to
his first affair.*

This is not information I ever needed to know.

*I am a forgiving person, Sugar, but here is the kicker: he
ISN'T sorry. I mean, I might be able to take all this new hid-
eous information—like he was fucking the housekeeper in the
eighties, for example—if he showed a drop of remorse, but he has
none. He claims that he's telling me and not my siblings because
he knew I "won't judge" him. What the hell gave him that idea?!*

*As warped as it is, I recognize it as his attempt to bond with
me. That being said, I would like him to shut up now. I suddenly
don't know how I feel about him living with me and spouting off
this bullshit every day. I am not sure what to do. I feel that it's
my responsibility to care for him, but am I allowed to establish
boundaries this late in the game?*

Trustee

Dear Trustee,

Yes, you are allowed to establish boundaries this late in the
game. In fact, this would be a good idea even if your father
hadn't become an unfortunate font of naughty narratives. An
elderly parent moving in with an adult·child is a major life
transition for both the parties (and in some cases, the adult
child's spouse and children as well). Even in the best of circumstances, it's wise to map out a family plan in which ground
rules and expectations are stated, concerns are discussed,
and a plan for conflict resolution is agreed upon. When two

households merge, roles of authority and responsibility must be rearranged—sometimes subtly, sometimes drastically—and they must be rearranged in a way that often reverses the long-established parent-child order. This is unquestionably a complicated thing.

That your father has chosen to further complicate it by becoming the mad sex confessor is no fun at all. I encourage you to simplify it immediately by telling him you do not want to hear another word about his sex life. Be clear. Be direct. Be unwavering. If he doesn't respect your wishes, cut him off at the quick. If he begins to speak of such things, tell him to stop. If he won't stop, walk out of the room or pull over to the side of the road or do whatever it takes to remove yourself from his company. If you're firm and consistent, he'll eventually get the point.

Once you've established this boundary, I encourage you to explore the underlying issues that may be compelling your father to speak to you so inappropriately. There's a chance that his confessions are connected to a medical condition. Some diseases of the brain cause personality changes. If you think there's even a chance this could be the case, and especially if you observe other changes in your father, I suggest you consult with his doctor.

A more likely scenario is what you suppose: these confessions are your father's warped way of bonding with you. Perhaps the best way to get him to stop telling you what you don't want to hear is to ask him about what you're willing to listen to. Maybe he simply needs to finally open up about his life to someone he loves. Why not try to engage him on a deeper level? Ask him to share with you other stories of his life—the ones that he's never been brave enough to tell. Surely he's got some that don't involve humping the housekeeper while your mother went to the grocery store.

For this, for both of you, I'll hope.

Yours,
Sugar

THE FUTURE HAS AN ANCIENT HEART

Dear Sugar,

I teach creative writing at the University of Alabama, where the majority of my students are seniors graduating soon. Most of them are English and creative writing majors/minors who are feeling a great deal of dread and anxiety about their expulsion from academia and their entry into "the real world." Many of their friends in other disciplines have already lined up postgraduate jobs, and many of my students are tired of the "being an English major prepares you for law school" comments being made by friends and family alike, who are pressuring them toward a career in law despite having little or no interest in it. I've been reading your columns to my students in an attempt to pep them up and let them know that everything is going to be all right.

Our school has decided to forgo a graduation speaker for the last five years or so, and even when we did have a graduation speaker, often they were leaders in business or former athletes, and so their message was lost on the ears of the majority of twenty-one- and twenty-two-year-olds. So, Sugar, I am asking you to deliver a graduation speech for our little class of writers. While we might have difficulty obtaining you an honorary PhD, believe me when I say that among us are some extremely talented writers, bakers, musicians, editors, designers, and video game players who will gladly write you a lyric essay, bake you a pie, write you a song, and perform countless other acts of kindness in exchange for your advice.

Fondly,
Cupcake & Team 408

Dear Cupcake & Team 408,

There's a line by the Italian writer Carlo Levi that I think is apt here: "The future has an ancient heart." I love it because it expresses with such grace and economy what is certainly true—that who we become is born of who we most primitively are; that we both know and cannot possibly know what it is we've yet to make manifest in our lives. I think it's a useful sentiment for you to reflect upon now, sweet peas, at this moment when the future likely feels the opposite of ancient, when instead it feels like a Lamborghini that's pulled up to the curb while every voice around demands you get in and drive.

I'm here to tell you it's okay to travel by foot. In fact, I recommend it. There is so much ahead that's worth seeing, so much behind you can't identify at top speed. Your teacher is correct: You're going to be all right. And you're going to be all right not because you majored in English or didn't and not because you plan to apply to law school or don't, but because all right is almost always where we eventually land, even if we fuck up entirely along the way.

I know. I fucked up some things. I was an English major too. As it happens, I lied for six years about having an English degree, though I didn't exactly mean to lie. I had gone to college and participated in a graduation ceremony. I'd walked across the stage and collected a paper baton. On that paper it said a bachelor's degree would be mine once I finished one final class. It seemed like such an easy thing to do, but it wasn't. And so I didn't do it and the years slipped past, each one making it seem more unlikely that I'd ever get my degree. I'd done all the coursework except that one class. I'd gotten good grades. To claim that I had an English degree was truer than not, I told myself. But that didn't make it true.

You have to do what you have to do. There is absolutely nothing wrong with law school, but don't go unless you want to be a lawyer. You can't take a class if taking a class feels like it's going to kill you. Faking it never works. If you don't believe me, read Richard Wright. Read Charlotte Brontë. Read Joy Harjo. Read Toni Morrison. Read William Trevor. Read the entire Western canon.

Or just close your eyes and remember everything you already know. Let whatever mysterious starlight that guided you this far guide you onward into whatever crazy beauty awaits. Trust that all you learned during your college years was worth learning, no matter what answer you have or do not have about what use it is. Know that all those stories, poems, plays, and novels are a part of you now and that they are bigger than you and they will always be.

I was a waitress during most of the years that I didn't have my English degree. My mother had been a waitress for many of the years that she was raising my siblings and me. She loved to read. She always wanted to go to college. One time she took a night class when I was very young and my father became enraged with her and cut her textbook into pieces with a pair of scissors. She dropped the class. I think it was biology.

You don't have to get a job that makes others feel comfortable about what they perceive as your success. You don't have to explain what you plan to do with your life. You don't have to justify your education by demonstrating its financial rewards. You don't have to maintain an impeccable credit score. Anyone who expects you to do any of those things has no sense of history or economics or science or the arts.

You have to pay your own electric bill. You have to be kind. You have to give it all you got. You have to find people who love you truly and love them back with the same truth. But that's all.

I got married when I was in college. I got divorced during the years that I was lying about having an English degree. When I met the man to whom I am now married, he said, "You know, I really think you should finish your degree, not because I want you to, but because I can tell that you want to." I thought he was sort of being an asshole. We didn't bring up the subject again for a year.

I understand what you're afraid of. I understand what your parents fear. There are practical concerns. One needs money to live. And then there is a deep longing to feel legitimate in the world, to feel that others hold us in regard. I felt intermittently ashamed during my years as a waitress. In my family, I was supposed to be the one who "made it." At times it seemed instead I had squandered my education and dishonored my dead mother by becoming a waitress like her. Sometimes I would think of this as I went from table to table with my tray, and I'd have to think of something else so I wouldn't cry.

Years after I no longer worked at the last restaurant where I waited tables, my first novel was published. The man who'd been my manager at the restaurant read about me in the newspaper and came to my reading. He'd often been rude and snappish with me and I'd despised him on occasion, but I was touched to see him in the bookstore that night. "All those years ago, who would've guessed we'd be here celebrating the publication of your novel?" he asked when we embraced.

"I would have," I replied.

And it was true. I always would have guessed it, even all the time that I feared it would never happen. Being there that night was the meaning of my life. Getting there had been my every intention. When I say you don't have to explain what you're going to do with your life, I'm not suggesting you lounge around whining about how difficult it is. I'm suggesting you apply yourself in directions for which we have no accurate measurement. I'm talking about work. And love.

It's really condescending to tell you how young you are. It's even inaccurate. Some of you who are graduating from college are not young. Some of you are older than me. But to those of you new college graduates who are indeed young, the old new college graduates will back me up on this: you are so goddamned young. Which means about eight of the ten things you have decided about yourself will over time prove to be false.

The other two things will prove to be so true that you'll look back in twenty years and howl.

My mother was young too, but not like those of you who are so goddamned young. She was forty when she finally went to college. She spent the last years of her life as a college student, though she didn't know they were her last years. She thought she was at the beginning of the next era of her life. She died a couple of months before we were both supposed to graduate from different schools. At her memorial service, my mother's favorite professor stood up and granted her an honorary PhD.

The most terrible and beautiful and interesting things

happen in a life. For some of you, those things have already happened. Whatever happens to you belongs to you. Make it yours. Feed it to yourself even if it feels impossible to swallow. Let it nurture you, because it will.

I have learned this over and over and over again.

There came a day when I decided to stop lying. I called the college from which I did not have an English degree and asked the woman who answered the phone what I needed to do to get one. She told me I had only to take one class. It could be any class. I chose Latin. I'd never studied Latin, but I wanted to know, at last, where so many of our words come from. I had a romantic idea of what it would be like to study Latin— the Romance languages are, after all, descended from it—but it wasn't romantic. It was a lot of confusion and memorization and attempting to decipher bizarre stories about soldiers marching around ancient lands. In spite of my best efforts, I got a B.

One thing I never forgot from my Latin class is that a language that is descended from another language is called a daughter language.

It was the beginning of the next era of my life, like this is of yours.

Years after I no longer lived in the state where my mother and I went to college, I traveled to that state to give a reading from my first novel. Just as my former boss had done in a different city mere weeks before, the professor who'd granted my mother a PhD at her memorial service read about me in the newspaper and came to the bookstore to hear me read. "All those years ago, who would've guessed we'd be here celebrating the publication of your novel?" she asked when we embraced.

"Not me," I replied. "Not me."

And it was true. I meant it as sincerely as I'd meant that I always would've guessed it when I'd been speaking to my boss. That both things could be true at once—my disbelief as well as my certainty—was the unification of the ancient and the future parts of me. It was everything I intended and yet still I was surprised by what I got.

I hope you will be surprised and knowing at once. I hope you'll always have love. I hope you'll have days of ease and a good sense of humor. I hope one of you really will bake me a pie (banana cream, please). I hope when people ask what you're going to do with your English and/or creative writing degree you'll say: *Continue my bookish examination of the contradictions and complexities of human motivation and desire;* or maybe just: *Carry it with me, as I do everything that matters.*

And then smile very serenely until they say, *Oh.*

Yours,
Sugar

FAUX FRIENDSHIP FOOTSIE

Dear Sugar,

I may be in love with my friend. He may be in love with me. At the very least, we love each other's company. We see each other every day, talk on the phone at least two or three times a day, and miss each other when we have to say goodbye. There's a high degree of sexual tension that quickly manifested in our friendship, which we tried to control by talking honestly to one another about it and discussing the reason it can't come to fruition: he's in a serious monogamous relationship with a kind, beautiful, loving woman that I also consider a friend.

At first we tried to brush off the mutual attraction as natural—we both find each other physically attractive. Whether it's natural or not, there were nights when it seemed unbearable not to touch, so we decided we should spend time apart. But attempting to stay apart only amplified how much we'd come to rely on each other. We'd only get a few hours into the day before one of us called the other. Then we tried to see each other only when his girlfriend was included as well. Horrifyingly, her presence didn't dispel the tension; it just made me feel guiltier. We've never kissed. We've never crossed a physical boundary. But something is happening.

He's not going to leave her, at least not right now, nor would I ask him to. As strongly as I may feel about him, I recognize they do genuinely love each other. We're not going to have an affair, as it would only end badly for everyone. We're probably not going to stop seeing one another. We've tried for the last two months and can't seem to make that happen. We are trying very, very hard to keep things platonic, but it shouldn't be this hard.

If we'd met at a different time, we'd probably be lovers. My friend is brilliant (but never condescending), kind, generous, talented, passionate, interesting, charming, funny, and warm. We spend hours talking. We're never bored. We can't stop smiling around each other. We really like each other. Our friendship means everything to me (and him), but it's not going to survive if we don't find a way to curtail the lust that only seems to grow stronger.

What do I do, Sugar? I love him. I respect and admire his girlfriend, and I want to do right by everyone. More than anything else, I want us to stay friends, so why doesn't that seem to be working?

"The Friend"

Dear "The Friend,"

It doesn't seem to be working because you aren't really friends with this man. You're having a sexually repressed, mildly deceitful romantic relationship with him. You're dry dating, and this particular version of dry dating sucks and will continue to suck until:

    a)   your friend breaks up with his girlfriend so the two of you can explore your feelings for each other without being lying jackasses, or

b) the two of you embrace the fact that we are all lying jackasses sometimes and you have an affair that includes sex, and not just the emotional affair you are so obviously having, so that you can see if this "tension" between you has a life beyond the don't touch/don't tell policy you've so achingly adopted, or

c) you break off your relationship with your friend because you are falling in love with him and he is unavailable.

A is out because you have no control over whether your friend will break up with his girlfriend.

B is out because you've already established (wisely) that you don't want to be a lying jackass (fun as that may be for a while).

But C is all yours, *mi amiga*. And from Sugar's candy-sweet vantage point it is so very crystal clear that it's what you need to do.

C is not fun. At first glance, parting ways with your seriously cool, smoking hot, but oh-so-very-attached wonder boy seems like the worst idea of all. But trust me when I say that it's the only route to get what you believe you want. Which is him. But it's all of him. Not him on the sly. Not him as a "friend" you want to sleep with but can't (and don't and won't).

To get what you want in a romantic relationship you must say what you want. Shall we say it together? *You want your friend to be free to fall in love with you for real if you are really going to fall in love.* This tortured, half-assed, overheated game of faux friendship footsie the two of you are playing simply won't do.

Maybe your decision to cut your friend loose will make it clear to him that he wants to explore what's possible with you and he'll do what needs to be done in his own life so you can. Maybe it will make it clear to him that losing a woman he loves in order to openly explore what's possible with you is too high of a price to pay. Either way, dear Friend, you win.

Yours,
Sugar

THE HUMAN SCALE

Dear Sugar,

I'm writing this from my little couch/bed in the Pediatric Intensive Care Unit at Egelston Children's Hospital in Atlanta. My husband and I just found out that our six-month-old daughter, Emma, has a tumor, and she is having brain surgery tomorrow. I am scared that I will lose her. I'm scared she could be paralyzed or her development will be messed up and she will have a hard life. I'm scared they will find out the tumor is cancerous and she will need chemo. She's only a little baby.

People have poured all their thoughts and prayers into us right now, but to be honest, God is farthest from my mind. I've never been super religious but now I find myself doubting His existence more than ever. If there were a God, why would he let my little girl have to have possibly life-threatening surgery, Sugar? I never in a million years thought that my husband and I would be in this situation.

I want to ask you to pray and all your readers to pray, to a God maybe I'm not sure I even believe in anymore. Pray that my baby will be okay. And that we can walk away from this and forget it even happened. I have written you before about different things, which now seem so stupid and silly. I just want to get through this with my husband and daughter and look back and thank God

that everything is okay. I want to believe in Him and I want to
believe all the prayers being said for us are working.

Abbie

Dear Abbie,

I have been thinking of you and Emma and your husband
nonstop since I read your email. Please know I'm holding you
in my deepest thoughts and wishing the best for Emma.

I would like to publish your letter and my reply, but I want
to be sure you sent it to me with that intent. If you didn't—if
you meant it as a personal email to me, that's fine and I won't
publish it. If you do want me to publish it, I want to make sure
you're okay with including the identifying details—Emma's
name, the name of the hospital, and such. If not, let me know
and either you or I can alter those details.

Sending you love, light, blessings, strength.

Love,
Sugar

Dear Sugar,

Thank you so much for replying. I would love for you to pub-
lish my letter. If you would like, you can also add this part to let
everyone know that the surgery went well. The doctors think the
tumor is benign. They had to leave one small, tiny part because
it was attached to a blood vessel and one wrong move could have
paralyzed her permanently. Emma has recovered so well that
even the doctors seem a bit surprised. We're most likely going
home tomorrow.

At this point I am hoping there is a God and that the power of prayer is what kept my little Emma safe and well. We had people all over the country praying for us. I hope that everyone will continue praying that the tumor will not come back and we can walk away from this. All my life I have been on the fence about God's existence. The hope He does exist and hears our prayers is something I think everyone has in them. To find out my six-month-old daughter had a tumor (cancerous or not) just put me right back to the part of me that says if God existed bad things wouldn't happen.

I want to take her surgery going well and the good news we have received so far as a sign He does exist, but I also don't want to assume such a large thing from what might be a coincidence. Whether He is there or not, or whether or not the prayers really work, I will keep praying for her speedy recovery and I hope all of your readers will join us in praying for Emma and all the children here at Egleston and everywhere else who go through such sad things early in life.

Feel free to post our names and locations. It won't bother me at all. I hope you will still run my letter. I would love to read what you have to say about the existence of God. I can't decide if I should take a leap of faith and believe since Emma is okay and attribute it to God.

> Thank you for thinking of us.
> Abbie

Dear Abbie,

I know everyone reading these words shares my relief that Emma came through her surgery so well. I'm sorry you've had to endure such a frightful experience. I hope that the worst of it is over and that you will be able to "walk away from this," as you put it, and to keep walking—far and fast—into a future that does not contain the words "tumor" and "surgery" and "cancer."

I agonized about whether to publish your letter. Not because it isn't worthy of a reply—your situation is as serious as it gets and your doubts about your faith in God are profound and shared by many. But I couldn't help but wonder who the hell I thought I was in daring to address your question. I wonder that often while writing this column, but I wondered it harder when it came to your letter. I'm not a chaplain. I don't know squat about God. I don't even believe in God. And I believe less in speaking of God in a public forum where I'm very likely to be hammered for my beliefs.

Yet here I am because there I was, finding it impossible to get your letter out of my head.

Nearly two years ago I took my children to the Christmas pageant at the big Unitarian church in our city. The pageant was to be a reenactment of the birth of Jesus. I took my kids as a way to begin to educate them about the non-Santa history of the holiday. Not as religious indoctrination, but as a history lesson.

Who is Jesus? they asked from the backseat of the car as we drove to the show, after I'd explained to them what we were about to see. They were four and nearly six at the time. They'd heard about Jesus in glimmers before, but now they wanted to know everything. I wasn't terribly literate in Jesus—my mother was an ex-Catholic who spurned organized religion in her adult life, so I had no religious schooling as a child—but I knew enough that I was able to cover the basics, from his birth in a manger, to his young adulthood as a proselytizer for compassion, forgiveness, and love, to his crucifixion and beyond, to the religion that was founded on the belief that Jesus, after suffering for our sins, rose from the dead and ascended to heaven.

After I finished with my narration, it was like someone had served my kids two triple-shot Americanos. *Tell me about Jesus!* became a ten-times-a-day demand. They weren't interested in his birth in the barn or his philosophies about how to live or even what he might be up to in heaven. They wanted only to know about his death. In excruciating detail. Over and over again. Until every ugly fact sank into their precious bones. For months I was compelled to repeatedly describe precisely how Jesus was flagellated, humiliated, crowned with thorns, and nailed at the hands and feet to a wooden cross to die an agonizing death. Sometimes I would do this while making my way in a harried fashion up and down the aisles of the hoity-toity organic grocery store where we shop and people would turn and stare at me.

My children were both horrified and enthralled by Jesus' crucifixion. It was the most appalling thing they'd ever heard. They didn't understand the story within its religious context. They perceived only its brutal truth. They did not contemplate Jesus' divinity, but rather his humanity. They had little interest in this business about him rising from the dead. He was not to them a Messiah. He was only a man. One who'd been nailed to a cross alive and endured it a good while.

Did it hurt his feelings when they were so mean to him? my son repeatedly asked. *Where was his mommy?* my daughter wanted to know.

After I told them about Jesus' death, I wondered whether I should have. Mr. Sugar and I had managed to shield them from almost all of the world's cruelty by then, so why, for the love of God (ahem), was I exposing them to this? Yet I also realized they had to know—their fascination with Jesus' agony was proof of that. I'd hit a nerve. I'd revealed a truth they were ready to know. Not about Christianity, but about the human condition: that suffering is part of life.

I know that. You know that. I don't know why we forget it when something truly awful happens to us, but we do. We wonder *Why me?* and *How can this be?* and *What terrible God would do this?* and *The very fact that this has been done to me is proof that there is no God!* We act as if we don't know that awful things happen to all sorts of people every second of every day and the only thing that's changed about the world or the existence or nonexistence of God or the color of the sky is that the awful thing is happening to *us*.

It's no surprise you have such doubt in this moment of crisis, sweet pea. It's perfectly natural that you feel angry and scared and betrayed by a God you want to believe will take mercy on you by protecting those dearest to you. When I learned my mom was going to die of cancer at the age of forty-five, I felt the same way. I didn't even believe in God, but I still felt that he owed me something. I had the gall to think *How dare he?* I couldn't help myself. I'm a selfish brute. I wanted what I wanted and I expected it to be given to me by a God in whom I had no faith. Because mercy had always more or less been granted me, I assumed it always would be.

But it wasn't.

It wasn't granted to my friend whose eighteen-year-old daughter was killed by a drunk driver either. Nor was it granted to my other friend who learned her baby is going to die of a genetic disorder in the not-distant future. Nor was it granted to my former student whose mother was murdered by her father before he killed himself. It was not granted to all those people who were in the wrong place at the wrong time when they came up against the wrong virus or military operation or famine or carcinogenic or genetic mutation or natural disaster or maniac.

Countless people have been devastated for reasons that cannot be explained or justified in spiritual terms. To do as you are doing in asking *If there were a God, why would he let my little girl have to have possibly life-threatening surgery?*— understandable as that question is—creates a false hierarchy of the blessed and the damned. To use our individual good or bad luck as a litmus test to determine whether or not God exists constructs an illogical dichotomy that reduces our capacity for true compassion. It implies a pious quid pro quo that defies history, reality, ethics, and reason. It fails to acknowledge that the other half of rising—the very half that makes rising necessary—is having first been nailed to the cross.

That's where you were the other night when you wrote to me, dear woman. Pinned in place by your suffering. I woke up at 3 a.m. because I could feel you pinned there so acutely that I—a stranger—felt pinned too. So I got up and wrote to you. My email was a paltry little email probably not too different from the zillions of other paltry little emails you received from others, but I know without knowing you that those emails from people who had nothing to give you but their kind words, along with all the prayers people were praying for you, together formed a tiny raft that could just barely hold your weight as you floated through those terrible hours while you awaited your daughter's fate.

If I believed in God, I'd see evidence of his existence in that. In your darkest hour you were held afloat by the human love that was given to you when you most needed it. That would have been true regardless of the outcome of Emma's surgery. It would have been the grace that carried you through even if things had not gone as well as they did, much as we hate to ponder that.

Your question to me is about God, but boiled down to its essentials, it's not so different than most of the questions people ask me to answer. It says: *This failed me* and *I want to do better next time.* My answer will not be so different either: *To do better you're going to have to try.* Perhaps the good that can come from this terrifying experience is a more complex understanding of what God means to you so the next time you need spiritual solace you'll have something sturdier to lean on than the rickety I'll-believe-he-exists-only-if-he-gives-me-what-I-want fence. What you learned as you sat bedside with Emma in the intensive care unit is that your idea of God as a possibly nonexistent spirit man who may or may not hear your prayers and may or may not swoop in to save your ass when the going gets rough is a losing prospect.

So it's up to you to create a better one. A bigger one. Which is really, almost always, something smaller.

What if you allowed your God to exist in the simple words of compassion others offer to you? What if faith is the way it feels to lay your hand on your daughter's sacred body? What if the greatest beauty of the day is the shaft of sunlight through your window? What if the worst thing happened and you rose anyway? What if you trusted in the human scale? What if you listened harder to the story of the man on the cross who found a way to endure his suffering than to the one about the impossible magic of the Messiah? Would you see the miracle in that?

Yours,
Sugar

PART THREE

CARRY THE WATER YOURSELF

If you had to give one piece of advice to people in their twenties, what would it be?

To go to a bookstore and buy ten books of poetry and read them each five times.

Why?

Because the truth is inside.

Anything else?

To be about ten times more magnanimous than you believe yourself capable of being. Your life will be a hundred times better for it. This is good advice for anyone at any age, but particularly for those in their twenties.

Why?

Because in your twenties you're becoming who you're going to be and so you might as well not be an asshole. Also, because it's harder to be magnanimous when you're in your twenties, I think, and so that's why I'd like to remind you of it. You're generally less humble in that decade than you'll ever be and this lack of humility is oddly mixed with insecurity and uncertainty and fear. You will learn a lot about yourself if you stretch in the direction of goodness, of bigness, of kindness, of forgiveness, of emotional bravery. Be a warrior for love.

Do you know who you are?

Yes.

How long did it take you to truly figure out who you are?

Thirty-some years, but I'm still getting used to myself.

BEAUTY AND THE BEAST

Dear Sugar,

I'm an average twenty-six-year-old man, exceptional only in that I'm incredibly ugly. I don't hate myself, and I don't have body dysmorphia. I was born with a rare blood disorder that has had its way with my body from a young age. It has left me with physical deformities and joint abnormalities. One side of my body is puny and atrophied compared to the other.

I would not have been a beauty even without this illness, but it's impossible to remedy the situation with normal exercise and physical therapy. I'm also overweight, which I admit I should be able to fix. I'm not an unhealthy eater, but like anyone, I could consume less. I'm not ugly in a mysterious or interesting way, like a number of popular actors. I look like what I am: a broken man.

My problem—and my problem with most advice outlets—is that there's not much of a resource for people like me. In movies, ugly characters are redeemed by being made beautiful in time to catch the eye of their love interest, or else their ugliness is a joke (and they aren't actually ugly). In practical life, we're taught that personality matters more than physicality, but there are plenty of attractive (or at least normal-looking) people who are also decent human beings.

What is there for people like me who will never be remotely attractive and who are just average on the inside?

I'm a happy person and have a very fulfilling life and good friends. I have a flexible job that allows me enough free time to pursue my hobbies, with employers who understand when I have to miss work for health reasons. But when it comes to romance, I'm left out in the cold. I don't want my entire life to pass without knowing that type of love.

Is it better to close off that part of myself and devote my time and energies to the aspects of my life that work, or should I try some novel approaches to matchmaking? My appearance makes online dating an absolute no-go. In person, people react well to my outgoing personality, but would not consider me a romantic option. I'm looking for new ideas or, if you think it's a lost cause, permission to give up. Thanks for your help.

Signed,
Beast with a Limp

Dear Beast,

Once upon a time I had a friend who was severely burned over most of his body. Six weeks after his twenty-fifth birthday, he didn't realize that there was a gas leak in the stove in his apartment, so he lit a match and his entire kitchen blew up. He barely survived. When he got out of the hospital four months later, his nose and fingers and ears were burnt nubs and his skin was more hide than flesh, like that of a pink lizard with mean streaks of white glazed over the top. I'll call him Ian.

"I'm a fire-breathing monster!" he roared to my kids the Thanksgiving before last, crouched beneath them near the edge of the bed. They shrieked with joy and fake fear, screaming, "Monster! Monster!" Ian looked at me and then he looked at Mr. Sugar and together we laughed and laughed.

You know why? Because he *was* a fire-breathing monster. My kids had never known him any other way and neither had their dad and I. I think it's true that Ian didn't know who he was before he was burned, either. He was a man made by the fire.

And because of the fire, he was also a rich man—he'd received a settlement from the gas company. He'd grown up lower middle class, but by the time I met him—when I was twenty-seven and he was thirty-one—he reveled in being a bit of a snob. He bought exquisite food and outrageously over-priced booze. He collected art and hung it in a series of hip and tony lofts. He wore impeccable clothes and drove around in fancy cars. He loved having money. He often said that being burned was the best thing that had ever happened to him. That if he could travel back in time he would not unlight that match. To unlight the match would be to lose the money that had brought him so much happiness. He had an incredible life, he said, and he was grateful for it.

But there was one thing. One tiny thing. He was sorry he couldn't have love. Romantic love. Sexual love. Love love. *Love.*

"But you *can!*" I insisted, though it's true that when I first met him I was skittish about holding his gaze because he was, in fact, a ghastly sight, his body a rough yet tender landscape of the excruciatingly painful and the distorted familiar. I met him when I was a waitress at a swank French bar where he was a regular. He sat near the place where I had to go to order and collect my drinks at the bar, and as I worked I took him in bit by bit, looking at him only peripherally. We chatted about books and art and shoes as he drank twenty-dollar shots of tequila and ate plates of meticulously constructed pâté and I zipped from the bar to the tables and back to the bar, delivering things.

After a while, he became more than a customer I had to be nice to. He became my friend. By then, I'd forgotten that he looked like a monster. It was the strangest thing, but it was true, how profoundly my vision of Ian changed once I knew him. How his burnt face became instead his bright blue eyes, his scarred and stumpy hands, the sound of his voice. It wasn't that I couldn't see his monstrosity anymore. It was still there in all its grotesque glory. But alongside it there was something else, something more ferocious: his beauty.

I wasn't the only one who saw it. There were so many people who loved Ian. And we all insisted over and over again that our love was proof that someday someone would love him. Not in the way *we* loved him—not just as a friend—but *in that way*.

Ian would not hear a word of it. To so much as contemplate the possibility of having a boyfriend was unbearable to him. He'd made the decision to close himself off to romantic love way back when he was still in the hospital. No one would love a man as ugly as him, he thought. When I argued with him, he said that I had no idea about the importance of physical appearance in gay culture. When I told him I thought there were surely a few men on the planet willing to love a burned man, he said he would make do with the occasional services of a prostitute. When I said I thought that his refusal to open himself up to romantic love was based on fear and conquering that fear was the last thing he had to heal from the trauma of his accident, he said the discussion was over.

And so it was.

One night after I got off work, Ian and I went to another

bar to have a drink. When we sat down he told me it was the anniversary of his accident and I asked him if he would tell me the entire story of that morning and he did. He said he'd just woken up and that he was gazing absently at a sleeve of saltine crackers on the counter the moment his kitchen flashed into blue flame. He was amazed to see the crackers and the sleeve disintegrate and disappear in an instant. It seemed to him a beautiful, almost magical occurrence, and then, in the next moment, he realized that he was engulfed in the blue flame and disintegrating too. He told me about falling down onto the floor and moaning and how his roommate had awakened but been too afraid to come to him, so instead he yelled words of comfort to Ian from another room. It was the people who'd been on the sidewalk down below and seen the windows blow out of his apartment who'd been the first to call 911. He told me about how the paramedics talked to him kindly as they carried him down the stairs on a stretcher and how one of them told him that he might die and how he cried out at the thought of that and how the way he sounded to himself in that cry was the last thing he remembered before he lost consciousness for weeks.

He would never have a lover.

He would be happy. He would be sad. He would be petty and kind. He would be manipulative and generous. He would be cutting and sweet. He would move from one cool loft to another and change all the color schemes. He would drink and stop drinking and start drinking again. He would buy original art and a particular breed of dog. He would make a load of money in real estate and lose another load of it on a business endeavor. He would reconcile with people he loved and estrange himself from others. He would not return my phone calls and he would read my first book and send me the nicest note. He would give my first child a snappy pair of ridiculously expensive baby trousers, and sigh and say he loathed children when I told him I was pregnant with my second. He would roar at Thanksgiving. He would crouch beneath the bed and say that he was a fire-breathing monster and he would laugh with all the grown-ups who got the joke.

And not even a month later—a week before Christmas, when he was forty-four—he would kill himself. He wouldn't even leave a note.

I've thought many times about why Ian committed suicide, and I thought about it again when I read your letter, Beast. It would be so easy to trace Ian's death back to that match, the one he said he would not unlight if he could. The one that made him appear to be a monster and therefore unfit for romantic love, while also making him rich and therefore happy. That match is so temptingly symbolic, like something hard and golden in a fairy tale that exacts a price equal to its power.

But I don't think his death can be traced back to that. I think it goes back to his decision to close himself off to romantic love, to refuse to allow himself even the possibility of something so very essential because of something so superficial as the way he looked. And your question to me—the very core of it—is circling around the same thing. It's not *Will I ever find someone who will love me romantically?*—(though in fact that question is there and it's one I will get to)—but rather *Am I capable of letting someone do so?*

This is where we must dig.

You will never have my permission to close yourself off to love and give up. Never. You must do everything you can to get what you want and need, to find "that type of love." It's there for you. I know it's arrogant of me to say so, because what the hell do I know about looking like a monster or a beast? Not a thing. But I do know that we are here, all of us—beasts and monsters and beauties and wallflowers alike—to do the best we can. And every last one of us can do better than give up.

Especially you. Anyone who has lived in the world for twenty-six years looking like what he is—"a broken man"—is not "just average on the inside." Because of that, the journey you take to find love isn't going to be average either. You're going to have to be brave. You're going to have to walk into the darkest woods without a stick. You aren't conventionally attractive or even, as you say, "normal-looking," and as you know already, a lot of people will immediately X you out as a romantic partner for this reason. That's okay. You don't need those people. By stepping aside, they've done you a favor. Because what you've got left after the fools have departed are the old souls and the true hearts. Those are the über-cool sparkle rocket mind-blowers we're after. Those are the people worthy of your love.

And you, my dear, are worthy of them. By way of offering up evidence of your didn't-even-get-started defeat, you mentioned movies in which "the ugly characters are redeemed by being made beautiful in time to catch the eye of their love interest," but that's not a story I buy, hon. We are way more ancient than that. We have better, truer stories. You know that fairy tale called "Beauty and the Beast"? Jeanne-Marie Le Prince de Beaumont abridged Gabrielle-Suzanne Barbot de Villeneuve's original "La Belle et la Bête" in 1756 and it is her version that most of us know today. There are many details that I'll omit here, but the story goes roughly like this:

A beautiful young woman named Belle lives with a beast in a castle. Belle is touched by the beast's grace and generosity and compelled by his sensitive intelligence, but each night when the beast asks Belle to marry him, she declines because she's repulsed by his appearance. One day she leaves the beast to visit her family. She and the beast agree that she'll return in a week, but when she doesn't the beast is bereft. In sorrow, he goes into the rose garden and collapses. That is how Belle finds him when she returns, half-dead from heartbreak. Seeing him in this state, she realizes that she truly loves him. Not just as a friend, but *in that way,* and so she professes her love and weeps. When her tears fall onto the beast, he is transformed into a handsome prince.

What I want you to note is that Belle loved the beast when he was still a beast—not a handsome prince. It is only once she loved him that he was transformed. You will be likewise transformed, the same as love transforms us all. But you have to be fearless enough to let it transform you.

I'm not convinced you are just yet. You say that people like you, but don't consider you a "romantic option." How do you know that? Have you made overtures and been rebuffed or are you projecting your own fears and insecurities onto others? Are you closing yourself off from the possibility of romance before anyone has the chance to feel romantically toward you? Who are you interested in? Have you ever asked anyone out on a date or to kiss you or to put his or her hands down your pants?

I can tell by your (articulate, honest, sad, strong) letter that you are one cool cat. I'm pretty certain based on your letter alone that a number of people would consider putting their hands down your pants. Would you let one of them? If the answer is yes, how would you respond once he or she got there? I don't mean to be a dirty smart-ass (though I am, in fact, a dirty smart-ass). I mean to inquire—without diminishing the absolute reality that many people will disregard you as a romantic possibility based solely on your appearance—about whether you've asked yourself if the biggest barrier between you and the romantic hot monkey love that's possible between you and the people who will—*yes! without question!*—be interested in you is not your ugly exterior, but your beautifully vulnerable interior. What do you need to do to convince yourself that someone might see you as a lover instead of a friend? How might you shut down your impulse to shut down?

These questions are key to your ability to find love, sweet pea. You asked me for practical matchmaking solutions, but I believe once you allow yourself to be psychologically ready to give and receive love, your best course is to do what everyone who is looking for love does: put your best self out there with as much transparency and sincerity and humor as possible. Both online and in person. With strangers and among your circle of friends. Inhabit the beauty that lives in your beastly body and strive to see the beauty in all the other beasts. Walk without a stick into the darkest woods. Believe that the fairy tale is true.

Yours,
Sugar

I CHOSE VAN GOGH

Dear Sugar,

I was sexually assaulted at seventeen. I was naïve and I didn't understand it. Anxiety became a deep part of my life, and it almost pulled me under. Trudging onward was all I could do. I've made peace with it.

I have been dating a great guy for about a year and a half. How do I tell him about my sexual assault? Do I need to? It doesn't affect my relationship or my day-to-day life, but it was a formative and intense thing and therefore played an important role in shaping who I am today. We've been through some emotionally intense events, so I know he's capable of hearing it. I would love your advice.

Signed,
Over It

Dear Over It,

I have a friend who is twenty years older than me who was raped three different times over the course of her life. She's a talented painter of some renown. When I learned about the rapes she'd endured, I asked her how she recovered from them, how she continued having healthy sexual relationships with men. She told me that at a certain point we get to decide who it is we allow to influence us. She said, "I could allow myself to be influenced by three men who screwed me against my will or I could allow myself to be influenced by van Gogh. I chose van Gogh."

I never forgot that. I think of that phrase "*I chose van Gogh*" whenever I'm having trouble lifting my own head up. And I thought of it when I read your letter, Over It. You chose van Gogh too. Something ugly happened to you and you didn't let it make you ugly. I salute you for your courage and grace. I think you should tell your boyfriend about your sexual assault and I think you should tell it straight. What happened. How you suffered. How you came to terms with the experience. And how you feel about it now.

You say this terrible experience no longer impacts your "day-to-day" life, but you also say it played an important role in shaping who you are. The whole deal about loving truly and for real and with all you've got has everything to do with letting those we love see what made us. Withholding this trauma from your boyfriend makes it bigger than it needs to be. It creates a secret you're too beautiful to keep. Telling has a way of dispersing things. It will allow your lover to stand closer inside the circle of you. Let him.

Yours,
Sugar

THE OTHER SIDE OF THE POOL

Dear Sugar,

My two grown sons, ages thirty-five and twenty-three, have returned to the nest, my home. They didn't ask. They simply showed up.

My younger son is going to college, but he hates it. He wants the financial aid money. He drinks, blows weed, watches daytime TV, and plays computer games. His eighteen-year-old girlfriend and their baby are going to move in soon, to fill out my already crowded spare bedroom. (Since the baby is my new grandchild, I'm kind of excited about that.)

My older son is also enrolled in college and is taking it seriously and getting good grades, but he drinks and is very moody and sarcastic to me. I've cleaned out my savings to make his car payments and cover his bills.

I'm a recovering alcoholic and have my own moods. I'm supporting the household with the dollars I can eke out as a writer, which is to say, not much. But I'm resourceful; I use coupons and shop at thrift stores.

My question is how do I get these men launched in life and out of my house? I want to write in privacy, pace the room in my underwear working out dialogue, research, sing, shake my ass, practice yoga, read, find my things where I left them the night before, enjoy a fragrant guest bathroom where the toilet seat remains down, eat tofu and oranges, drink green tea—not chips and hoagies. I don't want to have mayonnaise spilled down the front of the kitchen cabinet. I want to cry over romantic movies and hear Mozart's greatest hits, pay my bills, buy some bangle bracelets.

I'm stuck, Sugar. I love these kids. Their father, my ex-husband, died last year and I understand the loss and confusion my sons feel about this. I know the economy is hard. I recognize that building a life, finding someone to love, enjoying life's many pleasures, is hard work. But I'm afraid my sons are failing in the job of getting on with it. I'm afraid I won't be able to cover all the expenses. I'm afraid that what I want as I prepare to enter old age won't be attainable. I'm afraid my sons will never launch. I'm crowded with fear.

What do you think I should do?

Crowded

Dear Crowded,

One of my earliest memories is also one of my most vivid. I was three and enrolled in a swimming class at the local YMCA. On the first day, I, like all the three-year-olds, was issued what we called a bubble—a flotation device that buckled on around the shoulders and waist and featured an object about the size and shape of a football that was pressed up against my back. This would allegedly keep me afloat. "Don't worry!" my mother assured me over and over again. "Your bubble will hold you up!"

She said this same thing in various tones, with various degrees of patience and exasperation, week after week as

I clung to the side of the pool, but her words meant nothing. I would not be persuaded to join my peers in the water. I was terrified. I felt certain that if I let go of the wall, I would immediately drown, bubble or not. So each week, I stubbornly stationed myself there while watching my classmates kick themselves around the pool. "See!" my mother would point to them excitedly when they passed.

But I would not be swayed.

On the final day of the class, the parents were meant to swim with their children. My mother put on her suit and sat beside me on the side of the pool and together we dangled our feet in the water, watching the other kids perform the techniques they'd learned. When it was nearly time to leave, she said to me, "How about we just go in the water together? I'll hold you."

I was fine with that. That's how I'd always gone into the water, clinging to my mother, who might gently splash me or bob me up and down until I laughed. So into the water we went. When we got out to the middle of the pool, she convinced me to let her hold only my hands while dragging me through the water, and though, while she did this, I repeatedly begged, "Don't let me go, don't let me go," and she repeatedly promised, "I won't, I won't," in one sudden burst of power, she swirled me around and flung me away from her.

My memory of how it felt to glide through the water without my mother is still so fresh, so visceral, even though it was forty years ago. The sensations were both physical and intellectual. How strange and glorious it was to be anchored to nothing, to be free, in some particular way, for the first time in my life. How quickly I shifted from the shock of my mother's betrayal to the terror of my new reality to the pure delight of how it felt to swim. My mother had been right: my bubble held me up.

Of course, I didn't want to get out of the pool then. I swam around and around, circling my mother, as we laughed with joy and surprise, both of us wishing we'd known sooner that all it took for me to do this was for her to let me go. I swam so long that my mother got out while I swam to and fro, from where she sat on one side of the pool all the way over to the other side of the pool, which seemed then impossibly far. When I got there, I'd look back at her and yell, "I'm on the other side of the pool!" And she'd smile and say yes, there I was—all the way over on the other side of the pool!—and then I'd swim back to her and do it all over again.

I think you need to do a little something like my mom did after her weeks of patience, Crowded. You need to fling your sons away from you so they can learn how to swim. You must tell them to move out. They are not ill. They are not in crisis. They are not children. They are two adults capable of providing for themselves. Their bubbles will hold them up. You must demand that they trust that.

When you tell your sons you will no longer allow them to live in your house, it will probably come as a surprise to them. It is a shock to be flung away from the very person to whom one has clung to for so long. But I'm quite certain it will turn out to be a healthy shift for all of you. Much as your sons no doubt love you, it seems clear to me that they don't see you as truly separate from them. Your needs matter little because it barely occurs to them that you have any. They moved into your house without asking you because they don't really consider that house yours—they believe it's theirs too, that they have a right to it because it belongs to you, their mother. *Theirs.*

They have not separated themselves from you on a fundamental level. They want you to leave them alone and to refrain from telling them how to live, but they have not yet perceived that you have a life of your own too, one that their presence, at this point, thwarts. They don't yet see you as an adult with a right to privacy and self-determination.

This is not because they are bad men. It's that they need to go through that final stage of development—one in which the child truly separates from the parent—and it seems they need a push that only you can give. Remember when they were toddlers and everything was "Do it myself! Do it myself!"? I've never met your sons, but I'll guess that like most kids, at a certain stage of development it was important for them to perform tasks that you'd once done for them—opening doors, buckling seat belts, zipping up jackets. Children demand such things because they must, because their very survival depends on their ability to learn how to be self-sufficient.

For a mix of reasons I can only guess at—emotional immaturity, financial stress, your own enabling tendencies, grief over their father, youthful self-absorption—your sons have resisted the final stages of the *do it myself* impulse that begins in the toddler years. They've realized it's easier to let you do it for them. By asking them to move out of your house, you're telling them you know that they can do this too. You're doing your sons a service by asking them to leave. You're demonstrating your faith in the natural course of things: that they are now capable of thriving without you.

Evicting your sons from your house does not mean you are evicting them from your life. As their mother, what you owe them is unconditional love, emotional support, and respect. Asking them to move out of your house does not mean you will not help them in any number of ways over the years. Your son who's recently become a father, for example, may particularly need your support as a caregiver to your grandchild.

The point is, you get to choose what you wish to provide when it comes to money and resources now. You raised those boys into men. You paid your dues. It's time for you to allow your sons to pay theirs. It's only once you fling them away that they can do this, that they can see how it feels to float, how you look to them from that distance on the other side of the pool.

Yours,
Sugar

THE TRUTH THAT LIVES THERE

Dear Sugar,

I'm a twenty-six-year-old woman who has been married for nine months. My husband is forty. His wedding proposal was terribly romantic, like something out of a movie starring Audrey Hepburn. He is kind and funny. I do love him. And yet . . .

He's only the second person I've been in a serious relationship with. Throughout the wedding planning process I had second thoughts about settling down so young, but I didn't want to hurt or embarrass him by calling off the wedding. There are so many experiences I fear I'll miss out on by staying married to someone older. I want to apply for the Peace Corps, live all over the country, teach English in Japan, and yes, date other people. These are all things I was giving up when I said, "I do." But it's only hitting me now.

I feel stuck. I want to leave, but I'm also terrified of hurting my husband, who has been so good to me and who I consider my best friend. Sugar, I've always played it safe: I picked the safe major, accepted the safe job, went ahead with the wedding. I'm terrified that leaving my husband will mean I finally have no excuse for why I'm not living the bold, experience-rich life I've always dreamed of.

Sugar, please help me.

Playing It Safe

Dear Sugar,

I am a messed-up woman. I bear the scars of much emotional abuse, some physical abuse, and one sexual assault. I have an addictive personality, flirt with anorexia, OCD, and I don't know what it's like to live without the flush of adrenaline in my body from chronic stress. I'm vain, self-absorbed, depressed, angry, self-loathing, and lonely. Routinely.

I was raised to think I was a filthy person and God would only love me if I behaved. I mostly behaved. Then I met a man who told me God would love me anyway. I converted to fundamental Christianity and married the man. I was eighteen. That was seven years ago.

He is, for most intents and purposes, a good man. He means well and he loves me, but he suffers from the faults of most young men in our religion: the head-of-household syndrome. I'm expected to be a certain way, so I am. He doesn't realize he does this unless I tell him, and I've stopped bothering to tell him after so many years. But I am not really that person, and the longer we're married the more trapped and broken I feel about burying the real me, the messed-up person I already described. He knows all my scars, but as a Christian he doesn't understand mental illness at all. He pleads with me to trust God more. He says if I just try harder, he knows I can get better. He says I have such potential.

I don't blame him for my discontent (entirely). We were told we were too young to marry, but despite my own misgivings, I married to prove everyone wrong. We're both incredibly stubborn. I thought if I could be the person I was supposed to be, I would make myself okay. I would be better. It was a lie I told myself.

I love him. I don't want to hurt him. But I don't know how to stop this charade, how to heal, or how to make him understand. I spent a week in a psych ward for depression a few years ago because I just needed to put the brake on and knew that the only way to get through to him was something drastic: either I killed myself or I got help. I got help. However, the mask was back in place as soon as I was released, and my therapy was a joke. Nothing changed, and I feel myself reaching the breaking point again. I no longer have any urge to kill myself, and can recognize my own warning signs, but I do need a break. Pretending is tiring. My health has suffered over the past few months. We finally bought our first house, and most days I sit around it weeping.

I have thought of leaving so many times, but I don't want to hurt him. He has worked hard to allow me to stay home (though we have no children). If I left, he would become a pariah in our church community, where we are currently leaders. I don't want to do that to him. He does not believe in divorce, unless I cheated on him. I no longer know what I believe. I have tried talking about how I feel before, but we're on two different planets. If I confronted him about how I feel now, he would feel betrayed by me, and I would feel horrible. He in the past has refused counseling, saying our/my life is great and we don't need it, even if I do. My fear is that, as usual, if I say something, we seem better for a time, and the cycle continues. I am tired of the cycle.

Where is the line, Sugar? When you want the life you have to work but it doesn't, and you aren't sure it can, and when you want a completely different life, too, which way do you go? Do I stay and rub myself out until maybe I am the person I was always expected to be? Is this just what it means to be an adult? I never had a good example of a marriage until I was already married, in my in-laws, and we do not look like them. But could we, in time? How long do you try?

Signed,
Standing Still

Dear Sugar,

I am a woman in my late twenties who has dated the same guy for almost three years and lived with him for almost a year. All of my friends seem to be getting married, and I feel as though I should be considering marriage too. However, the thought of marrying my boyfriend makes me feel panicky and claustrophobic. He has mentioned once the possibility of us tying the knot, and I think he sensed I was not comfortable discussing it, so he didn't mention it again.

I've not had many boyfriends—one steady relationship in high school, a few very short-lived relationships post-college, and now this one. My boyfriend is the sweetest person you will ever find, and we have some things in common, but I find myself fantasizing about dating other people. I find my respect for my boyfriend waning. I don't know if this is a temporary feeling, or if this relationship is not meant to continue for the long term. I'm bored with him and I'm afraid I will get more bored as time goes on. I'm also afraid that there really is no one better out there for me, that I should be grateful for what I have, and that anyone I would be seriously interested in would be unlikely to be interested in me in the same way (seems to be the case, judging from experience). I hate feeling like I'm doing my boyfriend a disservice by not loving him as much as he loves me.

What do I do, Sugar?

Signed,
Claustrophobic

Dear Women,

I chose to answer your letters together because placed alongside each other I think they tell a story complete enough that they answer themselves. Reading them, it occurred to me that allowing you to read what others in a similar situation are struggling with would be a sort of cure for what ails you, though of course I have something to say about them too. I struggled with these very questions mightily in my own life, when I was married to a good man whom I both loved and wanted to leave.

There was nothing wrong with my ex-husband. He wasn't perfect, but he was pretty close. I met him a month after I turned nineteen and I married him on a rash and romantic impulse a month before I turned twenty. He was passionate and smart and sensitive and handsome and absolutely crazy about me. I was crazy about him too, though not absolutely. He was my best friend; my sweet lover; my guitar-strumming, political rabble-rousing, road-tripping sidekick; the co-proprietor of our vast and eclectic music and literature collection; and daddy to our two darling cats.

But there was in me an awful thing, from almost the very beginning: a small, clear voice that would no, no matter what I did, stop saying *go*.

Go, even though you love him.

Go, even though he's kind and faithful and dear to you.

Go, even though he's your best friend and you're his.

Go, even though you can't imagine your life without him.

Go, even though he adores you and your leaving will devastate him.

Go, even though your friends will be disappointed or surprised or pissed off or all three.

Go, even though you once said you would stay.

Go, even though you're afraid of being alone.

Go, even though you're sure no one will ever love you as well as he does.

Go, even though there is nowhere to go.

Go, even though you don't know exactly why you can't stay.

Go, because you want to.

Because wanting to leave is enough. Get a pen. Write that last sentence on your palm—all three of you. Then read it over and over again until your tears have washed it away.

Doing what one wants to do because one wants to do it is hard for a lot of people, but I think it's particularly hard for women. We are, after all, the gender onto which a giant *Here to Serve* button has been eternally pinned. We're expected to nurture and give by the very virtue of our femaleness, to consider other people's feelings and needs before our own. I'm not opposed to those traits. The people I most admire are in fact nurturing and generous and considerate. Certainly, an ethical and evolved life entails a whole lot of doing things one doesn't particularly want to do and not doing things one very much does, regardless of gender.

But an ethical and evolved life also entails telling the truth about oneself and living out that truth.

Leaving a relationship because you want to doesn't exempt you from your obligation to be a decent human being. You can leave and still be a compassionate friend to your partner. Leaving because you want to doesn't mean you pack your bags the moment there's strife or struggle or uncertainty. It means that if you yearn to be free of a particular relationship and you feel that yearning lodged within you more firmly than any of the other competing and contrary yearnings are lodged, your desire to leave is not only valid, but probably the right thing to do. Even if someone you love is hurt by that.

It took me ages to understand this. I still can't entirely explain why I needed to leave my ex. I was tortured by this very question for years because I felt like such an ass for breaking his heart and I was so shattered I'd broken my own. I was too young to commit myself to one person. We weren't as compatible as we initially seemed. I was driven by my writing, and he begrudged my success in equal measure to his celebration of it. I wasn't ready for long-term monogamy. He grew up upper middle class and I grew up poor and I couldn't keep myself from resenting him for that. My mother died and my stepfather stopped being a father to me and I was an orphan by the age of twenty-two and reeling in grief.

All of these reasons are true enough in their specificity, but they all boil down to the same thing: I had to leave. Because I wanted to. Just like all of you do, even if you aren't ready to do it yet. I know by your letters that you each have your own lists, but all those words on all of those lists boil down to one that says *go*. I imagine you'll understand that at some point. That when it comes down to it, you must trust your truest truth, even though there are other truths running alongside it—such as your love for the partners you want to leave.

I'm not talking about just up and walking out on your partners the moment the thought occurs to you. I'm talking about making a considered choice about your life. I desperately wanted to not want to leave my ex-husband. I agonized in precisely the ways you are agonizing, and I shared a fair piece of that struggle with my ex. I tried to be good. I tried to be bad. I was sad and scared and sick and self-sacrificing and ultimately self-destructive. I finally cheated on my former husband because I didn't have the guts to tell him I wanted out. I loved him too much to make a clean break, so I botched the job and made it dirty instead. The year or so I spent splitting up with him after I confessed my sexual dalliances was wall-to-wall pain. It wasn't me against him. It was the two of us wrestling together neck-deep in the muckiest mud pit. Divorcing him is the most excruciating decision I've ever made.

But it was the wisest one too. And I wasn't the only one whose life is better for it. He deserved the love of a woman who didn't have the word *go* whispering like a deranged ghost in her ear. To leave him was a kindness of a sort, though it didn't seem that way at the time.

It wasn't until I'd been married to Mr. Sugar a few years that I truly understood my first marriage. In loving him, I've come to see more clearly how and why I loved my first husband. My two marriages aren't so different from each other, though there's some sort of magic sparkle glue in the second that was missing in the first. Mr. Sugar and my ex have never met, but I'm certain if they did they'd get along swimmingly. They're both good men with kind hearts and gentle souls. They both share my passions for books, the outdoors, and lefty politics; they're both working artists, in different fields. I argue with Mr. Sugar about the same amount as I did with my former husband, at a comparable velocity, about similar things. In both marriages there have been struggles and sorrows that few know about and fewer still were and are capable of seeing or understanding. Mr. Sugar and I have been neck-deep together in the muckiest mud pit too. The only difference is that every time I've been down there with him I wasn't fighting for my freedom and neither was he. In our nearly sixteen years together, I've never once thought the word *go*. I've only wrestled harder so I'd emerge dirty, but stronger, with him.

I didn't want to stay with my ex-husband, not at my core, even though whole swaths of me did. And if there's one thing I believe more than I believe anything else, it's that you can't fake the core. The truth that lives there will eventually win out. It's a god we must obey, a force that brings us all inevitably to our knees. And because of it, I can only ask the three of you the same question: Will you do it later or will you do it now?

Yours,
Sugar

TOO MUCH PAINT

Dear Sugar,

Up until a few months ago, my dating life was always sort of black and white. I've either been in a serious, monogamous relationship or I've dabbled around with one-night stands or random, no-strings-attached romps with platonic male friends. Recently, I've entered the strange and magical world of casual, nonmonogamous dating. I've met a few guys who I enjoy on an intellectual level, as well as sexually. I'm learning a lot about my own sexuality through interacting with distinctly different partners, and I feel like I'm finally discovering that part of myself, which is awesome.

Maybe it's because I'm new to this whole nonmonogamous scene and it just doesn't come naturally to me (yet?), but sometimes I find myself feeling completely overwhelmed by the prospect of juggling these different men. One week, I went out with "Bill" on Monday, saw "Jack" on Tuesday, then had a no-strings-attached encounter with a friendly ex on Wednesday. It was lovely getting laid three nights in a row, but getting laid by three different dudes sort of made my head spin.

I don't want to have anonymous and/or completely meaningless sex, but neither do I want to home in on one guy and pursue a serious relationship right now. How can I navigate these new

waters without giving myself a nervous breakdown? Am I obliged
to tell the guys I'm seeing that they're not the only dude I'm sleep-
ing with?

Man Juggler

Dear Man Juggler,

I'll answer the easy question first: Yes, you are obliged to tell
the men you're sleeping with regularly that you're not sleeping with them exclusively. There are no exceptions to this rule.
Ever. For anyone. Under any circumstances. People have the
right to know if the people they are fucking are also fucking
other people. This is the only way the people fucking people
who are fucking other people can make emotionally healthy
decisions about their lives. It's clean. It's right. It's honest.
And it's a basic tenet of Sugar's hard-earned, didn't-do-it-the-
right-way-the-first-time-around Ethical Code to Loving Others as Well as Loving Oneself.

Plus, it seems like breaking this news is going to be rather
easy, Man Juggler. It sounds to me that the men on your current roster of lovers already know that you aren't sleeping with
them exclusively. (And yet, if they all knew this, why would
you ask the question?) Best be sure to slip it in rather soon. You
don't have to be overly specific or get all heavy and doe-eyed
and like, "Um . . . we really have to *talk.*" Just say, "Hey _____
(Bill/friendly ex/new romping partner I have acquired since I
wrote that question to Sugar), this has been superfun and I
want you to know that I'm seeing other people too."

Then smile. Just a little. And perhaps run your hand very
lightly up his dreamy hunk of hairy man arm.

Okay. Now. On to your question about how to navigate the

"strange and magical world of casual, nonmonogamous dating." I think it's excellent that you're having fun sleeping with people you like but don't love, who stimulate you both sexually and intellectually. And it's even better that this new (and likely temporary) era of your sex life is helping you discover a previously unexplored side of yourself. So all that's peachy, right? What's not so peachy is this business about how you feel "completely overwhelmed by the prospect of juggling these different men."

The beauty of your situation, Man Juggler, is that you don't have to juggle. Just because you can fuck a different man every night of the week doesn't mean you should. One of the basic principles of every single art form has to do not with what's there—the music, the words, the movement, the dialogue, the paint—but with what isn't. In the visual arts it's called the "negative space"—the blank parts around and between objects, which is, of course, every bit as crucial as the objects themselves. The negative space allows us to see the nonnegative space in all its glory and gloom, its color and mystery and light. What isn't there gives what's there meaning. Imagine that.

Sex with three different guys on three consecutive nights? It's too much paint. Don't do it again. Not because I told you so, but because *you told me so* when you used the phrases "head spin" and "nervous breakdown" in reference to that three-day run. Listen to yourself. And have fun.

Yours,
Sugar

TINY REVOLUTIONS

Dear Sugar,

I'm a woman in my mid-fifties. I read your column regularly and believe that my question is pedestrian but am humbly asking for your advice and support anyway as I sit in the pain of it all.

After a couple decades of marriage, my husband and I are separating. I'm at peace with it as I feel my marriage has essentially been dead for a while. My husband never was demonstrative emotionally or physically. I have spent many years feeling horribly lonely. No amount of trying to get from him what I needed brought change. It took a lot for me to finally believe that I was worthy of more and to make a step toward that possibility.

Of course the future terrifies me and excites me at the same time. I want to create more loving relationships in my life, both in friendship and romance. I want and need loving touches, loving words. And at the same time, I'm terrified that I'll never feel the tender touch of a man. Yesterday, as a friend was telling me about a wonderful intimate moment with his partner, I was frightened that I would never have that in my life.

I worry about sex. I haven't been with another man for a long time. The sex in my marriage was routine and uninspiring. At one point, I told my husband I wanted to have sex more often and he made a joke of it the next night. And I am afraid I am not very "good" at it. I would orgasm regularly with my husband so it isn't that. We hid behind what worked until it got to be boring. For years I imagined robust, adventurous sex, and yet I would allow the routine to continue. I am afraid that I will meet a man that I connect with and we'll have sex and I will not be any good in bed.

I need help. How does one go about changing that before it's too late?

And, then there is the issue of my body. With clothes on, I am presentable. Without clothes, my body reveals the story of significant weight gain and significant weight loss. I feel good about losing weight, but naked my body is droopy and I'm embarrassed by it. I try to imagine how I will be present sexually with all my insecurities in that department. Surgery is expensive and out of my means. My doctor says without it, my skin won't regain the same tightness. I imagine orchestrating ways to keep from being seen, but I know that probably won't work and I am so afraid of how a potential lover will react. I don't want to hide behind my fear, and yet I am so very frightened of exposing myself. I know you can't do it for me, Sugar, and yet I feel so alone in this place of fear.

Are there men my age who date women my age who will be accepting of my body? I know you really don't have the answer but I ask anyway. Emotionally, I am very brave. Sexually and being vulnerable with my body, I am not so much but want to be. And, of course, I am equally terrified that I won't have the opportunity to express myself and challenge myself in that way. Please help.

Signed,
Wanting

Dear Wanting,

When my daughter was five she overheard me complaining to
Mr. Sugar that I was a big fat ugly beast who looks terrible in
everything and immediately she asked with surprise, "You're a
big fat ugly beast who looks terrible in everything?"

"No! I was only joking!" I exclaimed in a falsely cheerful
tone. Then I proceeded to pretend, for the sake of my daughter's future self-esteem, that I did not believe myself to be a big
fat ugly beast who looks terrible in everything.

My impulse is to do the same for you, Wanting. In order to
protect you from a more complicated reality, I want to pretend that droopy-fleshed women in deep middle age are lusted
after by droves of men for their original and seasoned beauty.
"Looks don't matter!" I want to shout in a giddy, you-go-girl
tone. It wouldn't be a lie. Looks really don't matter. You know
they don't. I know they don't. All the sweet peas of Sugarland
would rise and ratify that statement.

And yet. But still. We know it's not entirely true.

Looks matter to most of us. And sadly, they matter to women
to a rather depressing degree—regardless of age, weight, or
place on the gorgeous-to-hideous beauty continuum. I don't
need to detail the emails in my inbox from women with fears
such as your own as proof. I need only do a quick accounting
of just about every woman I've ever known—an endless pha-
lanx of mostly attractive females who were freaked out because
they were fat or flat-chested or frizzy-haired or oddly shaped or
lined with wrinkles or laced with stretch marks or in some other
way imperfect when viewed through the distorted eyes of the
all-knowing, woman-annihilating, ruthless beauty god who has
ruled and sometimes doomed significant portions of our lives.

I say enough of that. Enough of that.

I've written often about how we have to reach hard in the direction of the lives we want, even if it's difficult to do so. I've advised people to set healthy boundaries and communicate mindfully and take risks and work hard on what actually matters and confront contradictory truths and trust the inner voice that speaks with love and shut out the inner voice that speaks with hate. But the thing is—the thing so many of us forget—is that those values and principles don't only apply to our emotional lives. We've got to live them out in our bodies too.

Yours. Mine. Droopy and ugly and fat and thin and marred and wretched as they are. We have to be as fearless about our bellies as we are with our hearts.

There isn't a shortcut around this. The answer to your conundrum isn't finding a way to make your future lover believe you look like Angelina Jolie. It's coming to terms with the fact that you don't and never will (a fact, I'd like to note, that Angelina Jolie herself will also have to come to terms with someday and probably already struggles with now).

Real change happens on the level of the gesture. It's one person doing one thing differently than he or she did before. It's the man who opts not to invite his abusive mother to his wedding; the woman who decides to spend her Saturday mornings in a drawing class instead of scrubbing the toilets at home; the writer who won't allow himself to be devoured by his envy; the parent who takes a deep breath instead of throwing a plate. It's you and me standing naked before our lovers, even if it makes us feel kind of squirmy in a bad way when we do. The work is there. It's our task. Doing it will give us strength and clarity. It will bring us closer to who we hope to be.

You don't have to be young. You don't have to be thin. You don't have to be "hot" in a way that some dumbfuckedly narrow mindset has construed that word. You don't have to have taut flesh or a tight ass or an eternally upright set of tits.

You have to find a way to inhabit your body while enacting your deepest desires. You have to be brave enough to build the intimacy you deserve. You have to take off all of your clothes and say, *"I'm right here."*

There are so many tiny revolutions in a life, a million ways we have to circle around ourselves to grow and change and be okay. And perhaps the body is our final frontier. It's the one place we can't leave. We're there till it goes. Most women and some men spend their lives trying to alter it, hide it, prettify it, make it what it isn't, or conceal it for what it is. But what if we didn't do that?

That's the question you need to answer, Wanting. That's what will bring your deepest desires into your life. Not: *Will my old, droopy male contemporaries accept and love the old, droopy me?* But rather: *What's on the other side of the tiny gigantic revolution in which I move from loathing to loving my own skin?* What fruits would that particular liberation bear?

We don't know—as a culture, as a gender, as individuals, you and I. The fact that we don't know is feminism's one true failure. We claimed the agency, we granted ourselves the authority, we gathered the accolades, but we never stopped worrying about how our asses looked in our jeans. There are a lot of reasons for this, a whole bunch of Big Sexist Things We Can Rightfully Blame. But ultimately, like anything, the change is up to us.

The culture isn't going to give you permission to have "robust, adventurous sex" with your droopy and aging body, so you're going to have to be brave enough to take it for yourself. This will require some courage, Wanting, but courage is a vital piece of any well-lived life. I understand why you're afraid. I don't mean to diminish the enormity of what's recently ended and what now will begin, but I do intend to say to you very clearly that this is not the moment to wilt into the underbrush of your insecurities. You've earned the right to grow. You're going to have to carry the water yourself.

So let's talk about men. A whole bunch of them will overlook you as a lover because they want someone younger and firmer, but not all of them will. Some of them will be thrilled to meet a woman just exactly like you. The sexiest not-culturally-sanctioned-sexy people I know—the old, the fat, the differently abled, the freshly postpartum—have a wonderful way of being forthright about who they are and I suggest you take their approach. Instead of trying to conceal the aspects of your body that make you feel uncomfortable, how about just coming out with it at the outset—before you get into the bedroom and try to slip unnoticed beneath the sheets while having a panic attack? What would happen if you said to Mister Just-About-to-Do-Me: *I feel terribly self-conscious about how droopy my body is and I'm not sure if I even really know how to have good sex anymore, since I was frozen in a boring pattern with my ex for years on end.*

In my experience, those sorts of revelations help. They unclench the stronghold of one's fears. They push the intimacy to a more vulnerable place. And they have a spectacular way of revealing precisely the sort of person one is about to sleep with. Does he laugh and say he thinks you're lovely so just hush up, or does he clear his throat and offer you the contact information for his ex-wife's plastic surgeon? Does he confess his own insecurities or lecture you appallingly about yours? Is he the fellow you really want to share your body with or had you better walk away while the getting's good?

I know as women we're constantly being scorched by the relentless porno/Hollywood beauty blowtorch, but in my real life I've found that the men worth fucking are far more good-natured about the female body in its varied forms than is generally acknowledged. "Naked and smiling" is one male friend's only requirement for a lover. Perhaps it's because men are people with bodies full of fears and insecurities and short-comings of their own. Find one of them. One who makes you think and laugh and come. Invite him into the tiny revolution in your beautiful new world.

Yours,
Sugar

NOT ENOUGH

Dear Sugar,

Last year I met a guy who is wonderful, though I recognize he has a lot of growing up to do (he's twenty-four). We get along well, have a similar sense of humor, and have great sex. After nine months, I still get a tingle in my gut when I see him. Our relationship started casually, but over time we got to know each other and became ourselves around each other. We can cook together and be silly and go on adventures and read to each other and have sex on the floor and then make a cake and eat it in bed. In the beginning, I was okay with us not being monogamous, but once our relationship became more than a fling, I wanted a commitment. We talked and he told me that sleeping with just one person could get boring, but that he clearly likes me or else he wouldn't spend time with me. He said he was afraid I would change him somehow—turn him into someone he's not.

I didn't understand him then, and I still don't. Am I just dense? He likes me, but not enough to say he likes only me? Maybe it's that simple.

We still see each other pretty often, just now without the sex. I care for him, but I don't know if I'm foolish to stick around to see where it goes. Am I torturing myself by keeping him a part of my life?

Best,
Needs Direction

Dear Needs Direction,

I receive a lot of letters like yours. Most go on at length, describing all sorts of maddening situations and communications in bewildered detail, but in each there is the same question at its core: *Can I convince the person about whom I'm crazy to be crazy about me?*

The short answer is no.

The long answer is no.

The sad but strong and true answer is the one you already told yourself: this man likes you, but not the way you like him. Which is to say, not enough.

So now you get to decide what you want to do about that. Are you able to be friends—or even occasional lovers—with this man who is less crazy about you than you are about him without feeling:

    a)   bad about yourself,

    b)   resentful of him, or

    c)   like you're always longing for more?

If the answer is not yes on all three counts, I suggest you give your friendship a rest, even if it's just for the time it takes you to get over him. There are so many things to be tortured about, sweet pea. So many torturous things in this life. Don't let a man who doesn't love you be one of them.

Yours,
Sugar

NO IS GOLDEN

Dearest Sugar,

*I'm writing to you with half of the answer already in my heart.
I felt I should say this up front, since conventional wisdom says
that no matter what advice a mixed-up person gets, they always
end up following their own. My question is about my upcom-
ing wedding, which my fiancé and I are planning to have at his
father's house in Europe. Because I'm from the United States, my
guests will be far fewer and I have to think a lot harder about
who merits an invite.*

*At thirty, I feel like I've reached a point in my life where I'm
doing all of the things necessary to move forward without forget-
ting my past. I've been in therapy for the past year, trying to come
to terms with a childhood filled with all of the usual pitfalls that
cause kids to grow up into bitter, emotionally damaged adults.
Alcoholism, drug abuse, physical and emotional abuse—along
with a mother who depended on me from the time I was five to
assure her that my father wasn't dead in an accident on some
dark road somewhere—all caused me to live most of my twenties
on a precarious ridge between responsible living and disastrous
free fall.*

*But I got lucky. I got away from my family and lived in another
country. I found the forgiveness within me to reestablish a rela-*

tionship with my mother. I gathered the courage to achieve what I refer to as "normality." People underestimate the importance of normality. Normality means no one is screaming, fighting, or insulting one another. Normality means I'm not sobbing in my room. Normality means Christmas and other family holidays are a joy. Normality means, for some people, getting married.

And so here I am, getting married to a sincere, sensitive man with a perfectly normal family who will, for the first time, meet my dysfunctional, fractured, and still very unaware-of-it-all family members. This scares me to death.

But what scares me most is my father, who is the person at the source of most of the pain I felt as a child. I'm torn about whether I should invite him to my wedding.

After years of noncommunication, my father, though in possession of many, many, many faults, has recently found his way back into my life. He is a big part of my youngest brother's life. And now, my fiancé wants to include him in our wedding. The last time I saw my father, he was stoned out of his mind and drunk. He was supposed to drive my brother and me to the train station (and didn't).

So I'm conflicted. I don't expect my wedding day to be perfect. Part of me feels like, despite all of the drama that could occur, maybe this is an opportunity to include my father in an important part of my life and that this could be healing for him, and even cathartic to some extent. But then I imagine my mother's face when my father has drunk a few too many, while my fiancé's family looks on in horror. (My father isn't the friendly, funny kind of drunk.)

I want to turn the proverbial page, but my hand is frozen, unable to make a decision. The easiest thing to do would be to just not invite him, not run the risk, so I won't have to be *nervous on "our day." But I never have chosen the easiest thing. Please help!*

> Daughter with (Maybe)
> Expired Daddy Issues

Dear Daughter,

Every time I read your letter a terrible screeching alarm goes off in my head. Please don't invite your father to your wedding. There isn't one word in your letter that tells me that you want to or should.

Let us first dispatch with your fiancé, since he—*not you!*—is the one who'd like to include your father in your wedding. I presume he had good intentions when he proposed this— Hollywood-inspired visions of profound revelations and touching reunions brought on by the magic of the day, no doubt. But you know what? His opinion on this matter has no bearing whatsoever. The decision about whether to invite your father isn't even a tiny bit up to him. Your fiancé's suggestion tells me that he has neither a clear understanding of your familial history, nor an awareness of your deeply dysfunctional dad. I suggest you have an exhaustive conversation with him on these subjects rather soon. Like *now*.

I commend you for working so hard to come to terms with your childhood. I know how painful that is to do, and I know how very much richer your life is for having done so. But as you are surely aware, forgiveness doesn't mean you let the forgiven stomp all over you once again. Forgiveness means you've found a way forward that acknowledges harm done and hurt caused without letting either your anger or your pain rule your life or define your relationship with the one who did you wrong. Sometimes those we forgive change their behavior to the extent that we can eventually be as close to them as we were before (or even closer). Sometimes those we forgive continue being the jackasses that they always were and we accept them while keeping them approximately three thousand miles away from our wedding receptions.

It sounds to me like your father fits into the latter category.

Which means you need to look sharp. If the words *love, light, acceptance,* and *forgiveness* are written on one side of the coin you've earned by creating the beautiful life you have in the wake of your ugly childhood, on the other side of that coin there is written the word *no.*

No is golden. *No* is the kind of power the good witch wields. It's the way whole, healthy, emotionally evolved people manage to have relationships with jackasses while limiting the amount of jackass in their lives.

I'm talking, of course, about boundaries. I'm talking about taking a level gaze at "the man at the source of most of the pain" and making an informed decision about an important event in your life in which you put yourself and your needs and your desires front and center. It's really very clear when you think about it, isn't it? Your father wronged you as a child. He wronged you as a woman. And he will very likely wrong you on your wedding day if you give him the opportunity to do so.

This is not because he doesn't love you. But love doesn't make a mean drunk not a mean drunk or a narcissist not a narcissist or a jackass not a jackass. At your wedding, your father will most likely behave the way he has behaved for all the years you've known him. Even if he doesn't, what's the best-case scenario? That you spend your wedding day worrying that your father is going to make an ass of himself and humiliate you and enrage your mom and alienate your in-laws, *but he doesn't*? Does that sound like fun? Is that what you hoped for? Is that what you want?

Of course not. You want your father to be a prince. And if he can't be that, you at least want him to be a decent human being. You want the enormity of *your big day* to be bigger than whatever measly little shit shack he's been living in all of your life. I know this. I understand that ache. When I think about my own father for more than five seconds at a stretch, I can still feel my daddy sorrow all the way down to the very tips of my toes. Oh, but baby girl, your father is not going to do anything you want him to do because you want him to do it. Not one damn motherloving thing! You simply didn't get that kind of dad. You got the kind who will only do what he can.

That you've gone to the door of his shit shack and knocked is a noble act. The strength and faith you called upon when you sought to repair your relationship with your father will shine through your life, regardless of what happens between the two of you. That is a magnificent thing, Daughter. It was created entirely by your grit and your grace. It belongs to you. Let it be the thing that guides you when you speak to your father about why he isn't invited to your wedding. You wrote that not inviting him is the "easiest thing to do," but I encourage you to make it the hardest thing. Use your decision as an opportunity to have a frank conversation with him about how his behavior affects you and your ability to truly let him back into your life.

If your father is a man worthy of your deepening affection, he'll respect your decision even if his feelings are hurt. He'll understand that his exclusion is not a punishment, but rather a consequence of his lifetime of poor fathering and bad behavior. He'll tell you that there are other ways for him to celebrate your marriage and he'll find a way to do it.

If he's not a man worthy of your deepening affection, he'll throw a fit. He'll blame you for his failures. He'll tell you that you're selfish and mean. Possibly, he'll X you out of his life. Or maybe it won't mean anything to him that his conduct is so deplorable that his daughter has chosen to exclude him from her wedding. Perhaps he'll simply let this—like so much else—roll right on by.

But you know what? No matter what he does, one thing is certain: he won't screw up your wedding day. Which, really, should be perfect. Or as close to perfect as it can be. And hard and sad as it is, it's up to you alone to make it that way, just like it's been up to you to make your perfect life.

I know it will be, dear one. I don't even need an invitation to see.

Yours,
Sugar

ROMANTIC LOVE IS NOT A COMPETITIVE SPORT

Dear Sugar,

I'm a twenty-five-year-old woman who started dating a wonderful man a couple of months ago. He's smart, good-natured, funny, and he definitely turns me on. I'm extremely happy to have met him, and even happier that he likes me as much as I like him. Our sex life is great, but my man has this bad habit of mentioning past sexual experiences. He doesn't go into detail, and I don't think he realizes his stories bother me. I think he genuinely trusts me, and simply wants to talk about these things.

Recently, he started to tell me that he'd once been in an orgy. I stopped him and said, "I'm sorry, but I don't want to know anything about this." He was not upset, and he respected my request, but now this image is floating around in my head. Constantly. Haunting me. I keep imagining what it was like, what he was like, what the women were like, and it's making me sick: Sick with jealousy. Sick with insecurity. Sick with fear. It intimidates me, makes me feel crazy.

I'm not worried that he's going to cheat on me to go have an orgy, but I do worry that maybe I won't be enough to satisfy him. I don't know what to do. This image is still in my head—as are others—but I don't know if talking with him about it (i.e., find-

ing out more details, that my imaginative little mind will feast on in potentially terrible ways) will help or just make it worse.

Is this something that, if left alone, I'll eventually just realize is a natural part of his healthy sexual past or do I need to tell him how it makes me feel, at risk of sounding like an irrational, insecure, jealous woman who doesn't trust him, possibly pushing him away? And if I do have to talk to him about it, how can I keep from fanning the crazed fire that's already burning in my head?

Love,
Haunted by His Sexual Past

Dear Haunted by His Sexual Past,

Hmmm, so let me see. Your boyfriend is

1. Wonderful.

2. Extremely smart.

3. Good-natured.

4. Funny.

5. Terrific in bed.

6. As into you as you are into him.

7. Trusting.

8. Trustworthy.

9. Respectful.

10. Interested in talking intimately with you about his life.

Am I going to have to remove my silk gloves and bop you with them?

You aren't haunted by your boyfriend's sexual past. You're haunted by your own irrational, insecure, jealous feelings, and if you continue to behave in this manner you will eventually push your lover away.

I don't mean to be harsh, darling. I'm direct because I sincerely want to help you and because it's clear to me that you're an incredibly good egg. I know it's a kick in the pants to hear that the problem is you, but it's also fucking fantastic. You are, after all, the only person you can change.

So let us dismantle your mania.

You say that your knowledge of your lover's past sexual experiences makes you feel jealous and insecure and afraid that you won't be "enough to satisfy him." *Really?* One thing about love—especially free, unfettered, and uncommitted love such as the kind you and your man are in—is that people pretty much do what they want to do. If you weren't enough to satisfy him, you'd know it because he wouldn't be with you. The fact that he is means that he likes you. A lot. And he doesn't want to be with all the other women he's fucked. Or at least not all that much.

Contrary to what the Bachelor/Bachelorette television franchise and the entire spirit-decimating Hollywood Industrial Complex would have you believe, romantic love is not a competitive sport. Some of those women your boyfriend used to fuck have nicer asses than you. Some are smarter or funnier or fatter or more generous or more messed-up than you. That's okay. That has no bearing on you whatsoever. You're not up against those women. You're running your own race. We don't dig or not dig people based on a comparison chart of body measurements and intellectual achievements and personality quirks. We dig them because we *do*. This guy—your lover, my anxious little peach? *He digs you.*

Don't ruin it because at some point in time he dug other women too. Of course you're going to get a pinchy feeling inside when you think of those women rubbing up against your man! I get that. I know what that's like. It was not so long ago that I was standing in my basement and I came across an envelope addressed to Mr. Sugar, and when I picked it up, out fell about seven thousand little bits of glossy paper that if you put them all together would be a photograph of the woman who was the last woman Mr. Sugar had sex with who wasn't me. And this woman was not just any woman, but an impossibly lithe modern dancer, her body so tight and taut and bitch fiddle-esque I might as well be the Pillsbury Doughboy. And these seven thousand pieces were not the result of Mr. Sugar ripping up the photograph because he didn't want to see the image of the last woman he had sex with who wasn't me anymore. No. This was a love puzzle she made for him—I know because I also read the card inside, which basically said, *Come and get me, Tiger.*

So of course I stood there among the spiderwebs and laundry lint and put the seven thousand pieces together, until there she was—sculpted and bedazzling—in all her not-Sugar glory.

It felt a little like someone had stabbed me in the gut.

But that was all it did. By the time I scooped the seven thousand pieces of her into my palms and returned them to their rightful place in the envelope, that feeling was just a tiny punch. I took a walk with Mr. Sugar later that day and I told him what I had found and we laughed about it a little, and even though I already knew the story of the woman who was in seven thousand tiny pieces, I asked him about her again—what drew him to her, what they did together, and why he did with her what he did—and by the time we were done talking I didn't feel anything in my gut anymore. I only felt closer to him.

I felt that way because we *were* closer. Not because I more deeply understood the woman who makes me look like the Pillsbury Doughboy, but because I more deeply understood Mr. Sugar's inner sanctum. The jealous fire that's burning in you, Haunted—the one that speaks up when your man tries to share stories of his sexual past with you—is keeping you from being close to him. The women your lover knew and loved and fucked and had wild orgies with before you are pieces of his life. He wants to tell you about them because he wants to deepen his relationship with you, to share things about himself that he doesn't share with many others.

This is called intimacy. This is called *fuck yes*. When people do this with us, it's an honor. And when the people who do this with us also happen to be people with whom we are falling in love, it lets us into an orbit in which there is only admission for two.

Isn't that *cool*? It is. It really is, pumpkin. It's gratitude that you should be feeling in place of jealousy and insecurity and fear when your lover shares stories of his life with you. I encourage you to reach for that gratitude. It's located just a stretch beyond the "crazed fire" that's burning in your head. I'm certain that if you apply some effort you'll have it in hand.

Please read the letter you wrote to me out loud to your boyfriend. This will be embarrassing, but do it anyway. Tell him how you feel without making him responsible for your

feelings. Ask him what his motivations are for telling you stories of his sexual past. Ask him if he'd like to hear about your
own sexual experiences. Then take turns telling each other one
story that makes each of you feel a little bit like you've been
stabbed in the gut.

Let yourself be gutted. Let it open you. Start there.

Yours,
Sugar

A BIG LIFE

Dear Sugar,

My question is not about love or sex, but rather one of identity and striving for the best quality of life possible. I, as many other Americans, am struggling financially. Student loans are continuously on my mind and are the cause of almost every stress in my life.

My parents graciously co-signed for my student loans, however, I am being forced to consolidate in order to relieve them of this duty. I realize this is more out of necessity than spite, yet the situation greatly impacts my already poor financial situation and also my dream of attending graduate school. I'm so angry with my parents for putting me in this circumstance instead of supporting me to get a graduate degree for my dream job, and I feel selfish about that.

My relationship with my parents has always been rocky to the point that I've come to realize I'll never get any emotional support from them. I am grateful they were able to help me with an undergraduate degree. However, I have never been close to them, and am often wary of their intentions. Our phone conversations are 100 percent concerning student loans rather than me as a person.

I struggle with student loans often defining me. I know my education, student loans, and occupation will define me to an extent. However, I am more than my job and these items combined. I am a twenty-five-year-old woman who strives for the greatest possible quality of life and to be the best person she can be. But more often than not, I am defined by my "student loan" identity. It is on my mind when I grab a beer, buy new clothes, and in general live my life. I do not spend excessively and have always had careful money management. Yet this situation extends beyond any careful money management.

I have always reached to have a positive spin on life. I fell into a deep, dark hole a few years ago, and have crawled out slowly myself. I purposely changed what I didn't like about my life. It wasn't an easy process by any means, but I am finally in a place where I can breathe. Yet the stresses of student loans bear greatly, and I am having trouble keeping up any positive outlook.

Sugar, I would love your perspective on this situation. I wish my parents would see me for the vibrant woman I am. I wish I could see myself as the vibrant young woman I strive to be and would like to be in the future.

Sincerely,
Wearing Thin

Dear Wearing Thin,

I received zero funding from my parents for my undergraduate education (or from relatives of any sort, for that matter). It wasn't that my mother and stepfather didn't want to help me financially; it was that they couldn't. There was never any question about whether I'd need to fend for myself financially once I was able to. I had to. So I did.

I got a job when I was fourteen and kept one all through

high school. The money I earned went to things like clothes, school activity fees, a junked-out car, gas, car insurance, movie tickets, mascara, and so on. My parents were incredibly generous people. Everything they had they shared with my siblings and me. They housed me, they fed me, and they went to great lengths to create wonderful Christmases, but, from a very young age, if I wanted something I usually had to buy it myself. My parents were strapped. Most winters there would be a couple of months so lean that my mother would have to go to the local food bank for groceries. In the years that the program was in place, my family received blocks of cheese and bags of powdered milk from the federal government. My health insurance all through my childhood was Medicaid— coverage for kids living in poverty.

I moved out of my parents' house a month before my eighteenth birthday. With a combination of personal earnings, grants, scholarships, and student loans I funded the bachelor's degree in English and women's studies that I'm still paying for. As of today, I owe $4,876. Over the years I've taken to saying— sometimes with astonishment, other times with anger, but mostly with a sense of resigned, distorted glee: "I'll be paying off my student loans until I'm forty-three!"

But you know what? I'm waving to you from the shores of forty-three and the months are peeling away. It's looking extremely likely that I'll still be paying off my student loans when I'm forty-four.

Has this ruined my life? Has it kept me from pursuing happiness, my writing career, and ridiculously expensive cowboy boots? Has it compelled me to turn away from fantastically financially unsound expenditures on fancy dinners, travel, "organic" shampoo, and high-end preschools? Has it stopped me from adopting cats who immediately need thousands of dollars in veterinary care or funding dozens of friends' artistic projects on Kickstarter or putting $20 bottles of wine on my credit card or getting the occasional pedicure?

It has not.

I have carried the weight of my student loan debt for about half of my life now, but I have not been "defined by my 'student loan' identity." I do not even know what a student loan identity *is*. Do you? What is a student loan identity?

It is, I guess, exactly what you're stuck with if you can't get some perspective on this matter, sweet pea. It's the threadbare cape you've wrapped around yourself composed of self-pitying half truth. And it absolutely will not serve you.

You need to stop feeling sorry for yourself. I don't say this as a condemnation—I need regular reminders to stop feeling sorry for myself too. I'm going to address you bluntly, but it's a directness that rises from my compassion for you, not my judgment of you. Nobody's going to do your life for you. You have to do it yourself, whether you're rich or poor, out of money or raking it in, the beneficiary of ridiculous fortune or terrible injustice. And you have to do it no matter what is true. No matter what is hard. No matter what unjust, sad, sucky things have befallen you. Self-pity is a dead-end road. You make the choice to drive down it. It's up to you to decide to stay parked there or to turn around and drive out.

You have driven out at least once already, Wearing Thin. You found yourself in a "deep, dark hole" a while back and then you courageously crawled out. You have to do it again. Your student loans will only hold you back if you allow them to. Yep, you have to figure out how to pay them. Yep, you can do that. Yep, it's a pain in the ass. But it's a pain in the ass that I promise will give you back more than you owe.

You know the best thing about paying your own bills? No one can tell you what to do with your money. You say your parents are emotionally unsupportive. You say you're wary of their intentions. You say they don't see you for the vibrant woman that you are. Well, the moment you sign that paper absolving them of their financial obligation to your debts, you are free. You may love them, you may despise them, you may choose to have whatever sort of relationship you choose to have with them, but you are no longer beholden to them in this one particular and important way. You are financially accountable only to yourself. If they express disdain for the jobs you have or the way you spend your money, you can rightly tell them it's none of their damn business. They have absolutely no power over you in this regard. No one does. That's a mighty liberating thing.

And it's a hard thing too. I know, honey bun. I really, really, really do.

Many years ago, I ran into an acquaintance I'll call Kate a few days after we both graduated college (though, in my case, I'm using the word "graduated" rather liberally—see the chapter "The Future Has an Ancient Heart"). Kate was with her parents, who'd not only paid for her entire education, but also for her junior year abroad in Spain, and her summer "educational opportunities" that included unpaid internships at places like *GQ* magazine and language immersions in France and fascinating archaeological digs in God knows what fantastically interesting place. As we stood on the sidewalk chatting, I was informed that (a) Kate's parents had given her a brand-new car for her graduation present, and (b) Kate and her mother had spent the day shopping for the new wardrobe Kate would need for her first-ever job.

Not that she had one, mind you. She was applying for jobs while living off her parents' money, of course. She was sending out her glorious résumé that included the names of foreign countries and trendy magazines to places that were no doubt equally glorious and I knew without knowing something simply glorious would be the result.

It was all I could do not to sock her in the gut.

Unlike Kate, by then I'd had a job. In fact, I'd had sixteen jobs, not including the years I worked as a babysitter before I could legally be anyone's employee. They were janitor's assistant (humiliatingly, at my high school), fast-food restaurant worker, laborer at a wildlife refuge, administrative assistant to a Realtor, English as a Second Language tutor, lemonade cart attendant, small town newspaper reporter, canvasser for a lefty nonprofit, waitress at a Japanese restaurant, volunteer coordinator for a reproductive rights organization, berry picker on a farm, waitress at a vegetarian restaurant, "coffee girl" at an accounting firm, student-faculty conflict mediator, teacher's assistant for a women's studies class, and office temp at a half a dozen places that by and large did not resemble offices and did not engage me in work that struck me as remotely "officey," but rather involved things such as standing on a concrete floor wearing a hairnet, a paper mask and gown, goggles, and plastic gloves and—with a pair of tweezers—placing two pipe cleaners into a sterile box that came to me down a slow conveyor belt for eight excruciating hours a day.

During those years, I sometimes wept with rage. My dream was to be a writer. I wanted it so badly that it made my insides hurt. And to be a writer—I felt sure—I needed to have a big life. Which at the time meant to me amazing experiences such as the sort Kate had. I needed to *experience culture* and *see the world*. I needed to speak French and hang out with people who knew people who worked at *GQ*.

Instead I was forced, by accident of birth, to work one job after another in a desperate attempt to pay the bills. It was so damn unfair. Why did Kate get to study in Spain her junior year? Why did she get to write the word "France" on her résumé? Why did she get her bachelor's degree debt-free and then, on top of that, a new car? Why did she get two parents who would be her financial fallback for years to come and then—decades into a future, which has not yet come to pass— leave her an inheritance upon their deaths?

I didn't get an inheritance! My mother died three months before I "graduated" college and all I got was her ancient, rusted-out Toyota that I quickly sold to a guy named Guy for $500.

Bloody hell.

So here's the long and short of it, Wearing Thin: There is no why. You don't have a right to the cards you believe you should have been dealt. You have an obligation to play the hell out of the ones you're holding. And, dear one, you and I both were granted a mighty generous hand.

Your parents helped you pay for your undergraduate education while you were a student and, presuming you didn't graduate at twenty-five (a presumption which may or may not be correct), they also helped you during the years immediately following your graduation. They've declined to continue to assist you not because they wish to punish you, but because doing so would be difficult for them. This strikes me as perfectly reasonable and fair. You are an educated adult of sound mind, able body, and resilient spirit who has absolutely no reason not to be financially self-sufficient, even if doing so requires you to earn money in ways you find unpleasant.

Your parents' inability to continue paying your student loans will prevent you from realizing your "dream of attending graduate school" only if you let it. Are you really not going to pursue your dream because you now have one more bill than you had before? Are you truly so cowed by adversity?

You don't mention what you'd like to study, but I assure you there are many ways to fund a graduate education. I know a whole lot of people who did not go broke getting a graduate degree. There is funding for tuition remission at many schools, as well as grants, paid research, and teaching assistantships, and—yes—the offer of more student loans. Perhaps more importantly in your case, there are numerous ways to either cancel portions of your student loan debt or defer payment. Financial difficulty, unemployment, attending school at least half-time (i.e., graduate school!), working in certain professions, and serving in the Peace Corps or other community service jobs are some ways that you would be eligible for debt deferment or cancellation. I encourage you to investigate your options so you can make a plan that brings you peace of mind. There are many websites that will elucidate what I have summarized above.

What I know for sure is that freaking out about your student loan debt is useless. You'll be okay. It's only money. And it was money well spent. Aside from the people I love, there is little I value more than my education. As soon as I pay off my undergraduate debt, Mr. Sugar and I intend to start saving for college for the baby Sugars. My dream is that they'll have college experiences that resemble Kate's more than mine. I want them to be able to focus on their studies instead of cramming them in around jobs. I want them to have a junior year abroad wherever they want to go. I want them to have cool internships that they could only take with parental financial support. I want them to go on cultural exchanges and interesting archaeological digs. I want to fund all that stuff I never got to do because no one was able to fund me. I can imagine all they would gain from that.

But I can also imagine what they won't get if Mr. Sugar and I manage to give them the college experience of my dreams.

Turns out, I learned a lot from not being able to go to France. Turns out, those days standing on the concrete floor wearing a hairnet, a paper mask and gown, goggles, and plastic gloves and—with a pair of tweezers—placing two pipe cleaners into a sterile box that came to me down a slow conveyor belt for eight excruciating hours a day taught me something important I couldn't have learned any other way. That job and the fifteen others I had before I graduated college were my own, personal "educational opportunities." They changed my life for the better, though it took me a while to understand their worth.

They gave me faith in my own abilities. They offered me a unique view of worlds that were both exotic and familiar to me. They kept things in perspective. They pissed me off. They opened my mind to realities I didn't know existed. They forced me to be resilient, to sacrifice, to see how little I knew, and also how much. They put me in close contact with people who could've funded the college educations of ten thousand kids and also with people who would've rightly fallen on the floor laughing had I complained to them about how unfair it was that after I got my degree I'd have this student loan I'd be paying off until I was forty-three.

They made my life big. They contributed to an education that money can't buy.

Yours,
Sugar

THE KNOWN UNKNOWNS

Dear Sugar,

I dated this girl for a while only to reach the realization she was a self-absorbed crazy. Last year she and her best friend got into an argument and they stopped being friends. My ex's friend called me up one night and asked me to hang out with her at her house. One thing led to another and I ended up sleeping with her. A few days later, this former best friend of my ex tells me she's engaged. She wears this weird short-haired wig while she breaks off our friends-with-benefits relationship. The thing is, I connected better with her in the two weeks we hung out than I did with my ex in months. Please help me figure out if I should never talk to either one of them again. I'm not a smart man but I do know what love is.

Gump

Dear Gump,

I'd rather be sodomized by a plastic lawn flamingo than vote for a Republican, but as I consider your situation, I can't help but quote the former secretary of defense Donald Rumsfeld, who quite wisely said: "There are known knowns. There are things we know we know. We also know there are known unknowns. That is to say, we know there are some things we do not know. But there are also unknown unknowns, the ones we don't know we don't know."

Shall we start with the known knowns, when it comes to your little triangular quagmire, Gump?

a)   You found your ex-girlfriend to be crazy and broke up with her.

b)   You fucked your ex-girlfriend's ex–best friend for a fortnight and felt "connected."

c)   In spite of such connection, your ex-girlfriend's ex–best friend donned a wig and announced that she has no interest in continuing to fuck you, claiming to be on the brink of a (presumably) monogamous and eternal connection to someone else.

Which brings us to the known unknowns:

a)   Why the wig? And if the wig, why the unnervingly short hair?

b)   Is the ex-girlfriend's ex–best friend actually engaged to be married or is this simply a grandiose ruse to shake you from her disinterested but chickenshit tail?

c)   How can it be that so many people's ex-girlfriends are crazy? What happens to these women? Do they eventually go on to birth babies and care for their elderly parents and scramble up gigantic pans of eggs on Sunday mornings for oodles of lounge-abouts who later have the nerve to inquire about what's for dinner, or is there some corporate Rest Home for Crazy Bitches chain in cities across the land that I am unaware of that houses all these women who used to love men who later claim they were actually crazy bitches?

Lastly, there are the unknown unknowns, the things, Gump, that you don't know you don't know.

a) You have nothing for these women.

b) These women have nothing for you.

c) And yet.

d) *And yet!*

e) You are loved.

Yours,
Sugar

ON YOUR ISLAND

Dear Sugar,

I'm transgender. Born female twenty-eight years ago, I knew I was meant to be male for as long as I can remember. I had the usual painful childhood and adolescence in a smallish town because I was different—picked on by other kids, misunderstood by my (otherwise loving) family.

Seven years ago I told my mom and dad I intended to have a sex change. They were furious and disturbed by my news. They said the worst things you can imagine anyone saying to another human being, especially if that human being is your child. In response, I cut off ties with them and moved to the city where I live now and made a new life living as a man. I have friends and romance in my life. I love my job. I'm happy with who I've become and the life I've made. It's like I've created an island far away and safe from my past. I like it that way.

A couple weeks ago, after years of no contact, I got an email from my parents that blew my mind. They apologized for how they'd responded when I told them about my plans for a sex change. They said they were sorry they never understood and now they do—or at least enough that we could have a relationship again. They said they miss me and they love me.

Sugar, they want me back.

I cried like crazy and that surprised me. I know this might sound odd, but I believed I didn't love my parents anymore or at least my love had become abstract, since they had rejected me and because we've not been in touch. But when I got that email a lot of emotions that I thought were dead came back to life.

This scares me. I have made it because I'm tough. I'm an orphan, but I was doing great without my parents. Do I cave and forgive them and get back in touch and even go visit them as they have asked me to do? Or do I email them and say thank you, but letting you back into my life is out of the question, given our past?

Orphan

Dear Orphan,

Please forgive your parents. Not for them. For you. You've earned the next thing that will happen if you do. You've remade yourself already. You and your mom and dad can remake this too—the new era in which they are finally capable of loving the real you. Let them. Love them back. See how that feels.

What they did to you seven years ago is terrible. They now know that. They're sorry. They've grown and changed and come to understand things that confounded them before. Refusing to accept them for the people they've become over these years of your estrangement isn't all that different from them refusing to accept you for who you are. It's fear-based and punishing. It's weak rather than tough.

You're tough. You've had to ask impossible questions, endure humiliations, suffer internal conflicts, and redefine your life in ways that most people don't and can't even imagine. But you know what?

So have your parents. They had a girl child who became

what they didn't expect. They were cruel and small when you needed them most, but only because they were drowning in their own fear and ignorance.

They aren't drowning anymore. It took them seven years, but they swam to shore. They have arrived at last on your island.

Welcome them.

Yours,
Sugar

PART FOUR

YOU DON'T HAVE TO BE BROKEN FOR ME

If love were an animal, what species would it be and could you train it?

Love would be two animals: a hummingbird and a snake. Both are perfectly untrainable.

What's a weird thing that happened to you?

One time I was hiking up a mountain in New Mexico. It was March, the trail still covered with snow in places. There was no one around but me for hours until I came upon two people—a man and a woman—who had just come upon each other. We were three strangers who met on a mountain in New Mexico. We got to talking and somehow within the first five minutes of knowing each other we figured out that we all had the same birthday, and not only that, we were born in three consecutive years. As we were talking, three feathers blew up to us on the snow. We picked them up.

What do you do when you don't know what to do about something?

I talk to Mr. Sugar and my friends. I make lists. I attempt to analyze the situation from the perspective of my "best self"—the one that's generous, reasonable, forgiving, loving, bighearted, and grateful. I think really hard about what I'll wish I did a year from now. I map out the consequences of the various actions I could take. I ask what my motivations are, what my desires are, what my fears are, what I have to lose, and what I have to gain. I move toward the light, even if it's a hard direction in which to move. I trust myself. I keep the faith. I mess up sometimes.

What are your spiritual beliefs?

I do not believe in God as most people conceive of God, but I believe there is a divine spirit in each of us. I believe there is something bigger than our individual selves that we can touch when we live our lives with integrity, compassion, and love.

What would you like to tell us about sex?

Snakes. Hummingbirds. Perhaps a polar bear.

THE MAGIC OF WANTING TO BE

Dear Sugar,

I am a sixty-four-year-old man who has been single for the past five years. My most recent romantic relationship lasted ten years—eight of which were wonderful. My ex had four adult children and three grandchildren. I liked her children a lot and I loved her grandkids. The year after our relationship ended was the most painful time of my life. (This, even though I'd lost my father in high school, spent a year in Vietnam, and watched another lover die of cancer.)

To survive my heartbreak, I started to do lots of community volunteer work. In the past four years, I've been involved with hospice, I've served on the board of directors of a nonprofit agency that provides services to survivors of domestic violence and sexual assault, I've tutored students at a middle school, and I've worked at an AIDS hotline. During this time, I've had a few dates with women I've met via Internet dating services, and found one good friend among them, but no romance. I've had one sexual encounter since my ex and I broke up, which I paid for. It wasn't very satisfying. I miss sex a lot but I also miss having someone to talk with over a meal or coffee.

There's a new volunteer coordinator at the AIDS hotline where I volunteer and she's wonderful. She is so exciting that I overcame my fears and asked her out to see a play with me. She said she couldn't go because she had a friend visiting from out of town. I believed that. I know I should ask her out again since she seemed willing, but one of my fears is that I am old enough to be her father. I don't want to be a dirty old man!

My counselor said just be light at first—start easy and be funny. Be Cary Grant! she said. But I don't know if I can do that, Sugar.

I give to lots of people, but I have emotional needs too. I want sex, affection, and emotional closeness. I want someone to care about me. I know people do care about me already, but I want someone special. I want to be loved and to receive love; to have someone there for me. My hunger for this is so great that I fear it's too much to ask anyone for. I'm afraid that if the volunteer coordinator did go out with me, I'd share all this with her at once, and though she'd be compassionate, she'd be scared off because she'd perceive me as needy. Of course I know that even if the volunteer coordinator and I did start seeing each other, she may not be the person for me or I the person for her.

But I want to take that chance and see. I don't want my fear to get in the way. What do you think, Sugar?

Fear of Asking Too Much

Dear Fear of Asking Too Much,

Of course you want someone special to love you. A majority of the people who write to me inquire about how they can get the same thing. Some are "hot, smart, and twenty-five," others are "forty-two, a bit chubby, but lots of fun," and others "awesome, but in a muddle." Many are teens and early twenty-somethings whose hearts have just been seriously broken for the first time and they are quite convinced they'll never find a love like that again. A few are seasoned, experienced grown-ups like you whose faith in the prospect is waning. Unique as every letter is, the point each writer reaches is the same: *I want love and I'm afraid I'll never get it.*

It's hard to answer those letters because I'm an advice columnist, not a fortune-teller. I have words instead of a crystal ball. I can't say when you'll get love or how you'll find it or even promise that you will. I can only say you are worthy of it and that it's never too much to ask for it and that it's not crazy to fear you'll never have it again, even though your fears are probably wrong. Love is our essential nutrient. Without it, life has little meaning. It's the best thing we have to give and the most valuable thing we receive. It's worthy of all the hullabaloo.

It seems to me that you're doing everything right, darling. I plucked your letter out of the enormous how-do-I-get-love pile because I was struck by the integrity with which you describe your situation. You're looking for love, not letting that keep you from living your life. In the face of your most recent (and considerable) heartbreak, you opted not to wallow. Instead, you gave generously of yourself by committing to work that's meaningful to you and important to your community. It's no surprise to me that it was in the course of that work you've met someone who genuinely sparks your interest.

So let's talk about her. The "exciting" volunteer coordinator. I agree with you that you shouldn't let your fears get in the way of asking her out. Just don't allow yourself to take it too personally if she says no. I can think of two reasons she might turn you down. One is your significant age difference—many women will date outside their age bracket, but some won't.

The other is your status as a volunteer for the agency that employs her—she may be constrained by workplace policies that prohibit her from dating you, or she may have a personal boundary about doing so (she does, after all, hold a position of professional authority in relation to you).

You won't know either until you find out. I suggest you ask her on a date without specifying the day or time or occasion, so you can avoid the uncertainty of another impossible-to-interpret "I'd love to but . . ." scenario. Just tell her that you think she's great and you wonder if she'd like to go out with you sometime. She'll either say yes or no or okay, but only as friends.

I agree with your counselor that light and easy is the way to begin—with her and with any woman you ask out—even if you have to fake it for a while.

Which happens to be precisely what Cary Grant did.

He wasn't born a suave and bedazzling movie star. He wasn't even born Cary Grant. He was a lonely kid whose depressed mother was sent to a madhouse without his knowledge when he was nine or ten. His father told him she'd gone on an extended vacation. He didn't know what became of her until he was well into his thirties, when he discovered her still institutionalized, but alive. He was kicked out of school in England at fourteen and by sixteen he was traveling across the United States, performing as a stilt-walker and acrobat and mime. Eventually he found his calling as an actor and changed his name to the one we know him by—the name your counselor invoked because it's synonymous with male charisma and charm and fabulousness, but he was always still that boy inside. Of himself Grant said, "I pretended to be somebody I wanted to be and I finally became that person. Or he became me. Or we met at some point."

I suggest you take that approach. It's not about becoming a movie star. It's about the down-in-the-dirt art of inhabiting the person you aspire to be while carrying on your shoulders the uncertain and hungry man you know you are. Your longing for love is only one part of you. I know that it feels gigantic when you're all alone writing to me, or when you imagine going out on that first date with a woman you desire. But don't let your need be the only thing you show. It will scare people off. It will misrepresent how much you have to offer. We have to be whole people to find whole love, even if we have to make it up for a while.

I remembered a younger version of myself as I pondered your letter, FOATM. I recalled a time fifteen years ago, when I was sitting in a café with Mr. Sugar. We'd only been lovers for a month, but we were already in deep, thick in the thrall of the you-tell-me-everything-and-I'll-tell-you-everything-because-I-love-you-so-madly stage, and on this particular afternoon I was telling him the harrowing tale of how I'd gotten pregnant by a heroin addict the year before and how I'd felt so angry, sad, and self-destructive over having an abortion that I'd intentionally sliced a shallow line in my arm with a knife, even though I'd never done that before. When I got to the part about cutting myself, Mr. Sugar stopped me. He said, "Don't get me wrong. I want to hear everything about your life. But I want you to know that you don't need to tell me this to get me to love you. You don't have to be broken for me."

I remember that moment precisely—where he was sitting in relation to where I was sitting, the expression on his face when he spoke, the coat I was wearing—because when he said what he said it felt like he'd scooped a hunk of my insides out and shown it to me in the palm of his hand. It wasn't a good feeling. It had never before occurred to me that I thought in order to get a man to love me I had to appear to be broken for him. And yet when he said it, I recognized it—immediately, humiliatingly—as true. Like truly-uly true. Like how-could-I-have-not-known-this-about-myself-before true. Like what-hole-can-I-go-and-die-in-now true. Because here was a man—a good, strong, sexy, kind, astounding, miraculous man—finally calling my bluff.

You don't have to be broken for me.

I didn't have to be broken for him, even though parts of me were. I could be every piece of myself and he'd love me still. My appeal did not rely on my weakness or my need. It relied on everything I was and wanted to be.

Yours does too, sweet pea. Bring your needy self when you go on that next date with a potential lover, but bring all your other selves too. The strong one. The generous one. The one who became fatherless too young and survived a war and lost one lover to cancer and another to the challenges of a decade together, but came out wiser and more tender for it. Bring the man you aspire to be, the one who already has the love he longs for. Play every piece of yourself and play it with all you've got until you're not playing anymore.

That's what Cary Grant did. The lonely boy who lost his mom in the fog of his father's deceit found himself in the magic of wanting to be. His name was Archibald Leach.

Yours,
Sugar

A GLORIOUS SOMETHING ELSE

Dear Sugar,

My older brother has terrorized me for as long as I can remember. The worst physical abuse was probably the time he gave me a concussion when I didn't answer the door quickly enough, after he rang the bell because he was locked out (I was eight, he was twelve). The worst mental abuse was probably the time he killed my pet rat by cutting her neck and stomach open, then put her on my pillow (I was eleven, he was fourteen). There were all kinds of mini-cruelties in between. I literally have no happy memories between us—I have happy memories of my childhood, but none between us. The closest I felt to a brother-sister love was the time he called me a fat greedy cow for eating the last of the cheese. I either hadn't eaten the cheese, or was trying to deflect his anger, because I protested that it wasn't me, and he replied that he knew it was me because I was "the person in the house who most loved cheese." I remember that exactly, because I was shocked that he knew that about me (I did love cheese, still do). So deep was his disdain for me that the realization that I even existed to him when he wasn't berating or beating me blew my little mind.

My parents did what they could, punishing him when they saw it, but I learned quickly that telling was worse than not telling. If he was punished by them, I'd be punished by him. His behavior worsened as he got older, and it also extended beyond me. He had his first trouble with the law in his early teens, got into drugs, dropped out of high school, and has been in and out of jail, rehab, and mental institutions. By the time I was eighteen, my brother had been arrested multiple times. He had one child and another on the way. I went to college across the country partly to get away from the havoc he wrought.

Now I'm twenty-nine. About a year ago—after ten years of living away from home and learning that just because my brother doesn't love me doesn't mean I'm unlovable (something he would often tell me, by the way)—I moved back to my hometown. I'd been living in a big city, with no hope of moving up in a soul-crushing career. I love my parents and my niece and nephew and I missed them. My hometown has a good master's program in a field I'm interested in and I enrolled. It's been great. I feel energized living again in a town I love.

My brother hasn't changed, but I don't have any contact with him unless he calls me for money or needs help with the kids. My parents aren't so lucky. They support him in every way possible. He has horrible credit, so they bought a house for him to "rent" from them (of course he never pays). He can't get a job with his felony record, so they buy him food and pay for day care and anything his kids need (their moms are okay, but can't support them alone). My parents even bought back the iPods they gave to my niece and nephew for Christmas last year after my brother pawned them.

Of course, he treats my parents just as you would expect a meth/cokehead sociopath to treat people. He steals from them, calls them names, threatens to physically harm them, lies to them about everything and anything. My parents get upset, draw the line, call everything the last straw, but they always give him a *second chance because he is their son. Always. He manipulates them with kindness as easily as he manipulates them with terror, and when he does that, things are fine for a week, then get bad again.*

Last week it got the worse it's ever been. My mom wouldn't give him money—she'd just given him $100 the day before and had nothing more to give—so he threw a wine bottle at her, spit in her face, threw plates on the floor, rampaged through the house, threw their cat against the wall, and destroyed furniture. He left when my mom called the cops, though he stopped to steal beers from the fridge as he went.

Things were strict for a few days: my parents would not return his calls and they would not allow him into the house again, only interacting with his baby mamas in regards to the kids. But, as always, he weaseled his way back in without an apology or even acknowledgment of the incident. Seriously, Sugar, that's what gets me! These things happen, and he calls them for a favor the next day and pretends nothing was wrong. My parents have long tried to get him help for anything and everything that could help him stop being a lunatic, but he refuses. It's the rest of the world that has a problem, not him. My parents blame drugs because they didn't see the worst of him as a kid, like I did. I think he's just an evil person.

Yet, I would forgive him the nastiness of his brotherhood. Yes, it was beyond anything normal, but we're adults now, and if he was apologetic and had grown out of his "bullying," I would have been fine. I would have welcomed a relationship. But I can't forgive what he's done to my parents. If anyone else treated them this way, there would be restraining orders and court dates.

This is a long story, Sugar, for a simple question about Christmas.

I want my brother out of my life. I think about what he's done to my parents and I feel such an impotent rage. While writing this letter to you, I had to leave the computer at points to calm down because my fingers were shaking. I don't want to sit across the table from someone who's called my mother a fucking cunt. But as long as my parents let him in, I feel I can't cut him out. We always have a family Christmas, but this year I want to put my foot down. I want to say that I won't be there when he is. I'll do whatever my parents want, because I love them, but I won't do anything involving him, because I love them. I cannot abide anyone who would hurt them. He's stolen their peace of mind, their belief in themselves as good people, and their identities: literally—having committed such fraud via their credit cards and bank accounts; because they refuse to press charges, their credit is shot.

I worry that refusing to see my brother at Christmas would be an empty gesture and that it would only cause more drama and pain in my parents' lives. I would miss my niece and nephew on Christmas and I want to make a normal day for them (though I see them all the time, since my parents take care of them 99 percent of the time when my brother has custody). But I don't know what else I can do.

I feel so powerless—the same way I felt as an eleven-year-old living with someone who threatened to kill me on a weekly basis. I can't do anything to help my parents, and they won't do anything to help themselves. I can't talk to friends about this, because they don't understand why my parents don't cut him off. My parents have been told by lawyers, cops, therapists, and friends—and me—that they are enabling my brother and that they should cut ties with him, but they won't. I've given up on trying to change their approach. I just want to feel in control of who I have in my life. I don't think I should have to pretend to love someone who hurts my parents. Yet I know my parents would be hurt if I refuse to have Christmas with them and my brother. They'd see it as a judgment on them. Sugar, what should I do?

Love and kisses,
C.

Dear C.,

Screw Christmas. Something far more important is at stake. That would be your emotional well-being, as well as the dignity and grace and integrity of your life. It's such a cliché, but it's true: you must set boundaries.

Fucked-up people will try to tell you otherwise, but boundaries have nothing to do with whether you love someone or not. They are not judgments, punishments, or betrayals. They are a purely peaceable thing: the basic principles you identify for yourself that define the behaviors that you will tolerate from others, as well as the responses you will have to those behaviors. Boundaries teach people how to treat you, and they teach you how to respect yourself. In a perfect world, our parents model healthy personal boundaries for us. In your world, you must model them for your parents—for whom boundaries have either never been in place or have gone gravely askew.

Emotionally healthy people sometimes behave badly. They lose their tempers, say things they either shouldn't have said or could have said better, and occasionally allow their hurt, fear, or anger to compel them to act in inappropriate, unkind ways. They eventually acknowledge this and make amends. They are imperfect, but essentially capable of discerning which of their behaviors are destructive and unreasonable, and they attempt to change them, even if they don't wholly succeed. That's called being human.

The situation you describe is different, C. It's a deeply embedded family system that's entirely off-kilter. Your story reads like a hostage tale, one in which your destructive and irrational brother is holding the gun. He has taught you and your parents how to treat him and you all obey, even when it's nuts to do so. In what universe does a man assault his mother, abuse her cat, and ransack her house?

Yours. Which means you must exile yourself from it or you will suffer forever. You must make a world of your own. You can take the first steps now, but the internal weeding out of so much familial dysfunction is going to be a years-long process, no doubt. I strongly encourage you to seek counseling.

So let's talk about Christmas.

What a terrible situation you're in. Your brother is a socio-path and your parents are his suckers. There is no way to extricate yourself from this without extricating yourself. You want to cut off all ties with your brother, so do that. Remember what I said about boundaries not having anything to do with whether you loved someone or not? Here's where that part comes in. Your parents are good people who have lost themselves in a nightmare. I don't agree with their continued support of your brother, but I understand their impulse to do so. Your brother is their son, the boy they'd have died for prob-ably from the minute he was born. But they didn't have to die for him. He's killing them instead.

You mustn't stand by, a willing onlooker. I'm not telling you that. *You're* telling me that. So don't stand by. Tell your parents you love them and then simply *love them*. Give to them all the gorgeous daughterness you have inside of you. But do not participate in their self-destruction. Inform them that you will be cutting off all ties with your brother and map out a plan for seeing them on Christmas and beyond. Don't let them try to talk you out of your decision, even if your decision means you spend Christmas alone. Let this be the first step of many in your liberation from the tyranny of your brother.

As for your niece and nephew, I hope you can continue to be a presence in their lives. How about approaching their mothers to make arrangements to see them when they are not under your brother's care? (You didn't ask about this, but I'm terribly worried about those kids. You say their mothers are "okay," but you also say your brother—who is not okay—has partial custody of his children. Even if your parents take care of them "99 percent of the time," it doesn't sound to me like your brother should be the legal custodian of anyone right now, even for a little while. I encourage you to investigate ways you can protect those children by working with your niece's and nephew's mothers, and possibly your parents, to legally limit your brother's contact with them.)

Your fear about your parents being hurt by your choices is valid. They will likely feel some pain when you tell them about your plans. Your cooperation in their wildly co-dependent behaviors has no doubt been a consolation to them. When you set new boundaries there is often strife and sorrow, but your life will be changed for the better. And maybe—just maybe— the example you set will motivate your parents to make some changes of their own.

Lastly, what I'd like to impress upon you is this: In spite of the complexity of your situation, it's notable that you didn't waver when it came to what you know to be the right thing to do. That's because you know the right thing to do. So do it.

It's hard, I know. It's one of the hardest things you'll ever have to do. And you're going to bawl your head off doing it. But I promise you it will be okay. Your tears will be born of grief, but also of relief. You will be better for them. They will make you harder, softer, cleaner, dirtier. Free.

A glorious something else awaits.

Yours,
Sugar

A TUNNEL THAT WAKES YOU

Dear Sugar,

I think (know) I have a serious problem with alcohol. It freaks me out; it even wakes me up in my sleep because I am terrified of this tunnel I keep going further into. No one has ever said anything to me about it, because I've always been professional, calm, laid-back, and in control. I don't think I have control anymore, and it seriously scares me. I drink before work, when I wake up, drink during lunch, and drink as soon as I get home to fall asleep, when no one can see me doing it.

But I also drink out socially, with my friends, and they are impossible NOT to drink around, and they actually prefer to see me "on," which is the only state I seem to be comfortable with now. I don't think I can give up drinking out socially, because without my friends, I would probably just end up drinking more at home alone.

I know you are not a psychologist, but I would like to get some unbiased advice about this. I have tried to approach some people about this before (including therapy), but it has proved fruitless, and also really embarrassing. I guess I am hoping you have the magic, easy solution to this, and I am going to assume there probably isn't one.

Thanks.
Drinker

Dear Drinker,

My unbiased advice is that you know you're addicted to alcohol and you need help. You're right that there is no "magic, easy solution" to this, sweet pea, but there is a solution. It's that you stop using alcohol. Privately. Socially. Morning. Noon. Night. And probably forever.

You will do this when you're ready to do this. To be ready you need only the desire to change your life. To succeed, most people need a community of support. Alcoholics Anonymous is a good place to begin. There, you will find those who struggle in the same ways you do; people who once told themselves the same lies about what was "impossible."

Addiction is a tunnel that wakes you up in the middle of the night. Everything else happens out here in the light.

Yours,
Sugar

HOW THE REAL WORK IS DONE

Dear Sugar,

I am newly civilly unioned. I love my spouse (wife?) dearly, though we have our issues. What appears to me to be our biggest problem—the one that keeps me up some nights—is that she won't get a job.

We're a quite poor couple in our mid-twenties, both in school. We've been together for four years, and in that time my girl has had three jobs: one she was laid off from because the job ended, one she quit, and one she was fired from. All these jobs lasted fewer than six months.

She's made halfhearted attempts to placate me in the year and a half she's been unemployed. Mostly though? We fight, she cries, she shuts down, she lies and says she's been trying to find a job, even though I know she hasn't. She has moderate social anxiety issues and says she can't work any jobs involving other people because of it. She doesn't even offer up excuses for not applying to any number of other jobs I've suggested (throwing newspapers! work-study in a low-traffic area of her school! selling her lovely quirky crafts online! dishwashing!). At one point, she suggested that she would rather donate plasma every week than get a job.

Sugar, I'm a full-time student working two jobs. We're barely getting by on what I'm bringing in. We frequently must rely on my parents for money, and they're rapidly losing their ability to keep up with my financial needs in addition to their own. I worry so much about this. I worry that my partner will never be motivated enough to hold a job. I worry about what her job prospects are going to be when she reaches thirty in a few years without ever actually having held a long-term job. I worry that, though she sees my struggles, she will never feel guilty enough to get things kicked into gear.

What can I possibly do to get her to take job searching seriously? She's emotionally fragile, due to years of social anxiety, sexual and emotional abuse from her father, and a recurring eating disorder. Because of that, I don't want to threaten her with any ultimatums, because I wouldn't mean any of them and I fear it would do more harm than good. My girl's got a good heart, but she is so afraid of failure that she willfully ignores how much I sacrifice to keep our rent paid. I love her, and she loves me, yet I feel I'm without a partner in this. I don't know what to do next. Please help.

Working for Two

Dear Sugar,

My husband makes me laugh every day, EVERY day, multiple times. He's been my best friend for years and is still my favorite person in the world. He's enriched my life in so many innumerable ways, and he has told me that I have reciprocated that enrichment. I do love him so. SO. And I am quite certain he loves me.

The issue is that he's been unemployed for over three years. He did try to find a job for a while (and I believe he still occasionally does), but now I think he feels unqualified for anything other than the job he used to hate and also that he has no reason to be hired for anything else. Inertia has taken him over. He wants to write, but feels unworthy, so he doesn't write. He is brilliant and funny and erudite, but he sees none of that. He doesn't paint/ sculpt/whatever might give him fulfillment or do anything that would move him forward in his life. I would be happy with him doing anything (and I truly mean that), yet he seems to be stuck. He's also bipolar and self-hating and all of that.

Fortunately, my job carries us financially, but only barely. The house is clean, the laundry is done, the dog is walked, but in three years he hasn't been able to figure out a way to financially contribute to our household. He's stressed out about the fact that we have trouble paying our bills, but he does nothing (truly nothing) to change it. If I had plenty of money, I'd be fine with this, but I don't. I've been carrying this load alone for a long time. I have repeatedly tried to talk to him about this, to no avail.

I love him so much and I'm so sad about this. I think my staying with him may be ruining both our lives. Perhaps my support is keeping him from fulfilling his dreams. What do you think, Sugar?

Responsible One

Dear Women,

As I'm sure you both know, there is nothing inherently wrong with a spouse who makes no money. The most common scenario in which it makes sense for one spouse to earn an income while the other does not is when the couple has a child or children who must be cared for, which goes along with a domestic life that requires constant vigilance of the cleaning, shopping, cooking, washing, folding, tidying up, taking-the-cat-to-the-vet-and-the-kids-to-the-dentist variety. In this situation and others like it, the "nonworking" spouse is often doing more work, hour for hour, than the "working" spouse, and though on paper it appears that the one with the job is making a greater financial contribution to the household than the one who "stays at home," if you ran the numbers and figured out what it would cost to employ someone to do the work of the "nonworking" spouse, it becomes apparent that one should probably shut their big trap when it comes to who is contributing what.

There are other reasons, usually more fleeting, that one spouse may not be earning money in any given period: if he or she is unemployed or seriously ill or attending school full-time or caring for an infirm or dying parent or working in a field in which the money comes only after an extended period of what may or may not turn out to be unpaid labor.

Neither of you appears to be in any of those circumstances. While it's technically true that both of your spouses are unemployed, it seems clear that something more complex is at play here. Your spouse, Working for Two, has such a spotty and brief record of employment that unemployment is her customary mode rather than a temporary state of affairs. Your spouse, Responsible One, has apparently drifted into a post-unemployment funk and has given up the search for a job. You both feel overly burdened and seriously bummed out. You're both desperate for change. You've both shared your feelings with your partners and been met with compassionate indifference (i.e., *I feel terrible, sweetie, but I'm not going to do a damn thing about it*).

What a mess.

I hope it's not going to be news to you when I say you can't make your partners get jobs. Or at least you can't make them get jobs by doing what you've done so far—appealing to their better nature regarding what's fair and reasonable, imploring them to act out of their concern for you and your wishes, as well as your collective financial well-being. Whatever dark angst is keeping your spouses from taking responsibility for their lives—depression, anxiety, a loss of self-confidence, a fear-based desire to maintain the status quo—it's got a greater hold on them than any angry fits you've pitched about being the only one bringing in any dough.

It's a truism of transformation that if we want things to be different we have to change ourselves. I think both of you are going to have to take this to heart the way anyone who has ever changed anything about their lives has had to take it to heart: by making it not just a nice thing we say, but a hard thing we *do*. Your spouses may or may not decide to get jobs in response to your changes, but that is out of your control.

The way I see it, there are two paths out of your misery. They are:

a)   accept the fact that your partner won't get a job (or even seriously delve into the reasons he/she won't seek one), or

b)   decide your partner's refusal to contribute financially is unacceptable and end the relationship (or at least break it off until circumstances change).

So let's say you went with option A. Both of you express love and adoration for your partners. You don't want to lose them. How might you accept your deadbeat darlings for who they are at this era of their lives? Is this possible? Is what they give you worth the burden they place upon you? Are you willing to shelve your frustrations about your partner's fiscal failings for a period of time? If so, how long? Can you imagine feeling okay with being the sole employed member of your union a year from now? Three years? Ten? Might you together agree to downsize and reduce expenses so that your single income becomes more feasible? What if you rethought the whole thing? What if instead of lamenting the fact that your partner is unemployed, the two of you embraced it as a choice you made together? Reframing it as a mutually agreed upon decision, in which you are the breadwinners and your partners are the significantly supportive, non-income-earning helpmates, would give you a sense of agency that's lacking now.

Working for Two, you don't mention if your partner does more than her share around the house, but Responsible One, you state that "the house is clean, the laundry is done, the dog is walked." That's something. In fact, it's quite a lot. It's not money, but your husband is positively contributing to your lives by seeing to those things. Oodles of people with jobs would be deeply pleased to return to a clean house that doesn't contain mountains of dirty laundry and a dog demanding to go out. Many people pay people to do those things for them or they return from work only to have to work another, domestic shift. Your husband's unpaid work benefits you. With that in mind, what other ways could your partners lighten your burden if they refuse to lighten it financially? Might you draw up a list of your household and individual needs—financial, logistical, domestic, and administrative—and divide the responsibilities in a manner that feels equitable, in terms of overall workload, that takes your job into account?

While I encourage you to sincerely consider coming to peace with your spouses' perpetual unemployment, I'll admit I'm presenting this option with more optimism than I feel. One thing I noted about both of your letters is that—while money is a major stress point—what worries you most deeply isn't money. It's how apathetic your partners are, how indifferent they are to their ambitions, whether they be income-earning or not. It would be one thing if your partners were these happy, fulfilled people who simply believed their best contribution to your coupledom would be as homemakers and personal assistants, but it seems clear that your partners have used home and the security of your relationships as a place to retreat and wallow, to sink into rather than rise out of their insecurities and doubts.

So let's talk about option B. Working for Two, you say that you won't give your partner an ultimatum, but I encourage you to rethink that. Perhaps it will help if you come to see what I see so clearly now: that you and Responsible One are the ones who've been given ultimatums, at least of an unstated, passive-aggressive sort.

Ultimatums have negative connotations for many because they're often used by bullies and abusers, who tend to be comfortable pushing their partners' backs against a wall, demanding that he or she choose this or that, all or nothing. But when used by emotionally healthy people with good intentions, ultimatums offer a respectful and loving way through an impasse that will sooner or later destroy a relationship on its own anyway. Besides, the two of you have been up against the wall for years now, forced by your partners to be the sole financial providers, even when you have repeatedly stated that you will not and cannot continue to be. You've continued. Your partners have made their excuses and allowed you to do what you said you don't want to do, even though they know it makes you profoundly unhappy.

Your ultimatum is simple. It's fair. And it's stating your own intentions, not what you hope theirs will be. It's: *I won't live like this anymore. I won't carry our financial burdens beyond my desires or capabilities. I won't enable your inertia. I won't, even though I love you. I won't, because I love you. Because doing so is ruining us.*

The difficult part is, of course, what to do in the wake of those words, but you don't have to know exactly what it will be right away. Maybe it will be breaking up. Maybe it will be mapping out a course of action that will save your relationships. Maybe it will be the thing that finally forces your partners to change. Whatever it is, I strongly advise you both to seek answers to the deeper questions underlying your conflicts with your partners while you figure it out. Your joint and individual issues run deeper than someone not having a job.

You can do this. I know you can. It's how the real work is done. We can all have a better life if we make one.

Yours,
Sugar

THE GHOST SHIP THAT DIDN'T CARRY US

Dear Sugar,

For those of us who aren't lucky enough to "just know," how is a person to decide if he or she wants to have a child? I'm a forty-one-year-old man and have been able thus far to postpone that decision while I got all the other pieces of my life in order. Generally speaking, I've enjoyed myself as a childless human. I've always had a hunch that as I continued on my path my feelings about parenthood would coalesce one way or the other and I would follow that where it took me. Well, my path has taken me here, to the point where all of my peers are having children and expounding on the wonders (and, of course, trials) of their new lives, while I keep enjoying the same life.

I love my life. I love having the things that I know will be in shorter supply if I become a parent. Things like quiet, free time, spontaneous travel, pockets of nonobligation. I really value them. I'm sure that everyone does, but on the grand gradient of the human condition, I feel I sit farther to one end than most. To be blunt, I'm afraid to give that up. Afraid that if I become a parent, I will miss my "old" life.

As a male, I know that I have a little more leeway in terms of the biological clock, but my partner, who is now forty, does not.

*She is also on the fence about a child, and while the finer points
of our specific concerns on the subject may differ, we are largely
both grappling with the same questions. At this point, we're trying to tease out the signal from the noise: Do we want a child
because we really want a child, or are we thinking about having
one because we're afraid we will regret not having one later? We
both now accept that the time for deferment is coming to a close
and we need to step up and figure it out.*

*When I try to imagine myself as a father, I often think back
to my two wonderful cats that I had from the age of twenty-two
until I buried them in the backyard almost two years ago. They
were born prematurely to a mother that was too sick to care for
them. I bottle-fed them, woke up in the middle of the night to
wipe their bottoms, was there for every stage of their growth from
kitten to cat, and basically loved the bejeezus out of them for their
entire lives. I raised them to be trusting, loving creatures. And
I did it consciously, even thinking at the time that it was great
training for the day I had a child if that felt like the right thing. I
really was their dad. And I loved it. Yet I also loved it that I could
put an extra bowl of food and water on the floor and split town
for a three-day weekend.*

*So here I am now exploring the idea of becoming a father.
Exploring it for real and deeply. Sugar, help me.*

*Signed,
Undecided*

Dear Undecided,

There's a poem I love by Tomas Tranströmer called "The Blue
House." I think of it every time I consider questions such
as yours about the irrevocable choices we make. The poem

is narrated by a man who is standing in the woods near his house. When he looks at his house from this vantage point, he observes that it's as if he'd just died and he was now "seeing the house from a new angle." It's a wonderful image—that just-dead man among the trees—and it's an instructive one too. There is a transformative power in seeing the familiar from a new, more distant perspective. It's in this stance that Tranströmer's narrator is capable of seeing his life for what it is while also acknowledging the lives he might have had. The poem strikes a chord in me because it's so very sadly and joyfully and devastatingly true. Every life, Tranströmer writes, "has a sister ship," one that follows "quite another route" than the one we ended up taking. We want it to be otherwise, but it cannot be: the people we might have been live a different, phantom life than the people we are.

And so the question is who do you intend to be. As you've stated in your letter, you believe you could be happy in either scenario—becoming a father or remaining childless. You wrote to me because you want clarity about which course to take, but perhaps you should let that go. Instead, take a figurative step into the forest like that man in the poem and simply gaze for a while at your blue house. I think if you did, you'd see what I see: that there will likely be no clarity, at least at the outset; there will only be the choice you make and the sure knowledge that either one will contain some loss.

You and I are about the same age. I have two children, whom I birthed in close succession in my mid-thirties. If a magic baby fairy had come to me when I was childless and thirty-four and promised to grant me another ten years of fertility so I could live a while longer in the serene, feline-focused, fabulously unfettered life I had, I'd have taken it in a flash. I, too, had spent my adult years assuming that someday, when it came to becoming a mother, I'd "just know." I, too, placed myself on the leave-me-the-hell-alone end on the "grand gradient of the human condition." I decided to become pregnant when I did because I was nearing the final years of my fertility and because my desire to do this thing that everyone said was so profound was just barely stronger than my doubts about it were.

So I got knocked up. With a total lack of clarity. On this, Mr. Sugar and I were in complete accord. Though we were generally pleased to be having a baby, we were also deeply alarmed. We liked to have sex and ramble around foreign countries in decidedly un-baby-safe ways and spend hours reading in silence on two couches that faced each other across the living room. We liked to work for days without interruption on our respective art forms and take unscheduled naps and spend weeks backpacking in the wilderness.

We did not, throughout my pregnancy, have many conversations about how awesome it was going to be once our baby was born and doing these things would become either indisputably or close to impossible. Mostly, we had ambivalent, mildly sickening talks about how we hoped we hadn't made a dreadful mistake. *What if we love the baby but not as much as everyone says we will?* I'd ask him every couple of weeks. *What if the baby bores us or annoys us or grosses us out? What if we want to ride our bicycles across Iceland or hike around Mongolia? Fuck. We do want to ride our bicycles across Iceland or hike around Mongolia!*

My point is not that you should have a baby, Undecided. It's that possibly you expect to have a feeling about wanting to have a baby that will never come and so the clear desire for a baby isn't an accurate gauge for you when you're trying to decide whether or not you should have one. I know that sounds crazy, but it's true.

So what, then, *is* an accurate gauge?

You say that you and your partner don't want to make the choice to become parents simply because you're afraid you "will regret not having one later," but I encourage you to reexamine that. Thinking deeply about your choices and actions from the stance of your future self can serve as both a motivational and a corrective force. It can help you stay true to who you really are as well as inspire you to leverage your desires against your fears.

Not regretting it later is the reason I've done at least three-quarters of the best things in my life. It's the reason I got pregnant with my first child, even though I'd have appreciated another decade from the magic baby fairy, and it's also the reason I got pregnant with my second child, even though I was already overwhelmed by the first. Because you are content in your current childless life, attempting to determine what you might regret later strikes me as the best way for you to meaningfully explore if having a child is important to you. So much so, that I suspect that whether you'll regret it later is the only question you must answer. It is the very one that will tell you what to do.

You already know the answers to everything else. You know you're open to becoming a father and that you're also open to remaining childless. You know you've gotten pleasure and satisfaction from nurturing the lives of others (in the form of your dear cats) and also that you get deep satisfaction from the freedom and independence a child-free life allows.

What don't you know? Make a list. Write down everything

you don't know about your future life—which is everything, of course—but use your imagination. What are the thoughts and images that come to mind when you picture yourself at twice the age you are now? What springs forth if you imagine the eighty-two-year-old self who opted to "keep enjoying the same life" and what when you picture the eighty-two-year-old self with a thirty-nine-year-old son or daughter? Write down "same life" and "son or daughter" and underneath each make another list of the things you think those experiences would give to and take from you and then ponder which entries on your list might cancel each other out. Would the temporary loss of a considerable portion of your personal freedom in middle age be significantly neutralized by the experience of loving someone more powerfully than you ever have? Would the achy uncertainty of never having been anyone's father be defused by the glorious reality that you got to live your life relatively unconstrained by the needs of another?

What is a good life? Write "good life" and list everything that you associate with a good life, then rank that list in order of importance. Have the most meaningful things in your life come to you as a result of ease or struggle? What scares you about sacrifice? What scares you about not sacrificing?

So there you are on the floor, your gigantic white piece of paper with things written all over it like a ship's sail, and maybe you don't have clarity still, maybe you don't know what to do, but you feel something, don't you? The sketches of your real life and your sister life are right there before you and you get to decide what to do. One is the life you'll have; the other is the one you won't. Switch them around in your head and see how it feels. Which affects you on a visceral level? Which won't let you go? Which is ruled by fear? Which is ruled by desire? Which makes you want to close your eyes and jump and which makes you want to turn and run?

In spite of my fears, I didn't regret having a baby. My son's body against mine was the clarity I never had. The first few weeks of his life, I felt honestly rattled by the knowledge of how close I'd come to opting to live my life without him. It was a penetrating, relentless, unalterable thing, to be his mother, my life ending and beginning at once.

If I could go back in time I'd make the same choice in a snap. And yet, there remains my sister life. All the other things I could have done instead. I wouldn't know what I couldn't know until I became a mom, and so I'm certain there are things I don't know because I can't know because I did. Who would I have nurtured had I not been nurturing my two children over these past seven years? In what creative and practical forces would my love have been gathered up? What didn't I write because I was catching my children at the bottoms of slides and spotting them as they balanced along the tops of low brick walls and pushing them endlessly in swings? What did I write because I did? Would I be happier and more intelligent and prettier if I had been free all this time to read in silence on a couch that sat opposite of Mr. Sugar's? Would I complain less? Has sleep deprivation and the consumption of an exorbitant number of Annie's Homegrown Organic Cheddar Bunnies taken years off my life or added years onto it? Who would I have met if I had bicycled across Iceland and hiked around Mongolia and what would I have experienced and where would that have taken me?

I'll never know, and neither will you of the life you don't choose. We'll only know that whatever that sister life was, it was important and beautiful and not ours. It was the ghost ship that didn't carry us. There's nothing to do but salute it from the shore.

Yours,
Sugar

YOUR INVISIBLE INNER TERRIBLE
SOMEONE

Dear Sugar,

I'm twenty-nine and dating a man that I adore; we're planning to move in together soon. I have a stable job that I hate, but I hope that I'll one day find something I enjoy. I have family and friends and hobbies and interests and love. So much love. And I'm desperately afraid that I'm going to have cancer.

I'm terrified that sooner or later, I'll be diagnosed. My mother had breast cancer when I was in college. She survived hers, but in some ways, she didn't. It broke her, Sugar. My father died of liver cancer when I was in high school—he was never lucky enough to be counted "a survivor." My grandmother had a brain tumor when I was a newborn; she didn't live to see my first birthday. As much as I take care of my health, as much as I try to be careful, I have this niggling doubt that my genes are setting me up for failure.

I know you can't tell me whether or not I will have cancer, and I know you can't tell me when. But what I'm struggling with— what I need help figuring out—is how to make the decisions in my life while keeping this possibility in mind. You know the decisions I mean: the Big Ones.

How do I decide whether or not to get married? How do I

look into the face of this man I adore and explain to him what he might have to go through if I am diagnosed? And worse, if I don't make it? I've already decided not to have children. How can I saddle a child with something that I don't even think I can face myself? How do I plan for the future when there may be no future to plan for? They say "Live your life to the fullest because there may be no tomorrow," but what about the consequences of "no tomorrow" on the people that you love? How do I prepare them for what I might have to go through? How do I prepare myself?

Scared of the Future

Dear Scared of the Future,

There's a crazy lady living in your head. I hope you'll be comforted to hear that you're not alone. Most of us have an invisible inner terrible someone who says all sorts of nutty stuff that has no basis in truth.

Sometimes when I'm all pretzeled up inside and my own crazy lady is nattering on, I'll stop and wonder where she got her information. I'll ask her to reveal her source. I'll demand some proof. Did her notions come from actual facts based in reason or did she/I dredge them up from the hell pit that burns like a perpetual fire at the bottom of my needy, selfish, famished little soul?

Is there credible evidence that my friends secretly don't like me very much or were they all simply deep in conversation when I walked into the room and it took them a beat to say hello? Was the acquaintance who said "With class sizes that big, I'd never send my son to public school" actually saying that I was a second-rate mother, recklessly destroying my children because there are thirty kids in their classes, or was she simply sharing her own complex parenting decisions with me? When I receive letters from people who disagree passionately with a particular piece of advice I've given in this column, is it true that it would be absolutely impossible for every reader to agree with me on every point or that I'm a stupid piece of know-nothing shit who should never write again?

If you asked me to draw a picture of myself, I'd draw two. One would be a portrait of a happy, self-confident, regular-looking woman, and the other would be a close-up of a giant gaping mouth that's ravenous for love. Many days I have to silently say to myself: *It's okay. You are loved. You are loved even if some people don't love you. Even if some people hate you. You are okay even if sometimes you feel slighted by your friends or you sent your kids to school someplace that someone else would not send her kid or you wrote something that riled up a bunch of people.*

I have to cut the crazy lady to the quick rather often. Over the years, my emotional well-being has depended on it. If I let her get the upper hand, my life would be smaller, stupider, squatter, sadder.

So will yours if you let it. You have my deepest sympathy and my most sincere understanding, but you're not thinking clearly on this. You're granting the crazy lady way too much power. Your sorrow and fear has clouded your ability to be reasonable about your mortality. And if you continue in this vein, it's going to rob you of the life you deserve—the one in which your invisible inner terrible someone finally shuts her trap.

You do not need to look into your lover's eyes and "explain to him what he might have to go through" should you be diagnosed with cancer. Tell him about your family's experiences with cancer and about how you made it through those difficult times. Share your fears with him, and your grief. But don't make the illogical line from your relatives' real illnesses to your nonexistent one. Only the crazy lady is pretty convinced you'll get cancer and die young. All the rest of us are entirely in the dark. Yes, you need to be aware of your risks and monitor your health, but do so while remembering that in most cases a genetic history of any given disease is only one predictor of your own likelihood of getting it.

Any of us could die any day of any number of causes. Would you expect your partner to explain what you might have to go through should he die in a car accident, of heart failure, or by drowning? Those are things that could happen too. You are a mortal being like every human and June bug, like every black bear and salmon. We're all going to die, but only some of us are going to die tomorrow or next year or in the next half century. And, by and large, we don't know which of us it will be, when, and of what.

That mystery is not the curse of our existence; it's the wonder. It's what people are talking about when they talk about the circle of life that we're all part of whether we sign up to be or not—the living, the dead, those being born right this moment, and the others who are fading out. Attempting to position yourself outside the circle isn't going to save you from anything. It isn't going to keep you from your grief or protect those you love from theirs when you're gone. It isn't going to extend your life or shorten it. Whatever the crazy lady whispered in your ear was wrong.

You're here. So be here, dear one. You're okay with us for now.

Yours,
Sugar

WAITING BY THE PHONE

Dear Sugar,

In this age of Facebook and Twitter, how are we supposed to get over our exes (who we're trying to be friends with) while being slammed with status updates and tweets (or, as I like to call them, li'l 140 characters of pain)?

> *Yours,*
> *Constantly Hitting Refresh*

Dear Constantly Hitting Refresh,

We aren't supposed to get over our exes by tracking their every move on Facebook and Twitter, sweetie. Facebook and Twitter are heartbreak torture machines. Back in Sugar's youth the goddamn telephone was torture enough. Here's how it went:

Would it ring? It would not ring.

Should you call? You should not call.

But you always called. You couldn't help but call because your heart was crushed and you thought maybe if you talked it out *one more time* the person who crushed your heart would change his/her mind and uncrush it.

So you'd sit for a while with the phone in your hand and it would feel like the phone was literally on fire with your pain and longing, and finally you'd dial and it would ring and ring, until at last the answering machine picked up and there would be his/her voice—so cheerful! so flip! so excruciatingly out of reach!—and the beep would beep and you'd start speaking into the silence, sounding remotely like the cool, strong, reasonably detached person you used to be before the beloved owner of the answering machine crushed your heart, but within about four seconds your voice would go all high and shaky and desperate and you'd stammer something out about how you just wanted to call to say hi because you missed him/her so much and because, after all, you were still friends and because, well, you just *wanted to talk* even though there was really nothing more to say and you'd finally shut up and hang up and a millisecond later you'd burst into gasping sobs.

Then you'd sob and sob and sob so hard you couldn't stand up until finally you'd go quiet and your head would weigh seven hundred pounds and you'd lift it from your hands and rise to walk into the bathroom to look at yourself solemnly in the mirror and you'd know for sure that you were dead. Living but dead. And all because this person didn't love you anymore, or even if he/she loved you he/she didn't want you and what kind of life was that? It was no life. There would be no life anymore. There would only be one unbearable minute after another and during each of those minutes this person you wanted would not want you and so you would begin to cry again and you'd watch yourself cry pathetically in the mirror until you couldn't cry anymore, so you'd stop.

You'd wash your face and brush your hair and apply lip balm even though you now looked like a tropical blowfish and you'd float out to your car in the jeans that were suddenly two sizes too big because your heart was so positively crushed that you hadn't eaten in a week. (No worries—those same jeans will soon be two sizes too small, once you hit the binge phase of your broken heart.) You'd get in your car and begin to drive and as you drove you'd think *I have no idea where I'm even going!*

But of course you'd know. You always knew. You'd drive past his/her house *just to see.*

And there he/she would be, visible through the front window; lit by the lamp you once switched off and on with a casual and familiar ease. You'd see him/her for only a fleeting moment, but that image would sear itself into your brain. He/she would be laughing a little, obviously in conversation with someone maddeningly out of view. And you'd want to stop, to investigate, to watch, but you couldn't stop because what if he/she looked out and saw you?

So you'd drive home and sit in the dark near the phone.

You would not hit refresh. You would not read that the man/woman who crushed your heart is now "friends" with anyone who has an incredibly hot-sounding name (Monique/Jack). You would not view photographs of your ex standing disturbingly and drunkenly close to strange, good-looking men/women at parties or read veiled references to anything that might possibly be a blow job. There would be no exposure to declarations about what sort of fun was recently had or about to be had or agitating lamentations about the single life. There would be no LOLs or TMIs or ROTFLMFAOs or sassily winking symbols composed of a period and a semicolon from people named Jack or Monique.

There would be nothing. There would be only you in the

dark near the phone that won't ever ring and the dawning realization that you have to move on.

In order to get over your ex, you have to move on, Constantly Hitting Refresh. And at least temporarily unfriending and unfollowing him/her will help you do so. Being friends with someone who once broke your heart is fine and dandy, but it's almost always a good idea to take a breather between this and that. I strongly encourage you to resist the temptation to devour your ex's every musing, darling. Shutting off that cyber feedbag will feel like hell those first few days, but I'm certain you'll soon realize how much better you can breathe when you're not constantly breathing in the fumes of your ex's life without you.

Yours,
Sugar

WE ARE ALL SAVAGES INSIDE

Dear Sugar,

I'm jealous. I'm jealous of people who succeed at what I do (write literary fiction). I'm jealous of them even if I love them or like them or respect them. Even when I pretend to be happy when my writer friends get good news, the truth is I feel like I swallowed a spoonful of battery acid. For days afterwards I go around feeling queasy and sad, thinking, Why not me?

So why not, Sugar? I'm thirty-one. I've written a novel that I'm currently revising while searching for an agent (which is turning out to be more difficult than I imagined). I received a first-rate education, holding a BA from a prestigious college and an MFA from another prestigious college. Several people in my social and literary orbit have gotten the sort of six-figure book deals that I dream of getting. A couple of these people are jerks, so I don't feel guilty for resenting their good fortune, but a few of them are good people whom I like and respect and, worst of all, one is a woman I count among my very best friends.

It makes me sick that I don't feel happy for them, especially when it comes to my close friend, but there it is. When I think of their successes, it only reminds me of what I don't have. I want what they have, but it's more than that: them having what I want pains me. When other writer friends are met with failure (rejections from agents or publishing houses, for example), I admit I feel a tiny lift inside. The feeling is more relief than glee—you know that old saying about misery enjoying company? I don't truly wish others bad. But neither do I honestly wish them well.

I know this makes me a shallow, awful person. I know I should be grateful that I have a decent job that allows me time to write, good friends, wonderful parents who are supportive of me both emotionally and financially (they paid my tuition for the above-mentioned colleges and have helped me in countless other ways), and a generally great life. But I find it impossible to focus on these things when I hear the news that another friend or acquaintance or former grad school peer has sold a book for X amount of dollars.

How do I deal with this, Sugar? Is jealousy simply part of a writer's life? Are my feelings what everyone is feeling, even when they pretend otherwise? Is it possible to purge these negative feelings and feel other, positive things when I hear someone else's fabulous news? Talk to me about jealousy, please. I don't want it to rule my life, or at least if it's going to rule my life I want to be reassured that it's ruling everyone else's life (secretly) too.

Signed,
Awful Jealous Person

Dear Awful Jealous Person,

We are all savages inside. We all want to be the chosen, the beloved, the esteemed. There isn't a person reading this who hasn't at one point or another had that *why not me?* voice pop into the interior mix when something good has happened to someone else. But that doesn't mean you should allow it to rule your life. It means you have work to do.

Before we get into it, I want to talk about what we're talking about. We are not talking about books. We're talking about book deals. You know they are not the same thing, right? One is the art you create by writing like a motherfucker for a long time. The other is the thing the marketplace decides to do with your creation. A writer gets a book deal when he or she has written a book that (a) an editor loves, and (b) a publisher believes readers will purchase. The number of copies a publisher believes people will purchase varies widely. It could be ten million or seven hundred and twelve. This number has pretty much nothing to do with the quality of the book, but rather is dictated by literary style, subject matter, and genre. This number has everything to do with the amount of your book deal, which is also related to the resources available to the publishing house that wants to publish your book. The big presses can give authors six-figure advances for books they believe will sell in significant numbers. The small ones cannot. Again, this has no relationship whatsoever to the quality of the books they publish.

I feel compelled to note these facts at the outset because my gut sense of your letter is that you've conflated the book with the book deal. They are two separate things. The one you are in charge of is the book. The one that happens based on forces that are mostly outside of your control is the book deal. You could write the world's most devastatingly gorgeous book of poems and nobody would give you $200,000 to publish it. You could write the world's most devastatingly gorgeous novel and maybe get that. Or not.

My point is, the first thing you need to do is get over yourself, Awful Jealous Person. If you are a writer, it's the writing that matters and no amount of battery acid in your stomach over who got what for what book they wrote is going to help you in your cause. Your cause is to write a great book and then to write another great book and to keep writing them for as long as you can. That is your only cause. It is not to get a six-figure book deal. I'm talking about the difference between art and money; creation and commerce. It's a beautiful and important thing to be paid to make art. Publishers who deliver our books to readers are a vital part of what we do. But what we do—you and I—is write books. Which may garner six-figure book deals for the reasons I outlined above. Or not.

You know what I do when I feel jealous? I tell myself to not feel jealous. I shut down the *why not me?* voice and replace it with one that says *don't be silly* instead. It really is that easy. You actually do stop being an awful jealous person by stopping being an awful jealous person. When you feel terrible because someone has gotten something you want, you force yourself to remember how very much you have been given. You remember that there is plenty for all of us. You remember that someone else's success has absolutely no bearing on your own. You remember that a wonderful thing has happened to one of your literary peers and maybe, if you keep working and if you get lucky, something wonderful may also someday happen to you.

And if you can't muster that, you just stop. You truly do. You do not let yourself think about it. There isn't a thing to eat down there in the rabbit hole of your bitterness except your own desperate heart. If you let it, your jealousy will devour you. Your letter is evidence that it has already begun to do so. It has depleted your happiness, distracted you from your real work, and turned you into a crappy friend.

You know that woman you mentioned who recently got the book deal—the one you describe as among your best friends?

She knows you're not truly happy for her. She knows it even if she's convinced herself that she doesn't know it; even if she's tried to explain away whatever weird vibe you emitted when you pretended to be happy for her about her good news. She knows because you can't fake love and generosity of spirit. It's either there or it isn't. The fact that when someone you profess to care deeply about shared with you something excellent that happened to her you had to fake your joy sucks way more than the fact that you haven't yet gotten the five- or six-figure book deal you're so convinced you deserve. And if you want to have a real, true, deep, authentic, satisfying, kickass, righteous life, I advise you to get that shit straightened out first.

I know it's not easy being an artist. I know the gulf between creation and commerce is so tremendously wide that it's sometimes impossible not to feel annihilated by it. A lot of artists give up because it's just too damn hard to go on making art in a culture that by and large does not support its artists. But the people who don't give up are the people who find a way to believe in abundance rather than scarcity. They've taken into their hearts the idea that there is enough for all of us, that success will manifest itself in different ways for different sorts of artists, that keeping the faith is more important than cashing the check, that being genuinely happy for someone else who got something you hope to get makes you genuinely happier too.

Most of those people did not come to this perspective naturally. And so, Awful Jealous Person, there is hope for you. You, too, can be a person who didn't give up. Most of the people who didn't give up realized that in order to thrive they had to dismantle the ugly jealous god in their heads so they could instead serve something greater: their own work. For some of them, it meant simply shutting out the *why not me* voice and moving on. For others, it meant going deeper and exploring why exactly it pained them so much that someone else got good news.

I hate to tell you, but my guess is that you're in the latter group. A large part of your jealousy probably rises out of your outsized sense of entitlement. Privilege has a way of fucking with our heads the same way as lack of it does. There are a lot of people who'd never dream they could be a writer, let alone land, at the age of thirty-one, a six-figure book deal. You are not one of them. And you are not one of them quite possibly because you've been given a tremendous amount of things that you did not earn or deserve, but rather that you received for the sole reason that you happen to be born into a family who had the money and wherewithal to fund your education at two colleges to which you feel compelled to attach the word "prestigious."

What is a prestigious college? What did attending such a school allow you to believe about yourself? What assumptions do you have about the colleges that you would not describe as prestigious? What sorts of people go to prestigious colleges and not prestigious colleges? Do you believe that you had a right to a free "first-rate" education? What do you make of the people who received educations that you would not characterize as first-rate? These are not rhetorical questions. I really do want you to take out a piece of paper and write those questions down and then answer them. I believe your answers will deeply inform your current struggle with jealousy. I am not asking you these questions in order to condemn or judge you. I would ask a similar series of questions of anyone from any sort of background because I believe our early experiences and beliefs about our place in the world inform who we think we are and what we deserve and by what means it should be given to us.

It is a way of going back to the roots of the problem, as it were. And I imagine you know I'm a big fan of roots.

You might, for example, be interested to know that the word "prestigious" is derived from the Latin *praestigiae*, which means "conjuror's tricks." Isn't that interesting? This word that we use to mean honorable and esteemed has its beginnings in a word that has everything to do with illusion, deception, and trickery. Does that mean anything to you, Awful Jealous Person? Because when I found that out, every tuning fork inside of me went *hum*. Could it be possible that the reason you feel like you swallowed a spoonful of battery acid every time someone else gets what you want is because a long time ago— way back in your own very beginnings—you were sold a bill of goods about the relationship between money and success, fame and authenticity, legitimacy and adulation?

I think it's worth investigating. Doing so will make you a happier person and also a better writer, I know without a doubt.

Good luck selling your novel. I sincerely hope you get six figures for it. When you do, write to me and share the wonderful news. I promise to be over the moon for you.

Yours,
Sugar

THE LUSTY BROAD

Dear Sugar,

I'm a spry forty-seven-year-old feisty broad. For the past three years I've been deeply in love with a woman. The timing of our meeting was atrocious. Her father was dying, she was recently downsized, and we were both nurturing recent heartbreaks. But once she quoted John Donne over my naughty bits after making love, I was done for. She pushed me away over and over again, and then started inviting me more frequently into her heart.

We've struggled ever since. Her sex drive has vanished (we've done it all—doctors, therapists, reading). She cannot fully commit, and she is consumed by fear (she's a classic love-avoider).

With her I find the highest of highs and the lowest of lows. We've broken up and reunited more times than I can count, and we are currently on an absolute restriction from each other for thirty days, which we've never managed. We are deeply KNOWN by each other in a spiritual, sacred way I've never been known before. Addictive, yes. Hence the break.

I should say she loves me deeply and, in some ways, when I demanded the full break, she took it harder than me.

I believe, as a midwestern lesbian, that I will never find this again and thus, I stay and tolerate her "rules," her angst, her sexual anorexia despite being a lusty broad. Yes, I've tried taking lovers. It simply does not work for me. Though our lovemaking is rare (four to five times per year), when we've made love it has been transcendent.

I'm a quirky unusual complex woman and it is hard to find a match. What the hell? What do YOU think?

Signed,
Should I Stay or Should I Go Now?

Dear Should I Stay or Should I Go Now,

What the hell, indeed. It sounds pretty crazy to me. Breaking up and getting back together more times than you can count? Sexual anorexia and "rules"? Your use of the word "addiction"? All those things unsettle me. But you know what unsettles me the most? This business about your lover being the only one who has "KNOWN" you in a "spiritual, sacred way," coupled with your conviction that you will "never find this again and thus" you stay.

Find what, pray tell? A sexually and emotionally withholding lover who is terrified of commitment and intimacy? If you and I were sitting at your kitchen table composing your ad for lustybroadslookingforlove.com, is this what you'd ask for?

You would not. I encourage you to contemplate why you're accepting that now. This relationship isn't meeting your needs; it's pushing your buttons. Namely, the big button that says *I'm a forty-seven-year-old midwestern lesbian, so I'd better take what I can get.* You write about your lover's fear, but it's your own fear that's messing with your head. I know it's hard to be alone, darling. Your anxieties about finding another partner are understandable, but they can't be the reason to stay. Desperation is unsustainable. It might have gotten you through until now, but you're too old and awesome to fake it anymore.

This doesn't necessarily mean you and your lover are doomed. Good couples sometimes get off to an appalling start. Perhaps the two of you will make it through, but you won't if you continue as you are. I know your connection feels powerful, rare, and incendiary. I know it seems like this woman is your own personal intimacy messiah. But you're wrong. True intimacy isn't a psychodrama. It isn't the "highest highs and lowest lows." It isn't John Donne whispered into your crotch followed by months of not-exactly-agreed-upon celibacy. It's a tiny bit of those things on occasion with a whole lot of everything else in between. It's communion and mellow compatibility. It's friendship and mutual respect. It's not having to say we must have an "absolute restriction on each other" for thirty days.

That isn't love, Lusty Broad. It's a restraining order. You don't have intimacy with this woman. You have intensity and scarcity. You have emotional turmoil and an overwrought sense of what the two of you together means.

I believe you know that. I could put most of the letters I receive into two piles: those from people who are afraid to do what they know in their hearts they need to do, and those from people who have genuinely lost their way. I'd put your letter in the former pile. I think you wrote to me because you realize you need to make a change, but you're scared of what that change will mean. I sympathize. Neither of us can know how long it will be before you find love again. But we do know that so long as you stay in a relationship that isn't meeting your needs, you're in a relationship that isn't meeting your needs. It makes you miserable and it also closes you off to other, potentially more satisfying romantic relationships.

I am not a religious person. I don't meditate, chant, or pray. But lines from poems I love run through my head and they feel holy to me in a way. There's a poem by Adrienne Rich I first read twenty years ago called "Splittings" that I thought of when I read your letter. The last two lines of the poem are: "I choose to love this time for once / with all my intelligence." It seemed such a radical thought when I first read those lines when I was twenty-two—that love could rise from our deepest, most reasoned intentions rather than our strongest shadowy doubts. The number of times *I choose to love this time for once with all my intelligence* has run through my head in the past twenty years cannot be counted. There hasn't been a day when those lines weren't present for me in ways both conscious and unconscious. You could say I'm devoted to them, even in times when I've failed profoundly to live up to their aspirations.

I suggest that you devote yourself to them too. The question isn't whether you should stay or go. The question is, How would your life be transformed if you chose to love this time for once with all your intelligence?

I'm not talking to your crotch, sister. I'm looking you in the eye.

Yours,
Sugar

THE BAD THINGS YOU DID

Dear Sugar,

For many years, to varying degrees, I stole compulsively. For many of the years I stole, I was on a "cocktail" of psychotropic drugs for depression, anxiety, and insomnia. In retrospect, I think the drugs made me powerless to fight against the compulsion to take things. An impulse would arise in my head—say, to take this pair of jeans from my friend, that book from that friend, or the abandoned flower pots that sat on the porch of an empty house. I even once took money out of the wallet of my future mother-in-law. When the ideas arose to take whatever it was, I would try to talk myself out of it, but I couldn't stop myself ultimately.

I don't do it anymore. I've been off all the meds for about six years, and I'm able to control the impulse, which, in fact, I rarely have now. I can't totally blame the meds because before I was taking them I also had the impulse to steal and did on occasion succumb to it. I blame myself. I think, because of my complicated psychology—my abusive childhood (my mother screaming at me from time immemorial that I was a liar, a cheat, and a thief)—I was not only trying to fulfill my mother's prophecy, but maybe trying to get people to hate and reject me for taking from them, for being a liar and a thief. I have also compulsively told whopping lies to people, over-the-top stories. They seemed to just come out.

I loathe myself for these acts. I don't know how to wipe the slate clean. I am terrified that friends and loved ones who I deceived and stole from—whether by taking a material possession or by making up some story—will find out what I did. I am not that person anymore and I haven't been for years. My greatest wish is to be able to forgive myself; to stop hating myself for these betrayals. I have tried to forgive myself for a long while, but I'm finding I'm no closer. I read a lot about this topic and I am back in therapy after years of being out of it, but I still hate myself for what I've done.

I know I will not take from anyone again in any way. Is that enough? Do I have to admit to those I stole from that I did? Or can I forgive myself without admitting to people how I wronged them? I know they would reject me if I were to admit what I'd done, even though I have not been a liar and a thief for a long, long time. I am so sorry for what I've done and would give anything not to have done what I have. Please help, Sugar. I'm tortured.

Signed,
Desperate

Dear Desperate,

Fifteen years ago I had a yard sale. I'd just moved to the city where I now live and I was literally down to my last twenty cents, so I put nearly everything I owned out on the lawn—my thrift-store dresses and books, my bracelets and knickknacks, my dishes and shoes.

Customers came and went throughout the day, but my primary companions were a group of preadolescent neighborhood boys who flitted in and out looking at my things,

inquiring about how much this and that cost, though they neither had the money to purchase nor an inclination to possess
the boring nonboy items I had to sell. Late in the afternoon
one of the boys told me that another of the boys had stolen
something from me—an empty retro leather camera case that
I'd once used as a purse. It was a small thing, a barely-worth-
bothering-about item that would've sold for something like
five bucks, but still I asked the accused boy if he'd taken it.

"No!" he yelled and stormed off.

The next day he returned wearing a big gray hoodie. He
lurked near the table where I'd set my things to sell and, when
he believed I wasn't looking, he pulled the camera case from
beneath his jacket and placed it where it had been sitting the
day before.

"Your thing is back," he said to me nonchalantly a while
later, pointing to the camera case as if he'd played no part in
its reappearance.

"Good," I said. "Why did you steal it?" I asked, but again he
denied that he had.

It was a sunny fall day. A few of the boys sat with me on the
porch steps, telling me bits about their lives. The boy who'd
stolen my camera case pulled up his sleeve and flexed his arm
so he could show me his biceps. He insisted in a tone more bel-
ligerent than any of the others that the cluster of shiny chains
he wore around his neck were real gold.

"Why'd you steal my camera case?" I asked again after a
while, but he again denied that he had, though he altered his
story this time to explain that he'd only taken it temporarily
because he was going to his house to get his money and then
he'd opted not to purchase it after all.

We talked some more about other things and soon it was

just the two of us. He told me about the mother he rarely saw and his much older siblings; about what kind of hot car he was going to buy the instant he turned sixteen.

"Why'd you steal my camera case?" I asked once more, and this time he didn't deny it.

Instead, he looked down at the ground and said very quietly but very clearly, "Because I was lonely."

There are only a few times anyone has been as self-aware and nakedly honest as that boy was with me in that moment. When he said what he said I almost fell off the steps.

I've thought about that boy so many times in these last fifteen years, perhaps because when he told me what he did about himself, he told me something about myself too. I used to steal things like you, Desperate. I had the inexplicable urge to take what didn't belong to me. I simply couldn't resist. I took a compact of blue eye shadow from my great-aunt in Philadelphia, a pretty sweater from a school friend, bars of soap in fancy wrappers from near-strangers' bathrooms, and a figurine of a white dog with his head askew, among other things.

By the time I met the lonely boy at my yard sale, I hadn't stolen for years, but like you, the things I'd taken haunted me. I'd meant no harm, but I had the horrible feeling that I'd caused it. And worse still, the intermittent urge to steal hadn't entirely left me, though I'd kept myself from acting on it since I was eighteen. I didn't know why I stole things and I still can't properly say, though "because I was lonely" seems about the rightest thing I've ever heard.

I think you were lonely too, sweet pea. And lonely isn't a crime. Maybe what happened in those years you were stealing and lying is you had a mother-sized hole to fill inside of you and so you stuffed a bunch of things into it that didn't belong to you and said a lot of things that weren't true because on some subconscious level you thought doing so would make the hole disappear. But it didn't. You came to understand that. You found a way to begin to heal yourself.

You need to heal better. Forgiveness is the next step, as you so acutely know. I don't think your path to wholeness is walking backward on the trail. The people you stole from don't need you to 'fess up. They need you to stop tormenting yourself over all those things you took that don't matter very much anymore. I'm not sure why you haven't been able to do that so far, but I imagine it has something to do with the story you've told yourself about yourself.

The narratives we create in order to justify our actions and choices become in so many ways who we are. They are the things we say back to ourselves to explain our complicated lives. Perhaps the reason you've not yet been able to forgive yourself is that you're still invested in your self-loathing. Perhaps not forgiving yourself is the flip side of your *steal-this-now* cycle. Would you be a better or worse person if you forgave yourself for the bad things you did? If you perpetually condemn yourself for being a liar and thief, does that make you good?

I don't like the thief part of my narrative either. I struggled mightily with whether or not I should write about it here—it's the first time I've written about it, ever. I've written about all sorts of other "bad things" I've done—promiscuous sex, drugs—but this seems worse, because unlike those other things, telling you that I used to steal things doesn't jibe with the person I want you to perceive me as being.

But it is the person I am. And I've forgiven myself for that.

Years after I stopped stealing things, I was sitting alone by a river. As I sat looking at the water, I found myself thinking about all the things I'd taken that didn't belong to me, and before I even knew what I was doing I began picking a blade of grass for each one and then dropping it into the water. *I am forgiven*, I thought as I let go of the blade that stood in for the blue eye shadow. *I am forgiven*, I thought for each of those fancy soaps. *I am forgiven*, for the dog figurine and the pretty sweater, and so on until I'd let all the bad things I'd done float right on down the river and I'd said *I am forgiven* so many times it felt like I really was.

That doesn't mean I never grappled with it again. Forgiveness doesn't just sit there like a pretty boy in a bar. Forgiveness is the old fat guy you have to haul up the hill. You have to say *I am forgiven* again and again until it becomes the story you believe about yourself, Desperate. I hope you will.

I don't know what ever became of that lonely boy at my yard sale. I hope he's made right whatever was wrong inside of him. That camera case he stole from me was still sitting on the table when I closed down my sale. "You want this?" I asked, holding it out to him.

He took it from me and smiled.

Yours,
Sugar

BEND

Dear Sugar,

*I have been with the same man off and on for twenty-one years—
we've been married for eleven. I consider him my soul mate and
the love of my life, hands down. About a year ago I met a man
who lives in my community and we developed an online flirtation that has gotten out of control. Why? A combination of reasons:*

1. *I was going through a bit of a midlife crisis (hello, forty!)
   and the attention of this particular man—who is attractive, sexy, successful, brilliant, etc.—was flattering.*

2. *My husband had recently had an online flirtation that I
   discovered accidentally and my feelings were hurt.*

3. *I'm a stay-at-home mom and I'm bored.*

*I am not and never was seriously interested in my online
crush. It was an ego stroke and a diversion. I have completely
cut off any contact with this man and sincerely want nothing
to do with him in the future, but recently I've been doing some
spiritual work and I've been advised to tell my husband the truth
because "what you hide owns you."*

I do think my husband and I could work through this if I told him the truth, as I did not have a full-blown affair with this man, was not in love with him, etc. At the same time, I know it would hurt my husband deeply, and since I have no intention or desire to leave him, I do not see the point.

As many say, "love is complicated," but mine for my husband is simple. I love him and want to be with him forever. Please advise.

Signed,
Can You Keep a Secret and
Still Feel Genuine About Your Love?

Dear CYKASASFGAYL,

I don't think you should tell your husband about your online flirtation gone off the rails. Love isn't the only thing that's sometimes complicated and sometimes simple. Truth is sometimes that way too.

Truth is simple in the la-la land where most of us first hatched our love. *Of course we'd never lie to each other!* we smugly believe in the early, easy days. But every now and then love gets more complicated in the thick of our real lives than a simple black-and-white interpretation of truth will allow.

I believe I've made it apparent that I'm not a fan of deception. Honesty is a core value in any healthy and successful relationship. To withhold the details of our lives from our intimate partners often leads to a hot mess. But there are rare situations in which the truth is more destructive than a confession would be.

If you'd had sex with this fellow; if emotional affairs were a pattern for you or even if you'd done this more than once;

if this experience made you realize you were no longer in love with your husband; if you were continuing the relationship you know to be deceitful and destructive; if your gut instinct told you that you should reveal this secret; if you believed that keeping this to yourself would be more destructive to you and your relationship than sharing it would—in each of these cases, I'd advise you to tell your husband about what happened.

But it doesn't sound to me like that's what's going on with you. Sometimes the greatest truth isn't in the confession, but rather in the lesson learned. What you revealed to yourself in the course of your experience with the other man will likely make your marriage stronger.

Isn't love amazing that way? How it can bend with us through the years? It has to. It must. Lest it break.

Yours,
Sugar

THE OBLITERATED PLACE

Dear Sugar,

1.   *It's taken me many weeks to compose this letter and even still, I can't do it right. The only way I can get it out is to make a list instead of write a letter. This is a hard subject and a list helps me contain it. You may change it to a regular letter if you wish to should you choose to publish it.*

2.   *I don't have a definite question for you. I'm a sad, angry man whose son died. I want him back. That's all I ask for and it's not a question.*

3.   *I will start over from the beginning. I'm a fifty-eight-year-old man. Nearly four years ago, a drunk driver killed my son. The man was so inebriated he drove through a red light and hit my son at full speed. The dear boy I loved more than life itself was dead before the paramedics even got to him. He was twenty-two, my only child.*

4.   *I'm a father while not being a father. Most days it feels like my grief is going to kill me, or maybe it already has. I'm a living dead dad.*

5.   *Your column has helped me go on. I have faith in my version of God and I pray every day, and the way I feel when I'm in my deepest prayer is the way I feel when I read your words, which feel sacred to me.*

6.   *I see a psychologist regularly and I'm not clinically depressed or on medication.*

7.   *Suicide has occurred to me (this is what initially prompted me to make an appointment with my psychologist). Given the circumstance, ending my life is a reasonable thought, but I can't do it because it would be a betrayal of my values and also of the values I instilled in my son.*

8.   *I have good friends who are supportive of me, my brother and sister-in-law and two nieces are a loving and attentive family to me, and even my ex-wife and I have become close friends again since our son's death—we'd been cold to one another since our divorce when our son was fifteen.*

9.   *In addition, I have a rewarding job, good health, and a girlfriend whom I love and respect.*

10. *In short, I'm going on with things in a way that makes it appear like I'm adjusting to life without my son, but the fact is I'm living in a private hell. Sometimes the pain is so great I simply lie in my bed and wail.*

11. *I can't stop thinking about my son. About the things he would be doing now if he were alive and also the things I did with him when he was young, my good memories of*

him, my wish to go back in time and either relive happy memories or alter those that are less happy.

12. *One thing I would change is when, at seventeen, my son informed me he was gay. I didn't quite believe him or understand, so I inquired in a negative tone: But how can you not like girls? I quickly came to embrace him for who he was, but I regret my initial reaction to his homosexuality and I never apologized to him for it. I believe he knew I loved him. I believe he knew I wanted him to be happy, no matter what path his happiness might take. But, Sugar, for this and other things, I am tormented anyway.*

13. *I hate the man who killed my son. For his crime, he was incarcerated eighteen months, then released. He wrote me a letter of apology, but I ripped it into pieces and threw it in the garbage after barely scanning it.*

14. *My son's former boyfriend has stayed in touch with my ex-wife and me and we care for him a great deal. Recently, he invited us to a party, where he informed us we would meet his new boyfriend—his first serious one since our son. We both lied and said we had other engagements, but the real reason we declined is that neither one of us could bear meeting his new partner.*

15. *I fear you will choose not to answer my letter because you haven't lost a child.*

16. *I fear if you choose to answer my letter people will make critical comments about you, saying you don't have the*

right to speak to this matter because you have not lost a child.

17. *I pray you will never lose a child.*

18. *I will understand if you choose not to answer my letter. Most people, kind as they are, don't know what to say to me, so why should you? I certainly didn't know what to say to people such as me before my son died, so I don't blame others for their discomfort.*

19. *I'm writing to you because the way you've written about your grief over your mother dying so young has been meaningful to me. I'm convinced that if anyone can shed light into my dark hell, it will be you.*

20. *What can you say to me?*

21. *How do I go on?*

22. *How do I become human again?*

Signed,
Living Dead Dad

Dear Living Dead Dad,

1. I don't know how you go on without your son. I only know that you do. And you have. And you will.

2.   Your shattering sorrowlight of a letter is proof of that.

3.   You don't need me to tell you how to be human again. You are there, in all of your humanity, shining unimpeachably before every person reading these words right now.

4.   I am so sorry for your loss. *I am so sorry for your loss.* Iamsosorryforyourloss.

5.   You could stitch together a quilt with all the times that that has been and will be said to you. You could make a river of consolation words. But they won't bring your son back. They won't keep that man from getting into his car and careering through that red light at the precise moment your son was in his path.

6.   You'll never get that.

7.   I hope you remember that when you peel back the rage and you peel back the idle thoughts of suicide and you peel back all the things you imagined your son would be but wasn't and you peel back the man who got into the car and drove when he shouldn't have and you peel back the man who the man your son loved now loves and you peel back all the good times you had and you peel back all the things you wish you'd done differently, at the center of that there is your pure father love that is stronger than anything.

8. No one can touch that love or alter it or take it away from you. Your love for your son belongs only to you. It will live in you until the day you die.

9. Small things such as this have saved me: How much I love my mother—even after all these years. How powerfully I carry her within me. My grief is tremendous but my love is bigger. So is yours. You are not grieving your son's death because his death was ugly and unfair. You're grieving it because you loved him truly. The beauty in that is greater than the bitterness of his death.

10. Allowing such small things into your consciousness will not keep you from your suffering, but it will help you survive the next day.

11. I keep imagining you lying on your bed and wailing. I keep thinking that hard as it is to do, it's time for you to go silent and lift your head from the bed and listen to what's there in the wake of your wail.

12. It's your life. The one you must make in the obliterated place that's now your world, where everything you used to be is simultaneously erased and omnipresent, where you are forevermore a living dead dad.

13. Your boy is dead, but he will continue to live within you. Your love and grief will be unending, but it will also shift in shape. There are things about your son's life and your own that you can't understand now. There are

things you will understand in one year, and in ten years, and in twenty.

14. The word "obliterate" comes from the Latin *obliterare*. *Ob* means "against"; *literare* means "letter" or "script." A literal translation is "being against the letters." It was impossible for you to write me a letter, so you made me a list instead. It is impossible for you to go on as you were before, so you must go on as you never have.

15. It's wrong that this is required of you. It's wrong that your son died. It will always be wrong.

16. The obliterated place is equal parts destruction and creation. The obliterated place is pitch black and bright light. It is water and parched earth. It is mud and it is manna. The real work of deep grief is making a home there.

17. You have the power to withstand this sorrow. We all do, though we all claim not to. We say, "I couldn't go on," instead of saying we hope we won't have to. That's what you're saying in your letter to me, Living Dead Dad. You've made it so long without your sweet boy and now you can't take it anymore. But you can. You must.

18. More will be revealed. Your son hasn't yet taught you everything he has to teach you. He taught you how to love like you've never loved before. He taught you how to suffer like you've never suffered before. Perhaps the

next thing he has to teach you is acceptance. And the thing after that, forgiveness.

19. Forgiveness bellows from the bottom of the canoe. There are doubts, dangers, unfathomable travesties. There are stories you'll learn if you're strong enough to travel there. One of them might cure you.

20. When my son was six he said, "We don't know how many years we have for our lives. People die at all ages." He said it without anguish or remorse, without fear or desire. It has been healing to me to accept in a very simple way that my mother's life was forty-five years long, that there was nothing beyond that. There was only my expectation that there would be—my mother at eighty-nine, my mother at sixty-three, my mother at forty-six. Those things don't exist. They never did.

21. Think: *My son's life was twenty-two years long.* Breathe in.

22. Think: *My son's life was twenty-two years long.* Breathe out.

23. There is no twenty-three.

24. You go on by doing the best you can. You go on by being generous. You go on by being true. You go on by offering comfort to others who can't go on. You go on by allowing the unbearable days to pass and allowing the pleasure in other days. You go on by finding a channel for your love and another for your rage.

25. Letting go of expectation when it comes to one's children is close to impossible. The entire premise of our love for them has to do with creating, fostering, and nurturing people who will outlive us. To us, they are not so much who they are as who they will become.

26. The entire premise of your healing demands that you do let go of expectation. You must come to understand and accept that your son will always be only the man he actually was: the twenty-two-year-old who made it as far as that red light. The one who loved you deeply. The one who long ago forgave you for asking why he didn't like girls. The one who would want you to welcome his boyfriend's new boyfriend into your life. The one who would want you to find joy and peace. The one who would want you to be the man he didn't get to be.

27. To be anything else dishonors him.

28. The kindest and most meaningful thing anyone ever says to me is: *Your mother would be proud of you.* Finding a way in my grief to become the woman who my mother raised me to be is the most important way I have honored my mother. It has been the greatest salve to my sorrow. The strange and painful truth is that I'm a better person because I lost my mom young. When you say you experience my writing as sacred, what you are touching is the divine place within me that is my mother. Sugar is the temple I built in my obliterated place. I'd give it all back in a snap, but the fact is, my

grief taught me things. It showed me shades and hues I couldn't have otherwise seen. It required me to suffer. It compelled me to reach.

29. Your grief has taught you too, Living Dead Dad. Your son was your greatest gift in his life and he is your greatest gift in his death too. Receive it. Let your dead boy be your most profound revelation. Create something of him.

30. Make it beautiful.

Yours,
Sugar

PART FIVE

PUT IT IN A BOX AND WAIT

You give a lot of advice about what to do. Do you have any advice about what not to do?

Don't do what you know on a gut level to be the wrong thing to do. Don't stay when you know you should go or go when you know you should stay. Don't fight when you should hold steady or hold steady when you should fight. Don't focus on the short-term fun instead of the long-term fallout. Don't surrender all your joy for an idea you used to have about yourself that isn't true anymore. Don't seek joy at all costs. I know it's hard to know what to do when you have a conflicting set of emotions and desires, but it's not as hard as we pretend it is. Saying it's hard is ultimately a justification to do whatever seems like the easiest thing to do—have the affair, stay at that horrible job, end a friendship over a slight, keep loving someone who treats you terribly. I don't think there's a single dumbass thing I've done in my adult life that I didn't know was a dumbass thing to do while I was doing it. Even when I justified it to myself—as I did every damn time—the truest part of me knew I was doing the wrong thing. Always. As the years pass, I'm learning how to better trust my gut and not do the wrong thing, but every so often I get a harsh reminder that I've still got work to do.

Do you think the advice you write in your column is always right?

I stand by the advice I've given. I don't take anything back. But I wouldn't claim that what I have to say to any given person is "right." Mostly because I don't think of the advice I give as necessarily on the right–wrong continuum. I sometimes state that I firmly believe a person should do one thing or another, but more often I try to help those who write to me see a third way. I'm not so much telling people what to do in my columns as I am attempting to either present a perspective that might be difficult for those who write to me to see on their own or to more complexly hash out the either/or options that the letter writer has posed. I think the answer to most problems is more often than not outside of the right/wrong binary that we tend to cling to when we're angry or scared or in pain. We are complicated people. Our lives do not play out in absolutes. I want my column to reflect that, but it's always only my opinion. There are others too.

A BIT OF SULLY IN YOUR SWEET

Dear Sugar,

I'm a twenty-nine-year-old woman who is engaged to be married. I'm very close to my sister. She's much older than me (fifty-three) and she's technically my "half" sister (we share a father who had one marriage very young, another quite old). My sister and I have always been close, but because of our age difference she's been more like an aunt to me, though over the past couple of years our relationship has shifted and we've become more like equals. Recently, we went on a weekend trip together, just the two of us, and I learned things about her life that make me feel . . . I don't even know what the word is, Sugar. Sad? Uncomfortable? Angry? Disappointed? A mix of all four. That's the reason I'm writing to you.

My sister has been married for twenty-five years. I love my brother-in-law almost as much as I love my sister. I've always considered them to be my "role model couple." They are still in love after all these years and still best friends. Everyone who knows them, including me, thinks they're the perfect couple. They are proof to me that happy marriages are possible. Or at least they were.

You see, what happened is that while I was away with my sister I asked her what the "secret to marriage" was, and during our conversation about it she revealed things that surprised and upset me. She said while it's true she and my brother-in-law are happy to be married to each other, there were several times over the years she doubted they'd make it. She confided that both she and my brother-in-law have cheated on each other. Several years ago, my brother-in-law had a full-blown affair that lasted a few months, and at another point my sister had a brief, "technically unconsummated fling" that she opted not to tell her husband about (she figured why hurt him when she'd "learned her lesson" and wasn't going to break up her marriage over it). Together, they eventually repaired these breaches, but it wasn't easy.

I know they've been happy too. They've raised two kids together, traveled, and shared many interests. It isn't as if everything I've seen in them is a facade. I understand that. But I can't help but admit my picture of them has changed and I'm having a hard time with that, as I plan to have them walk me down the aisle at my wedding. I know this might sound naïve and judgmental, but I'm shaken and bummed and now I don't know if people who cheated should play such a big role in my wedding.

I know couples have to work on their relationships, but my position on infidelity is that it's a deal-killer. My fiancé and I have agreed that if one of us ever cheated on the other it would be automatically over between us, no conversation required. When I told my sister about this she actually laughed and said we were being "too black and white," but, Sugar, I don't want to think that in twenty-five years I'll be saying that there were times I didn't think my husband and I would make it. I want healthy love.

From reading your column, I know you're married and I wonder what you think. It seems to me that you and Mr. Sugar are a perfect couple too. What's the secret to a good marriage? Have there been times you didn't believe your relationship would make it? Isn't infidelity a deal-killer? Can my sister and brother-in-law still be my role model couple now that I know they've failed to keep their vows at least at some points along the way? Should they walk me down the aisle? Why do I feel so let down? My heart feels heavy with the fear that marriage can't work for anyone if it can't work for them. Is marriage this horribly complex thing for which I'm ill prepared? Am I being stupid to ask why two people can't just love each other?

Signed,
Happily Ever After

Dear Happily Ever After,

One day about a year after Mr. Sugar and I moved in together, a woman called our house and asked to speak to Mr. Sugar. He wasn't home, I told her. Could I take a message? She hesitated in a way that made my heart beat faster than it had any right to. When she finally said her name, I knew who she was, though I'd never met her. She lived in a city thousands of miles away, where Mr. Sugar occasionally went to work. They weren't exactly friends, he'd told me when I'd inquired about her a few weeks before, after I'd found a postcard from her to him in our mailbox. "Acquaintance" was a better word, he'd said. Cool, I'd replied.

And yet as I held the phone, I got a funny feeling, in spite of my internal scoldings that I had no reason to feel funny. That Mr. Sugar was crazy in love with me was entirely apparent, both to me and to everyone who knew us, and I was likewise crazy in love with him. We were a "perfect couple." So happy. So meant to be together. So utterly in love. Two people who leapt from the same pond to miraculously swim down parallel streams. I was the only woman he'd ever called *the one*. And who was she? She was just a woman who sent him a postcard.

So I surprised even myself when, that afternoon as I held the phone, I asked in my gentlest, most neutral voice, while everything inside of me clanged, if she knew who I was.

"Yes," she replied. "You're Sugar. Mr. Sugar's girlfriend."

"Right," I said. "And this is going to seem odd, but I'm wondering about something. Have you slept with Mr. Sugar?"

"Yes," she said immediately. He'd come to her apartment the month before, when he'd been in town, she informed me. They had an "intense sexual attraction," she said with a breathy puff of pleasure. She was sorry if that hurt me.

"Thank you," I replied, and I meant it.

When I hung up the phone, I remember very vividly staggering around the room as if someone had shot me in the heart with an arrow that would forever be stuck in my chest.

Mr. Sugar and I hardly owned anything then. In our living room there was nothing but two ratty, matching couches we'd been given as hand-me-downs, each one lining an opposite wall. We referred to them as the *dueling couches* because they sat in an eternal face-off, the only things in the room. One of our favorite things to do was recline on the dueling couches— him on one, me on the other—for hours on end. Sometimes we'd read silently to ourselves, but more often, we'd read out loud to each other, whole books whose titles still make my heart swoon, so powerfully do they remind me of the tender intensity between us in those first years of our love: *Charlotte's Web, Cathedral and Other Stories, The Selected Poetry of Rainer Maria Rilke.*

All of that was a pile of shit now, I realized as I collapsed onto one of the dueling couches. By going off and fucking the woman who sent him a postcard and then not telling me about it, Mr. Sugar had ruined everything. My trust. Our innocence. My magical sense of myself as the only woman he could possibly desire. The pure and unassailable nature of our perfect coupledom. I was shattered and furious, but most of all I was shocked. How could he have done this?

When he walked in the door an hour later and I told him what I knew, he crumpled onto the dueling couch opposite me and we had the duel of our lives.

I didn't think we'd survive it. I was pretty sure to do so would be kind of sick. I wasn't the sort of person who took bullshit from men and I wasn't about to begin doing so now. I loved Mr. Sugar, but he could sincerely go and fuck himself. I'd been true and faithful to him, and in return, he'd broken the deal. The deal was killed. Even being in the same room with him felt humiliating to me.

But there I was, nonetheless, crying and yelling while he cried and apologized. I told him it was over. He begged me to stay. I told him he was a lying, selfish bastard. He agreed that's exactly what he was. We talked and talked and talked and talked and after an hour or so my rage and sorrow subsided enough that I went silent and listened while he told me everything: exactly how it went down with the woman who sent him the postcard; what I meant to him and what the woman he'd slept with meant; how and why he loved me; how he'd never been faithful to any woman in all his life, but how he wanted to be faithful to me, even though he'd already failed at that; how he knew his problems with sex and deception and intimacy and trust were bigger than this one transgression and rooted in his past; how he'd do everything in his power to understand his problems so he could change and grow and become the partner he wanted to be; how knowing me had made him believe he was capable of that, of loving me better, if only I would give him another chance.

As I listened to him talk, I alternated between sympathizing with him and wanting to punch him in the mouth. He was a jackass, but I loved him dearly. And the fact was, I related to what he said. I understood his explanations, infuriating as they were. I'd been a jackass too, given to failings of my own that hadn't manifested themselves in this relationship yet. When he said he had sex with the woman who sent him the postcard because he got a little bit drunk and wanted to have sex and it didn't have anything to do with me, even though of course it ultimately very much did, I knew what he meant. I'd had that sort of sex too. When he looked me in the eye and told me he was sorrier than a person has ever been and he loved me so much he didn't even know how to say it, I knew he was telling me a truer truth than he'd ever told anyone.

I'm going to guess this is roughly the sort of crossroads your own personal perfect role model couple was at a few times in their incredibly successful and loving decades-long-and-still-going-strong relationship, Happily Ever After. And I'm going to guess if you manage to live happily ever after with your honey you're going to be there a time or two as well, whether the precise issue be infidelity or not.

This isn't a spotless life. There is much ahead, my immaculate little peach. And there is no way to say it other than to say it: marriage is indeed this horribly complex thing for which you appear to be ill prepared and about which you seem to be utterly naïve.

That's okay. A lot of people are. You can learn along the way.

A good place to start would be to let fall your notions about "perfect couples." It's really such an impossible thing to either perceive honestly in others or live up to when others believe it about us. It does nothing but box some people in and shut other people out, and it ultimately makes just about everyone feel like shit. A perfect couple is a wholly private thing. No one but the two people in the perfect relationship know for certain whether they're in one. Its only defining quality is that it's composed of two people who feel perfectly right about sharing their lives with each other, even during the hard times.

I think that's what your sister was getting at when she revealed her relationship struggles in response to your question about the "secret to marriage." She wasn't trying to bum you out. She was actually trying to tell you the secret. In allowing you a more intimate view of her much-touted-but-flawed marriage, your sister was attempting to show you what a real perfect couple looks like: happy, humane, and occasionally all fucked up.

I can't imagine anyone more fitting to walk you down the aisle on your wedding day than your sister and her husband, two people who've kept their love and friendship alive for more than twenty-five years. That you're doubting this after learning not all of those years were easy tells me there's something deeper at work here that has nothing to do with their marriage and everything to do with your own insecurities and fears.

You appear to be focused on infidelity as the "deal-killer" that you believe would compel you to "automatically" dissolve your own future marriage, and that's fair enough. I understand the icky place in your gut where that impulse lives. There is probably nothing more hurtful and threatening than one partner breaking from an agreed-upon monogamous bond. A preemptive ultimatum against that allows at least the sense of control. But it's a false sense.

Painful as it is, there's nothing more common in long-term relationships than infidelity in its various versions (cheated, pretty much cheated, cheated a teeny bit but it probably doesn't quite count, came extremely close to cheating, want to cheat, wondering about what it would be like to cheat, is flirting over email technically even cheating? etc.). The letters in my inbox, the stories of many of my friends, and my own life are a testament to that. I'm not suggesting everyone cheats, of course, and perhaps you and your husband will never have to confront this issue. But if you really want to live happily ever after, if you honestly want to know what the secret to sustaining a lifelong "healthy love" is, it would be a good idea to openly grapple with some of the most common challenges of doing so, rather than pretending that you have the power to shut them down by making advance threats about walking out, "no conversation required," the moment a transgression occurs.

This will require a rethink about your own dark capacities, as well as those of your future husband, and the members of various couples you admire. Most people don't cheat because they're cheaters. They cheat because they are people. They are driven by hunger or for the experience of someone being hungry once more for them. They find themselves in friendships that take an unintended turn or they seek them out because they're horny or drunk or damaged from all the stuff they didn't get when they were kids. There is love. There is lust. There is opportunity. There is alcohol. And youth. There is loneliness and boredom and sorrow and weakness and self-destruction and idiocy and arrogance and romance and ego and nostalgia and power and need. There is the compelling temptation of intimacies with someone other than the person with whom one is most intimate.

Which is a complicated way of saying, it's a long damn life, Happily Ever After. And people get mucked up in it from time to time. Even the people we marry. Even us. You don't know what it is you'll get mucked up in yet, but if you're lucky, and if you and your fiancé really are right for each other, and if the two of you build a marriage that lasts a lifetime, you're probably going to get mucked up in a few things along the way.

This is scary, but you'll be okay. Sometimes the thing you fear the most in your relationship turns out to be the thing that brings you and your partner to a deeper place of understanding and intimacy.

That's what happened to Mr. Sugar and me a couple of years into our relationship, when I learned of his infidelity, and told him to go fuck himself, and then took him back. My decision to stay and work it out with him in the aftermath of that betrayal is way, way far up on the list of the best decisions of my life. And I'm not just grateful that I decided to stay. I'm grateful it happened. It took me years to allow that, but it's true. That Mr. Sugar cheated on me made us a better couple. It opened a conversation about sex and desire and commitment that we're still having. And it gave us resources to draw upon when we faced other challenges later on. The truth is, for all the sweet purity of our early love, we weren't ready for each other in that time during which we loved each other most sweetly. The woman who sent him the postcard pushed us down a path where we made ourselves ready, not to be a perfect couple, but to be a couple who knows how to have a duel when a duel needs to be had.

I hope that's what you get too, Happily Ever After. A bit of sully in your sweet. Not perfection, but real love. Not what you imagine, but what you'd never dream.

Yours,
Sugar

WE ARE HERE TO BUILD THE HOUSE

Dear Sugar,

I am a young woman in an American city. I'll be out of a job in a few weeks. Gulp. I'm in the process of entering into an arrangement with a man: we will rendezvous once or twice a week and he will pay me an "allowance" of $1,000 a month. About this, I have many conflicting thoughts. There are the practical questions: Is what I am doing illegal? Is what I am receiving taxable income? If so, how do I report it? Am I being paid fairly?

But also, more importantly: Is what I am doing immoral? The man is married. He told me that he loves his wife, he is going to take care of her forever, but she doesn't want sex like she used to; she's not the jealous type, and he'd tell her but he doesn't want to rub her face in it. To me this sounds cowardly. I am a person who believes in nonmonogamy; I believe in people making the choices that are the best for them. But I also believe in communication, respect, and integrity. Am I complicit in something awful?

And my last set of questions, Sugar. Is this something I can do? Is this something I should be doing? I am theoretically pro-sex, but I've never really enjoyed it. I have all sorts of ugly issues involved—I know we all do—and I don't know if this will make them better or worse. I am trying to approach the whole situation in a meta way, as an exploration of my feminist ideology—

but every time I think about him touching me I want to cry. And yet I am very poor and soon to be unemployed. How much can/ should I take my desperation into account?

I think I am going to go through with this, so I don't know what my question really is. I guess I just want to know how people negotiate all this shit, and how I am supposed to be okay. Thank you.

LTL

Dear LTL,

I said yes to this gig immediately. Within the hour, I realized I'd made a mistake. I was way too busy to be Sugar. The job pays nothing. I earn my living as a writer. Mr. Sugar also earns his living as an artist. There is not a steady job, trust fund, savings account, retirement plan, parent willing to pay any portion of our preschool bill, free babysitter, not-maxed-out credit card, employer-paid health insurance policy, paid sick day, or even a middle-class childhood between us. Between us there are only two beautiful children and ten mountains of debt.

I can't work for free. *I can't work for free.* Of course I can't work for free!

That was the mantra screaming through my head after I agreed to be Sugar. So, an hour after saying yes, I composed an email saying I'd changed my mind. The unsent email sat on my computer screen while I paced my living room thinking about all the reasons that it was perfectly unreasonable for me to write an advice column for no pay. Every reason was punctuated by a silent exclamation point. I had other writing to do! Writing for which I was being paid! Writing that would need to be pushed aside on a weekly basis so I could crank out a column! And what was a column anyway? I didn't write columns! I didn't know anything about giving advice! Plus, there were my kids! I was stretched thin already, my every not-writing moment consumed by caring for them! The whole Sugar idea was ridiculous from the start!

And yet I could not bring myself to send that email. I wanted to be Sugar. I was intrigued. Sparked. Something powerful overrode all the silent exclamation points in my head: my gut. I decided to trust it. I gave Sugar a shot.

I thought of this when I read your letter, sweet pea. It made me think about what's at stake when we ponder a gig. About what work means. About the fine balance of money and reason and instinct and the ideas we have about ourselves when we imagine we can be "meta" about our bodies and lives and the ways we spend our days. About what's at work when we attempt to talk ourselves into things we don't want to do and out of things we do. When we think a payoff comes from being paid and a price exacted from doing things for free. About what morality is. And who gets to say. What relation it has to making money. And what relation it has to desperation.

Your letter unsettles me. There is the husband predictably casting his decision to deceive his wife as a benevolent one. There is your naïveté about the logistics of prostitution— which is the correct term for the act of providing sex for money. Even if you refer to it as a rendezvous. But most of all there is you, dear fathomless bird of truth, telling me exactly what you know you must do. And then turning away from it.

You don't need me to tell you whether you should accept this offer. You need me only to show you to yourself. *I am theoretically pro-sex, but I've never really enjoyed it,* you write. *Every time I think about him touching me I want to cry,* you say. Do you hear that? It's your body talking to you. Do what it tells you to do. Be its employee. It doesn't matter what your head is working out—the monthly grand, the uncertainty of unemployment, the meta/feminist gymnastics. Putting faith in that stuff might pay the rent, but it's never going to build your house.

We are here to build the house.

It's our work, our *job*, the most important gig of all: to make a place that belongs to us, a structure composed of our own moral code. Not the code that only echoes imposed cultural values, but the one that tells us on a visceral level what to do. You know what's right for you and what's wrong for you. And that knowing has nothing to do with money or feminism or monogamy or whatever other things you say to yourself when the silent exclamation points are going off in your head. Is it okay to be a participant in deceit and infidelity? Is it okay to exchange sex for cash? These are worthy questions. They matter. But the answers to them don't tell us how to rightfully live our lives. The body does.

There might be women out there who can fuck men for money and be perfectly fine, but you are not one of them. You told me so yourself. You're simply not cut out for the job. When it comes to sex you say that you have "all sorts of ugly issues" and that you "know we all do," but you're wrong. We all don't. You do. I once did. Not everyone does. By generalizing your problems regarding sex and sexuality, you're running from yourself. You're covering your wounds with a classic it's-okay-if-I'm-fucked-up-because-everyone-is-fucked-up canard. It's a lie you've told yourself that has flattened down whatever hurts.

But what hurts remains. Something inside of you that has

to do with sex and men needs to be healed. And until you heal it you are going to have to open and patch and cover and deny that wound over and over again. This job offer is an opportunity, but not the sort you think it is. It's an invitation to do the real work. The kind that doesn't pay a dime, but leaves you with a sturdy shelter by the end.

So do it. Forget the man. Forget the money. It's your own sweet self with whom you must rendezvous.

Yours,
Sugar

THE EMPTY BOWL

Dear Sugar,

I could be worse. *That's one of my father's favorite sayings. Whenever we heard a story about a man beating his children, murdering his family, locking them away:* I could be worse. *It was as if the mere existence of vileness and depravity could exculpate him of any wrongdoing.*

He never hit my mother or me. He didn't rape me or threaten me. These are the first things that come to mind when we think of child abuse. But while my mother would have left him if he'd lifted a hand against me, words—painful, horrible words—were allowed. Instead of bruises and scrapes, I suffered from internal pain. My father is a narcissist: controlling, vain, volatile, and charming. If I wasn't cheerful enough, he didn't want to look at me and I was locked in my room for days; if I made a joke, he'd yell and curse at me for being insensitive. My room was my sanctuary, my books my closest friends. I could never be perfect enough, and yet I tried so hard to make him proud, to make him care. He was my dad, after all.

I never had anyone to talk to about it. I couldn't fully trust my friends, and my mother was too busy pacifying my father to realize how much it hurt. My mother and I were the only ones allowed to see that side of him. Counseling was out of the question, and extended family visited seldom.

He disowned me twice. They were over small things, slight disagreements that led him to denounce me as his child. When he decided that everything was fine again, I was expected to accept his change of heart—no apologies (unless they were mine), no further mention of the incident. Each time, I let my mother convince me to give him another chance.

But three months ago he went too far. He betrayed my mother, and in trying to support her, I was subjected to an angry diatribe. I was a fucking bitch for finding out about his infidelity. I had no right to invade his privacy.

This time, I disowned him. I moved out (at twenty, I'd been staying at home for the summer). I've ceased all contact. And though my mother is more understanding of my position than she once was, she's still trying to fix that broken relationship. While I know I could live happily without my father, and that I'm stronger than I've ever been since he's been gone from my life, it's like I can never fully escape him. My mother constantly talks about him, how he's changed. She wants to know when I'll be ready to be around him again. It's hard to explain that I really don't feel anything anymore.

In spite of my mother's claims, my father is still trying to control me, still so consumed by his image that he disregards my feelings. He found out that my therapist—an understanding, kind, and sympathetic counselor—was a woman he worked with and insisted I stop seeing her. Yet another attempt to keep me isolated, away from any outside support. Still, my mother is pressuring me (sometimes unconsciously) to make it work. But I no longer trust him, no longer trust my judgment when it comes to my father.

*We will never have a good relationship, but is it right for me
to sever it completely, Sugar? So many people insist that family is
too important, that it is my duty to forgive the man that gave me
life. He's the only father that I have. But is it worth the pain, the
self-doubt, and the depression?*

Could Be Worse

Dear Could Be Worse,

No, maintaining a relationship with your abusive father is not
worth the pain, the self-doubt, and the depression. In cutting
off ties with him, you have done the right thing. It's true that
he is the only father you will ever have, but that does not give
him the right to abuse you. The standard you should apply in
deciding whether or not to have an active relationship with
him is the same one you should apply to all the relationships
in your life: you will not be mistreated or disrespected or
manipulated.

Your father does not currently meet that standard.

I'm sorry your dad is an abusive narcissist. I'm sorry your
mother has opted to placate his madness at your expense.
Those are two very hard things. Harder still would be a life
spent allowing yourself to be abused. I know that liberating
yourself from your father's tyranny isn't easy or uncompli-
cated, but it's the right way. And it's also the only way that
might—*just might*—someday lead to a healthy relationship
between the two of you. By insisting that your father treat you
with respect, you are fulfilling your greatest duty, not only as a
daughter, but as a human. That you stopped interacting with
an abuser as powerful as your father is a testament to your
courage and strength. You have my respect.

I haven't had parents as an adult. I've lived so long without them and yet I carry them with me every day. They are like two empty bowls I've had to repeatedly fill on my own.

I suppose your father will have the same effect on you. In some ways, you're right: you probably won't ever "fully escape" your dad. He will be the empty bowl that you'll have to fill again and again. What will you put inside? Our parents are the primal source. We make our own lives, but our origin stories are theirs. They go back with us to the beginning of time. There is absolutely no way around them. By cutting off ties with your father, you incited a revolution in your life. How now are you going to live?

I said you were strong and brave to stop communicating with your father because you did something many people can never do. You set a boundary. You decided that you will not be mistreated and you acted upon that decision. That choice was born of anger and hurt. The territory beyond it is born of healing and transformation and peace—at least it is if you'd like to have a smashingly beautiful life.

What I mean to say is that you've left your father, but your relationship with him isn't over. It will take you years to fully come to terms with him (and also with your mother, by the way). There is so much work to do that has to do with forgiveness and anger, with acceptance and letting go, with sorrow and even perhaps a complicated joy. Those things do not move in a direct trajectory. They weave in and out of each other and wind back to smack you in the ass. They will punch you in the face and make you cry and laugh. You say you will never have a good relationship with your dad, but you don't know. You will change. Maybe he will too. Some facts of your childhood will remain immutable, but others won't. You may never make sense of your father's cruelty, but with work and with mindfulness, with understanding and heart, you will make sense of him.

I hope you have the guts to do it.

After my mother died when I was twenty-two, I wrote a letter to my dad. I hated him by then, but there was a bright crack in my hate that had been made entirely by my mother's love, into which my father could have slipped if he'd changed. In the letter, I told him my mother had suddenly died and also that I had always hoped that someday we could have a relationship. I said that in order for me to do that, he first had to explain to me why he'd done the things he'd done when we'd been together.

Sometimes I imagine my father opening that letter. It was twenty years ago and though just about everything in my life has changed in those twenty years, my imagining of my father receiving the letter with news of my mother's death has not. In my mind, he cries softly at the news. He realizes his three children are now orphans and here's his chance to make things right. Here's his chance to be our dad. It's not too late. We need him now.

But he didn't realize that. Instead, he got drunk and called to say that I was a lying bitch and that our mother had tainted our minds and turned my siblings and me against him. I hung up without saying goodbye.

Seventeen years passed.

Then one day the phone rang and there it was: my father's name on the tiny screen of my telephone. *He's dead,* was my first thought. I believed his third wife was calling to tell me that. I didn't pick up the phone. I only watched it ring. I listened to the message a few minutes later.

It wasn't my father's third wife. It was my father. "This is your father," he said, followed by his first and last name, in case I didn't know who my father was. He told me his phone number and asked me to call him.

It took me a week to do it. I was done with him. I had filled up the empty bowl of him over and over again. I had walked barefoot across a bunch of crap carrying it in my hands. I hadn't let anything slosh out. I didn't love him anymore. I only remembered that I had loved him. So long ago.

I dialed his number. "Hello," he said—his voice so familiar after all this time.

"This is your daughter," I said, followed by my first and last name, in case he didn't know who his daughter was.

"Do you watch Rachael Ray?" he asked.

"Rachael Ray?" I whispered, barely able to speak, my heart racing.

"Rachael Ray, you know. The cookbook writer. She has a talk show."

"Oh, yeah," I said.

And on it went, the most flabbergasting conversation I've ever had. My father spoke to me as if we spoke every week, as if nothing that had happened had happened, as if my whole childhood did not exist. We chatted about low-fat recipes and poodles; cataracts and the importance of sunscreen. I got off the phone fifteen minutes later, utterly bewildered. He wasn't delusional or ill or giving in to age-induced dementia. He was my father. The man he'd always been. And he was talking to me as if I was his daughter. As if he had a right.

But he didn't. Shortly afterwards he sent me a chatty note over email. When I replied, I said what I'd said in the letter I'd written to him years before—that I would consider having a relationship with him only after we spoke honestly about our shared past. He replied inquiring what it was I "wanted to know."

I had come so far by then. I had accepted the facts of my life. I was happy. I had two children and a partner I loved. I wasn't angry with my father anymore. I didn't want to hurt him. But I couldn't pretend to have a relationship with him if he refused to acknowledge our life. I was prepared to listen. I wanted his insight, to know what he thought, and also to see if by some wondrous turn of events, he'd become a different man—one who could at last be my dad.

I wrote the most generous, loving, true, fearless, painful, mature, and forgiving letter I could muster. Then I pasted it into an email and pressed Send.

My father's reply came so quickly it seemed impossible that he'd read the whole thing. In enraged words he wrote that I should never contact him again and that he was glad to be finally rid of me.

I didn't cry. I laced on my running shoes and went out my front door and walked through my neighborhood to a park and up a big hill. I didn't stop walking until I got all the way to the top and then I sat down on a bench that looked over the city. It was the week before my thirty-ninth birthday. I always think of my parents on my birthday, don't you? And I imagine it in the same way I imagine my father getting the letter I wrote to him after my mother died—it doesn't change, no matter what happened afterwards. I can conjure my mother and my father so clearly on the day I was born. How truly they must have loved me. How they must have held me in their arms and thought that I was a miracle. They must have believed they could be better people than they'd been before. They would be. They knew they would. They had to be. Because now there was me.

So it felt particularly acute to sit on that bench absorbing what had just transpired. I had that feeling you get—there is no word for this feeling—when you are simultaneously happy and sad and angry and grateful and accepting and appalled and every other possible emotion, all smashed together and amplified. Why is there no word for this feeling?

Perhaps because the word is "healing" and we don't want to believe that. We want to believe healing is purer and more perfect, like a baby on its birthday. Like we're holding it in our hands. Like we'll be better people than we've been before. Like we have to be.

It is on that feeling that I have survived. And it will be your salvation too, my dear. When you reach the place that you recognize entirely that you will thrive not in spite of your losses and sorrows, but because of them. That you would not have chosen the things that happened in your life, but you are grateful for them. That you have the two empty bowls eternally in your hands, but you also have the capacity to fill them.

That's what I did the week before I turned thirty-nine. I filled the empty bowl of my father one last time. I sat for so long on that bench looking at the sky and the land and the trees and the buildings and the streets, thinking: My father—*my father!*—he is finally, finally, finally rid of me.

Yours,
Sugar

TRANSCEND

Dear Sugar,

I'm torn. I feel like I have to decide between the two things I love the most. My wife and I have an eighteen-month-old daughter. Our marriage has been rocky for years. My wife is a heroin addict who relapsed (post-baby), after seven years of recovery. She had been breastfeeding and snorting opioids until the night I caught her.

I come from three generations of addiction from both my parents. I got sober myself when I was a teen and turned my life around while living at a boys' home, which I consider partially my home. I now work as a drug counselor at this very place. I have become a walking example for the Los Angeles street kids I work with, who are much like me. This work is my calling. It has even inspired me to write my novel, which has become the most stolen book at the boys' home where I work.

Here is where the tear in my soul begins. My wife is from a small city in the South. I met her there. My mother died when I was living there. My wife was there for me. That city healed me. Recently my wife got an opportunity for a job that's based in that city. All of my wife's family and support are there. She just had her second interview and is probably going to be offered this great job.

I'm confused about what to do. Things are progressing for me professionally. I'm halfway through my master's degree in social work and momentum is building in my life. Right before my wife got this job opportunity, she had confessed to being on methadone (prescribed by her doctor) for the last three months to wean her off her heavy addiction. She chose not to tell me even though I have been supportive and had been asking for connection since her relapse. It might not make sense, but I felt more betrayed by this than I do by her relapse. I just want her to have a connection with me.

If she gets the job, I don't know if I can make the commitment to go with her because of my lack of trust in her and the positive direction of my life here in Los Angeles. I want my wife to be happy and near her family (I don't have family to offer her as support), but I cannot even bear the thought of being away from my daughter. I don't want to be like my father.

I'm torn and distraught. Should I be with my daughter and my wife or continue the path of my calling with the boys' home among the LA street kids I love?

Please help me think this through, Sugar.

Signed,
Torn and Distraught

Dear Torn and Distraught,

I teach memoir writing occasionally. I always ask my students to answer two questions about the work they and their peers have written: *What happened in this story?* and *What is this story about?* It's a useful way to see what's there. A lot of times, it isn't much. Or rather, it's a bunch of what happened that ends up being about nothing at all. You get no points for the

living, I tell my students. It isn't enough to have had an interesting or hilarious or tragic life. Art isn't anecdote. It's the consciousness we bring to bear on our lives. For what happened
in the story to transcend the limits of the personal, it must be
driven by the engine of what the story means.

This is also true in life. Or at least it's true when one wishes
to live an ever-evolving life, such as you and I do, sweet pea.
What this requires of us is that we don't get tangled up in
the living, even when we in fact feel woefully tangled up. It
demands that we focus not only on what's happening in our
stories, but also what our stories are about.

There's a sentence in your letter that matters more than all
the other sentences: *I don't want to be like my father.* It's strange
that it matters since I don't know precisely what you mean by
it—nowhere in your letter do you tell me what your father is
like. And yet, of course I understand. *I don't want to be like my
father* is a story I know. It's code for a father who failed. It's
what your story is about.

If you do not want to be like your father, do not be like him.
There is your meaning, dear man. There is your purpose on
this earth. Your daughter is the most important person in your
life and you are one of the two most important people in hers.
That's more than a fact. It's a truth. And like all truths, it has
its own integrity. It's shiningly clear and resolute. If you are to
succeed in fulfilling your meaning, everything that happens in
your life must flow from this truth.

So let's talk about everything that's happening.

Your first obligation as a parent is to protect your child.
Allowing your daughter to move across the country without
you when you know that her mother is a drug addict who is
struggling mightily with her recovery is a bad idea no matter

how many grandmothers and uncles and cousins live across town. Until your wife is clean and strong in her recovery, she should not be the primary caregiver of your child. I don't question the profound love your wife no doubt has for your daughter. But I know addicts and you know addicts and we both know that no matter how wonderful and loving your wife may be, when she's in her addiction, she's not in her right mind. For that, your daughter will suffer and has suffered. It is your duty to shield her from this to the greatest extent possible.

The struggle your wife is engaged in right now is essential and monumental. Everything is at stake for her. Her ability to get and stay clean is directly connected to her ability to mother your child and remain your partner. Her addiction can't be cured by a job or a new town, though those things may ultimately play a role in her recovery. It can only be cured by her desire to stay clean and explore the underlying issues that compelled her to become an addict.

I strongly encourage the two of you to step back from the frazzled excitement of a possible job opportunity in a far-off and beloved town and focus instead on the monster that's hunkered down in your living room. What support and resources does your wife need? What role can and will you play in her recovery? Is your marriage salvageable? If it is, how will you as a couple reestablish trust and connection? In what city would you like to build your life together and what does that decision mean for each of you, professionally and personally? If your marriage isn't salvageable, how might you lovingly proceed in the direction of divorce? How will you negotiate custody of your daughter?

Those are the questions you need to be asking right now.

Not whether your wife and daughter should move across the country without you in the midst of this already tumultuous time. There are other jobs for your wife. There are other jobs for you (much as you love yours, there are boys all over the country who would benefit from your leadership and wisdom). There are other times one or both of you may decide to move back to her hometown or stay in LA.

Choosing not to ask these questions right now doesn't mean that you won't ask them later. It's only putting a pause button on what's happening in your story so you can figure out what it means instead. It's opting to transcend—*to rise above or go beyond the limits of*—rather than living inside the same old tale.

I know you know what it means to transcend. You did it in your own life when you made a whole man out of the fractured boy you once were. But the thing about rising is we have to continue upward; the thing about going beyond is we have to keep going.

You have only begun to understand what it means to not be like your father. Keep understanding. Do not fail yourself on this front. No matter what happens when it comes to your marriage or your work life or your geographical location, there is no being torn when it comes to your daughter unless you choose to rip the fabric yourself. She wins every time.

Yours,
Sugar

A SHIMMERING SLICE OF YOUR
MYSTERIOUS DESTINY

Dear Sugar,

I'm getting married in a few months. Why do I feel totally aggressive and angry? How does anyone get through this event?

Aggressive

Dear Aggressive,

My guess is you're the bride and that you feel aggressive and angry because you're in wedding planning hell and you're caught up in all the expectations, outdated fairy tales, overpriced products, and irrational beliefs that one adheres to when one believes it possible to flawlessly orchestrate the behaviors, conversations, drinking habits, and attire of a large group of in-laws, out-laws, friends, strangers, and co-workers while simultaneously having a meaningful and intimate exchange with your sweetheart in front of an audience. It is not.

Or at least it's not possible in exactly the way you're imagining now. I'm quite certain that whatever you're all worked up about these days—the colors of your napkins, the invitation that should or should not be sent to your mother's cousin

Ray—matters little and whatever will actually happen on that day when you get married will positively blow your mind.

Your wedding is going to be a kick, honey bun, but only after you accept that it isn't something to "get through." Perhaps it might help to stop thinking about it as the perfect "event," but rather a messy, beautiful, and gloriously unexpected day in your sweet life.

My own wedding was really something, though for a good stretch it appeared that everything had gone to hell. As our one hundred or so guests arrived, it was pouring rain and we'd made no rain contingency plans for our outdoor wedding. Mr. Sugar realized he'd forgotten his pants sixty miles away, back in the city where we lived, and I realized I'd forgotten the marriage license. My mother-in-law arrived dressed like a sheepherder from biblical times if sheepherders from biblical times wore teal, and one of my old friends pulled me aside to grill me about why I hadn't chosen her to be a bridesmaid. I couldn't find the bobby pins I'd brought to pin my veil to my hair and then once other bobby pins had been purchased, in a mad dash relay effort that involved two local drugstores, I and seven of my girlfriends couldn't get the goddamn veil to stay on my head.

Many of those things seemed calamitous at the time, but they are now among my most treasured memories of that day. If they hadn't happened, I'd have never run down the street in the rain holding Mr. Sugar's hand laughing and crying at the same time because I was going to have to marry him in a dingy library basement instead of on the banks of a beautiful river. I'd have never felt the way it feels when everyone you know volunteers to drive at an illegal speed to retrieve a pair of pants and a piece of paper. I'd have never known what a biblical-times sheepherder might look like in teal, and that important piece of information about my old friend. And I wouldn't have been so distracted by getting those goddamned bobby pins in my hair that I didn't realize the rain had stopped and Mr. Sugar had discreetly enlisted our guests to carry one hundred white wooden chairs a quarter mile, from the terrible library basement back to the grassy spot on the banks of the beautiful river, where I had hoped to marry him in the sunlight and did.

We all get lost in the minutiae, but don't lose this day. Make a list of everything that needs to be seen to and decided and worried about between now and your wedding day and then circle the things that matter the most to you and do them right. Delegate or decide on the other stuff and refuse to worry anymore.

Let your wedding be a wonder. Let it be one hell of a good time. Let it be what you can't yet imagine and wouldn't orchestrate even if you could. Remember why it is you've gone to so much trouble that you've been driven to anger and aggression and an advice columnist. You're getting married! There's a day ahead that's a shimmering slice of your mysterious destiny. All you've got to do is show up.

Yours,
Sugar

THE ORDINARY MIRACULOUS

Dear Sugar,

The general mystery of becoming seems like a key idea in many of your columns, of how you don't know what something will turn out to be until you've lived it. It's made me want to know more. Will you give us a specific example of how something has played out over years of your life, Sugar?

    Thank you.

Big Fan

Dear Big Fan,

The summer I was eighteen I was driving down a country road with my mother. This was in the rural county where I grew up and all of the roads were country, the houses spread out over miles, hardly any of them in sight of a neighbor. Driving meant going past an endless stream of trees and fields and wildflowers. On this particular afternoon, my mother and I came upon a yard sale at a big house where a very old woman lived alone, her husband dead, her kids grown and gone.

"Let's look and see what she has," my mother said as we passed, so I turned the car around and pulled into the old woman's driveway and the two of us got out.

We were the only people there. Even the old woman whose sale it was didn't come out of the house, only waving to us from a window. It was August, the last stretch of time that I would live with my mother. I'd completed my first year of college by then and I'd returned home for the summer because I'd gotten a job in a nearby town. In a few weeks I'd go back to college and I'd never again live in the place I called home, though I didn't know that then.

There was nothing much of interest at the yard sale, I saw, as I made my way among the junk—old cooking pots and worn-out board games; incomplete sets of dishes in faded, unfashionable colors; and appalling polyester pants—but as I turned away, just before I was about to suggest that we should go, something caught my eye.

It was a red velvet dress trimmed with white lace, fit for a toddler.

"Look at this," I said and held it up to my mother, who said, *Oh, isn't that the sweetest thing,* and I agreed and then set the dress back down.

In a month I'd be nineteen. In a year I'd be married. In three years I'd be standing in a meadow not far from that old woman's yard holding the ashes of my mother's body in my palms. I was pretty certain at that moment that I would never be a mother myself. Children were cute, but ultimately annoying, I thought then. I wanted more out of life.

And yet, ridiculously, inexplicably, on that day the month before I turned nineteen, as my mother and I poked among the detritus of someone else's life, I kept returning to that red velvet dress fit for a toddler. I don't know why. I cannot explain it even now except to say something about it called powerfully to me. I wanted that dress. I tried to talk myself out of wanting it as I smoothed my hands over the velvet. There was a small square of masking tape near its collar that said $1.

"You want that dress?" my mother asked, glancing up nonchalantly from her own perusals.

"Why would I?" I snapped, perturbed with myself more than her.

"For someday," said my mother.

"But I'm not even going to have kids," I argued.

"You can put it in a box," she replied. "Then you'll have it, no matter what you do."

"I don't have a dollar," I said with finality.

"I do," my mother said and reached for the dress.

I put it in a box, in a cedar chest that belonged to my mother. I dragged it with me all the way along the scorching trail of my twenties and into my thirties. I had a son and then a daughter. The red dress was a secret only known by me, buried for years among my mother's best things. When I finally unearthed it and held it again it was like being slapped and kissed at the same time, like the volume was being turned way up and also way down. The two things that were true about its existence had an opposite effect and were yet the same single fact:

My mother bought a dress for the granddaughter she'll never know.

My mother bought a dress for the granddaughter she'll never know.

How beautiful. How ugly.

How little. How big.

How painful. How sweet.

It's almost never until later that we can draw a line between this and that. There was no force at work other than my own desire that compelled me to want that dress. Its meaning was made only by my mother's death and my daughter's birth. And then it meant a lot. The red dress was the material evidence of my loss, but also of the way my mother's love had carried me forth beyond her, her life extending years into my own in ways I never could have imagined. It was a becoming that I would not have dreamed was mine the moment that red dress caught my eye.

My daughter doesn't connect me to my mother more than my son does. My mother lives as brightly in my boy child as she does in my girl. But seeing my daughter in that red dress on the second Christmas of her life gave me something beyond words. The feeling I got was like that original double whammy I'd had when I first pulled that dress from the box of my mother's best things, only now it was

My daughter is wearing a dress that her grandmother bought for her at a yard sale.

My daughter is wearing a dress that her grandmother bought for her at a yard sale.

It's so simple it breaks my heart. How unspecial that fact is to so many, how ordinary for a child to wear a dress her grandmother bought her, but how very extraordinary it was to me.

I suppose this is what I mean when I say we cannot possibly know what will manifest in our lives. We live and have experiences and leave people we love and get left by them. People we thought would be with us forever aren't and people we didn't know would come into our lives do. Our work here is to keep faith with that, to put it in a box and wait. To trust that someday we will know what it means, so that when the ordinary miraculous is revealed to us we will be there, standing before the baby girl in the pretty dress, grateful for the smallest things.

Yours,
Sugar

WE CALL THIS A CLUSTERFUCK

Note: The following two letters are from each of the women involved in the situation detailed in the letters.

Dear Sugar,

I recently had sex with a guy who has a complicated history with a friend of mine. I knew sleeping with him would hurt my friend's feelings, and so I told her I wouldn't. She didn't ask me not to sleep with him, but it was implied. She would make references to "his crush on me" and once asked him if we had had a threesome with this other girl. Long story short, I broke my promise. I meant what I said to my friend at the time, Sugar, but I failed.

The man in question is a good guy. I enjoyed spending time with him and let's just say my bed has been rather empty of late. My desire outweighed the potential hurt I knew my actions would cause. The guy and my friend have had many conversations since I slept with him, and they appear to have made up, whereas my friendship with her is still on shaky ground. I think it will normalize eventually, but I already feel like our friendship is something that's not that important to her. I don't even know if it's all that important to me either.

Very recently, my stepdad had a heart attack. It was his second. It made me think about gravity and consequence and trivialities, and that if this one night of problematic sex forever alters or negates all the other ways I've been a good friend to her, then so be it. If that's the case, our friendship wasn't meant to last, and I have more important things to worry about. But at the same time I can't help but wonder if I am losing my humanity a little. Because today an ex-friend of mine basically said she hadn't completely forgiven me for hurting her six years ago. I cheated on her like the dumb twenty-two-year-old I was, and I have apologized a thousand times since then. We weren't friends for a while, but we became good friends again eventually. Until today, I was operating under the assumption that we were okay. To hear her say she relates to me differently, that she withholds information from me because of how I behaved years ago, makes me profoundly sad and angry. What does it mean if someone forgives you, but never forgets?

I feel both horrible and stubborn. And I don't know how much of this anger is due to acknowledging potentially ugly truths about myself—that I value desire at the expense of my friendships; that I can't seem to learn from past mistakes; that I am a person others deem untrustworthy. The last one stings the worst, and is a doubt I expressed to the guy shortly after our tryst. "She never trusted you," he said, which was a confirmation of my fears, if not a self-fulfilling prophecy.

I would probably have done the same thing, given another opportunity. And I don't know if that should worry me or if it makes me some kind of pleasure addict or just a terrible friend. I don't regret my recent behavior, but should I? Am I throwing away solid friendships for stupid sexual gratification? Part of me feels selfish even writing to you, because I know you'll call me honey bun and make me feel better when I don't deserve it.

Friend or Foe

Dear Sugar,

I have two friends who I love dearly. One is a man I've known since we were teenagers. A few years ago, he and I started a brief nonmonogamous romance. He then fell in love with another woman, who he rightly chose over me. Though I knew we were meant to be friends instead of romantic partners, my feelings for him ran deep, so I was crushed. Eventually the pain subsided, and we became closer as friends.

The other friend is a woman I admire greatly as a writer and as a person. She's witty, sexy, brilliant. We support each other through romantic traumas and laugh constantly whenever we're together. She was there to comfort me when my male friend told me he had met someone else. She sat with me as I unabashedly cried in public in the middle of downtown San Francisco.

Recently, these two friends met and hit it off. He started joking about sleeping with her. (He is single now.) I told my male friend that this idea made me feel uncomfortable, but he dismissed my worries. I didn't press the issue because my female friend swore that she would never sleep with him. She said this to me repeatedly, emphatically, even when I didn't ask her. While I was over my attraction to this guy, the history was still a little too fresh, and I wasn't finished processing the heartbreak. She saw how it was still affecting me. I trusted her.

But it happened anyway. They slept together. When my male friend told me, I got very upset; I yelled at him for the way he'd dismissed my feelings in the past. We talked on several very long phone calls, and by the end of it I felt heard, valued, and respected. He also forced me to come to terms with my jealousy and lack of claim I have over others' actions. Since then, I've had to do a lot of hard looking at my own insecurity and desire for control.

Two weeks later, when my female friend apologized for breaking the promise she had made to me, I told her I no longer thought I'd had a right to that promise in the first place, even though it hurt and angered me when she broke it. She had done what she felt was right for her, and now I had to figure out what was right for me: taking time and space. Part of me felt at peace with this conclusion. But by that point, I also felt so emotionally exhausted by the whole situation, and so disgusted with myself, I wasn't even sure I deserved an apology from anyone.

Sugar, I'm conflicted. I know what they did wasn't morally wrong; I've felt desire before for the exes of friends, and the friends of exes. These two friends have a relationship that's independent of me. Still, I was so hurt. And the worst part is, I'm ashamed of my hurt. I'm ashamed of the jealousy I didn't know was still in me, even eighteen months after the romance ended. I want to be the person who can gracefully take joy in the fact that two people I love were able to share some sexy fun. I want to believe that the hurt is all in my possessive, competitive little brain, so I can just change myself and get over it. All I do now is beat myself up, for whatever choice I make. My internal compass on this matter is so broken. I need your wise, soothing words.

Love,
Triangled

Dear Women,

A couple of years ago the baby Sugars got into a vicious fight over the decapitated head of a black-haired plastic princess. My son was all but frothing at the mouth. My daughter screamed so hard for so long I thought the neighbors were going to call the cops. The decapitated head in question was about the size of a gumball, its neck not a proper neck, but rather an opening into which a tiny interchangeable torso was meant to be snapped. This torso was either the ancient female Egyptian my daughter was holding in her hand or the sultry skirted girl pirate my son was holding in his. Hence the uproar.

Neither of them could be convinced to relinquish their claim on the decapitated head of the black-haired plastic princess, no matter how gently or sternly or maniacally I explained that they could take turns, each of them attaching the head to "their torso" for short periods of time. Likewise, they refused to be consoled by any one of the countless items that clutter the room they share—not the bin of agates or the wooden daggers; not the stuffed kittens or the alphabet flashcards; not the foam swords or the half-trashed markers; not the ballerinas or the Roman warriors or monkeys or fairy statuettes or fake golden coins or movie-inspired action figures or unicorns or race cars or dinosaurs or tiny spiral-bound notebooks or any other damn thing in the whole motherloving universe but the decapitated head of the black-haired plastic princess.

It's mine, my daughter shrieked.

I was playing with it first, countered my son.

It's special to me, wailed my daughter.

She plays with my special toys all the time, my son bellowed.

I talked and reasoned and made suggestions that soon

became commands, but really, ultimately, there was nothing to be done. There was one head and two torsos. The indisputable fact of that was like a storm we had to ride out until all the trees were blown down.

I begin with this allegorical snippet from Chez Sugar not because I think your individual and joint struggles regarding your friendship are as infantile as a tussle over a toy, but rather because I think it's instructive to contemplate in essential terms our desire to have not only what is ours, but what also belongs to those we love, and not only because we want those things for ourselves, but because we want the other person not to have them. That fervor is age-old and endless and a gumball-sized piece at the core of what we're grappling with here and I invite you both to ponder it.

We all have a righteous claim to the decapitated head of the black-haired plastic princess. We believe she is ours alone to hold. We refuse to let her go.

Before we begin disentangling your situation in earnest, I'll say right out that I'm quite sure if the two of you continue talking silently to yourselves about this icky and weird thing that happened with the man I'm going to go ahead and call The Foxy Fellow you're going to regret it. And more than that, you're going to hatch a whole slew of increasingly distorted beliefs about *what went down* and *what that means* and *who did and said what* and it will not only make you miserable and sad and bitter, it will also rob you of a friend who you really should be sitting on a porch with ten years in the future, laughing about what knuckleheads you were back in the day.

You both did something you basically know wasn't so great. Your desires and fears and failings and unreasonable expectations and things you won't admit to yourselves clicked into each other as neatly as a plastic head does into a plastic torso and when you put them together you both got pinched. The same thing happened to you from different points of view. With whom should our sympathies lie? On which woman's shoulders should the blame be placed? In what directions do the arrows of your narratives flow? How best do you find your way out of this place?

These are the questions I asked myself as I considered your letters. Every time I tried to straighten the stories out in my head, they got all tangled up instead. I made charts and lists with bullet points. I took a piece of paper and drew a map. I turned your Foxy Fellow imbroglio into a pair of mathematical equations of the sort I never learned how to do properly in school (which utterly frees me to use them for my own whimsical literary purposes). Here's how they look:

Friend or Foe: "I solemnly swear that I will never fuck The Foxy Fellow because my friend still has tender and territorial feelings for him and I don't want to hurt her" + [I am a caring person and fucking The Foxy Fellow would compel me to question the sort of person I believe myself to be] + fucked The Foxy Fellow anyway = eek/ugh^2 × [but perhaps, when I really think about it, my friendship with this woman is "not that important"] ÷ and yet there was that time I sat with her in downtown San Francisco while she bawled unabashedly > so − fuck this shit! + how dare she be mad at me! + I was a good friend to her in every other way! + The Foxy Fellow has not even been her boyfriend for, like, EVER! + I am attracted to him! + he is attracted to me! + I'm not even thirty and my vagina is growing cobwebs! + who the hell is she to say who The Foxy Fellow and I get to have sex with in the first place? < I am a terrible person and a selfish sex fiend [will the damn-

ing ex-girlfriend please present her testimony to the court?]
÷ cheated, yes + lied, yes + to ever be trusted or forgiven, no,
never, not by any woman in any time for any reason whatsoever = you know what? Fuck those bitches! + I'd totally do The
Foxy Fellow again! ≠ Except. Well. [Damn]

Triangled: "The Foxy Fellow is a wonderful person" +
[we "broke up," though we were never really together, never
monogamous, even though he crushed my heart in this really
hard-to-exactly-define-way for which I do not fault him
because I didn't have expectations—why would I have expectations? etc.] ÷ it's pretty clear to me that he wants to fuck my
lovely woman friend who watched me bawl unabashedly over
him in downtown San Francisco and this makes me feel like
puking[2] + [what is the meaning of monogamy? what is love?
do we ever owe anyone anything when it comes to sex? why
do I feel like puking if The Foxy Fellow is "only my friend"?]
= accept adamant and profuse promises from my lovely
woman friend regarding her plans to not fuck The Foxy Fellow × [sisterhood!] − allow The Foxy Fellow to brush me off
when I express my wish he not fuck my lovely woman friend
= cry/rage when they fail to not fuck + [how could they? she
promised! I thought she was my friend! he never listened
to me!] < long, difficult, ultimately satisfying conversation
with The Foxy Fellow that makes me feel oddly closer to him
[and worse about my puny, insecure, control freak, jealous,
uncool, dumbass, competitive, needy self[2]] × short, unpro-
ductive, decidedly cool conversation with my lovely woman
friend [doesn't it seem like she should be sorrier than this?/
what right do I have to an apology? since when do I get to
say who fucks whom?/but she promised!] ÷ fantasize that my
lovely woman friend will take a long-term job in Korea + lis-

ten to my generation's equivalent of Lisa Germano's "Cancer of Everything" repeatedly while huddled into the pathetic ball of myself + [alternate with trying to cheerfully compose the phrase "to share some sexy fun" in relation to those two selfish assholes] ≠ Except. Well. [Damn.]

In the math-ignorant world of Sugarland, we call this a clusterfuck.

You are both wrong. You are both right. You both know you can do better than you did. The fact that you failed to do so equals nothing unless you learn something from this. So let's learn it, sweet peas.

Triangled, if it really hurts and enrages you that The Foxy Fellow fucks a friend of yours, he isn't your friend and you should not conduct yourself with him as such. He is your ex, the love you've yet to get over for reasons you may not be able to explain or justify even to yourself, the man who is an absolute no-go zone for anyone who's even remotely in your inner circle. Lose the but-we're-just-friends-now/free-love mumbo jumbo and own up to what you actually feel: if The Foxy Fellow is fucking anyone, you don't want to be hanging out with her. Not yet. Not now. Maybe not ever. At the very least, heal your heart before you go introducing The Foxy Fellow to your friends, especially those you'd describe as "witty, sexy, brilliant." And then brace yourself.

Though it may seem that Friend or Foe's choice to break her promise and fuck The Foxy Fellow is what caused all this pain, her actions are not at the root of your sorrow. What's at the root is the fact that you failed to recognize and honor your own boundaries. You tried to have it both ways. You wanted to be the woman who could be friends with a man she's not over, but you are not that woman. I understand why you want to be her, darling. She's one cool cat. She's the star of the show. She doesn't take anything personally. But you are not her. And that's okay. You are your own fragile, strong, sweet, searching self. You can be sad a guy you sort of fell for didn't fall for you. You don't have to be a good sport. You don't have to pretend you're okay with sharing your interesting and beautiful friends with The Foxy Fellow, even if you feel like a puny asshole not being okay with it. You can say no.

But the thing is, you have to say it. You have to be the woman who stands up and says it. Not only to the lovely friend who can't possibly keep the promises she's made to you while swimming in the shared waters of your wishy-washy ache for affirmation and orgasms, but also to the man himself. Yes, The Foxy Fellow. The one who is, but who is not, your friend. You have to live with the uncomfortable reality that it's from him that you need time and space. And then you have to take it, hard as it is, come what may.

Friend or Foe, you made a choice you knew would hurt someone who trusted you—a choice, it's worth noting, you explicitly vowed not to make—and afterwards you justified that choice with reasons you could've more thoughtfully discussed with her beforehand. This makes you neither "a pleasure addict" nor "a terrible friend." It makes you someone who did what most people would do in this situation at this moment in your life: a woman who took what she wanted instead of what she needed.

You are at once blameless in this and entirely responsible. You were sort of set up by Triangled and you were also basically a jerk to her. The reason all that other junk came up in your post–Foxy Fellow contemplations—(your ex, your feelings of being eternally punished for having wronged her, your sense that your friend never trusted you either)—is that, contrary to your claim that you don't regret what you did, you know you could have done this differently, better, or not at all. What's at stake here is not only your friendship with Triangled, but also your own integrity. You promised you would not hurt someone you cared for. You hurt her anyway. What do you make of that? What would you like to take forward from this, honey bun? Do you want to throw up your hands and say "Oh well," or do you dare to allow this experience to alter your view?

We all like to think we're right about what we believe about ourselves and what we often believe are only the best, most moral things—i.e., *Of course I would never fuck The Foxy Fellow because that would hurt my friend!* We like to pretend that our generous impulses come naturally. But the reality is we often become our kindest, most ethical selves only by seeing what it feels like to be a selfish jackass first. It's the reason we have to fight so viciously over the decapitated head of the black-haired plastic princess before we learn how to play nice; the reason we have to get burned before we understand the power of fire; the reason our most meaningful relationships are so often those that continued beyond the very juncture at which they came the closest to ending.

I hope that you'll do that, dear women, even if it takes you some time to stagger forward. I don't know if your friendship is built to last a lifetime, but I know the game is worth the candle. I can see you on that ten-years-off porch.

Yours,
Sugar

ARE YOU MY MOTHER?

Dear Sugar,

I moved to a new city a year ago and in the past few months have been feeling so at home and at ease after various bouts of loneliness. I've met some great women here, women I might have seen myself being able to date at some point, or at least sleep with for a while. What is the problem with this? Well, I am finding that I am gravitating toward women more from habit than from necessity. I pursue what is immediately available and then lose interest rapidly—sometimes before it even starts—but because I am a sensitive, sensual person, I have a hard time turning it away.

I guess what I am asking is, is this biological or emotional? I'm a male in my mid-twenties just starting what looks to be a promising career doing what I love. I feel so much love and gratitude in my life, and just typing that sentence made me feel a bit better. I really, really love women and don't know if I could ever just turn it off. I also don't want to end up another distant, difficult, noncommunicative male unsure of his own feelings.

I think part of the problem might be that I feel like I need physical love to be happy and am less of a person without it. Is it more self-affirmation I need? Do I need to convince myself that I will find someone that I really can love and not just pursue

*because they are available for me immediately? Does this have
anything to do with my mother?*

Anonymous

Dear Anonymous,

Have you ever read that book by P. D. Eastman called *Are You
My Mother?* In it, a baby bird hatches while his mother is away
from the nest and he decides to go out to find her. He can't
fly yet so he walks. He walks and he walks and he walks on
his tiny baby bird feet, constantly asking the question: *Are you
my mother?* Each time he asks the question, he's convinced
the answer is yes. But he's wrong. Nothing is ever his mother.
The kitten isn't his mother. The hen isn't his mother. The dog
isn't his mother. The cow isn't his mother. The boat isn't his
mother. The plane isn't his mother. The steam shovel that he
calls a Snort isn't his mother. But finally, when all hope is lost,
the baby bird gets himself back to the nest and along comes
his mother.

It's a children's book that isn't really about children. It's a
book about you and me and everyone else who has ever been
twentysomething and searching for the thing inside that allows
us to feel at home in the world. It's a story about how impossible it can be to recognize who we are and who we belong to
and who belongs to us. It's a fairly precise tale of the journey
you're on right now, Anonymous, and from it I encourage you
to take both heart and heed.

Of course you've slept with women you aren't actually
very interested in having a relationship with, honey bunch.
Of course you have! When you're single and in your twenties,
having sex with whoever comes along is practically your *job*.

It's biological. It's emotional. It's psychological. It's egomaniacal. And yes, some of those impulses just might have a little something to do with your mom (and your dad too, for that matter).

The conflicted feelings and thoughts you're having about love and sex and the occasionally contradictory actions you're taking with women are developmentally appropriate and they'll teach you something you need to know, so don't be too hard on yourself, but do take care not to get stuck. Not getting stuck is key to not becoming "another distant, difficult, non-communicative male unsure of his own feelings" who sleeps with every mildly interesting and interested woman he meets. We learn from experience, but no need to keep learning the same things from the same experiences over and over again, right?

You know what it feels like to say yes to women you don't ultimately dig, so how about seeing how it feels to say no? What space is filled up by sex with women you aren't all that into and what fills that space when you don't fill it with them? If you'd like to become the emotionally evolved man it seems so very clear to me that you are on the brink of becoming, you're going to have to evolve beyond asking every kitten you meet if she's your mother.

She isn't. You are. And once you figure that out, you're home.

Yours,
Sugar

TEN ANGRY BOYS

Dear Sugar,

I am a mother of two beautiful little girls, ages four and two. They are my reason for being; I love them more than words can express. I didn't think I wanted to be a mother and often said I had no affinity with children. But, my God, when my first was born, it was like a 360 spinout. I didn't know what hit me. I fell in love and was under her spell instantly. I bonded quickly with both girls and would call myself an attachment parent. The three of us are very close and we're a very affectionate family.

I'm aware of the importance of respecting my daughters' feelings and teaching them about expressing their feelings, not suppressing them. But lately I have been losing control of my temper, allowing this demonic THING to come out of me during times of stress. Don't get me wrong: I'm not flying off the handle over trivial things like not finishing dinner or being rowdy at the supermarket. It's more of a culmination where I'm tolerating one thing after another and then I explode.

I should also explain that my husband, who is an adoring father and husband, works long and unpredictable hours. This kills him because he misses being with us, but it's just the way it is. He is what I call a pure heart. He is the man who saved me, because before I met him I was a compulsive negative thinker. He is just pure "good" in the way that you don't see these days. He's so gentle and fun and loving with our girls and I'm so grateful for that, but he works long hours, so I'm often a single mom and I feel stretched thin. Most days are good, but when I lose it, it's like gangbusters.

The thing that frightens me, Sugar, is that I come from a very volatile family background. Not in the sense that my parents were raging alcoholics or freakishly abusive. They unfairly screamed their heads off and intimidated us and hit us a lot. We weren't allowed to make our own choices and were made to feel very powerless. My mother especially would unleash on my siblings and me, and often it was like negotiating through land mines. You just didn't know when she'd blow. She would say out loud that she wanted to run away, and on those nights I wouldn't sleep until she was in bed. I truly did think she was packing her bags. She had major issues that I've learned of recently. She comes from a dysfunctional background and other circumstances that will take too long to explain here. I think this caused her to go off on hour-long soliloquies about how her life sucked and her kids sucked, too.

Okay, so that's the backstory in a nutshell. I'm a woman with low self-esteem who just gritted her teeth through university, got a pretty good job, married a great guy, have a beautiful family, but now I'm scaring myself because of my temper. I'm doing things that I know are not acceptable. Tonight I grabbed my older girl out of her car seat and threw her onto our front yard. She was lying there in shock and started to cry. The prelude to this was a screaming adult tantrum during the drive home. It's almost like I can't come down until I've had my hit of rage.

I feel like I totally suck and don't deserve to be their mother because I know this is wrong but I can't stop. Today I asked my doctor for a referral to a therapist so I can start talking through these deeper issues. I'm just scared that I'll never be able to change, and this temper and need to explode is hardwired in me.

Yours,
Helpless Mom

Dear Helpless Mom,

I don't think you're helpless. I think you're a good mom who has on occasion been brought to the edge of her capacities for tolerance and patience and kindness and who needs to learn how to manage her anger and her stress. You're entirely capable of doing that. The part of your letter in which you state that you believe you may "never be able to change" concerns me more than the part of your letter in which you describe flinging your child onto the lawn in a rage. Given your situation as the primary caregiver of two very young children with little practical support from a partner, it comes as no surprise that you've lost it with your beloved kids from time to time. I have, for short stretches, parented my own two young children in circumstances very much like those you describe, and it is without question the most exhausting and maddening work I've ever done.

I've also behaved in ways toward my children that I regret. Find me a mother who hasn't.

I don't say this to let you off the hook, but rather—paradoxically—to place responsibility for change squarely on your shoulders. Parenting is serious business. It brings out the best and the worst in us. It demands that we confront our brightest and darkest selves. Your dear daughters have given you the opportunity to see yourself in full: you are the woman who has the ability to love more deeply than she ever thought possible and also the woman who has intermittent "screaming adult tantrums" directed at two people under the age of five.

The best thing you can do for your girls is to forgive yourself for what has passed, accept that your rages helped you to understand you have work to do in order to be the mother your children deserve, and then draw on every resource you can—both internal and external—to become her.

Your husband's job is demanding, but surely he's around often enough that he can give you regular breaks from the family fray. Does he? Do you take them? I know how hard it can be to pull yourself away, especially when you're hungry for the rare *we're-all-together-for-once!* family time, but I encourage you to find space for yourself too, even if you have to struggle to carve it out. It's amazing what an hour alone can restore, what rages a walk can quell. There are also other venues of support. A babysitting/playdate exchange with other parents; sending your children to a preschool a few mornings or afternoons a week, even if you don't have a "job" that demands you do so; a membership at a gym that provides child care while you work out or sit in the sauna paging through a magazine—these are all things that helped me through the thick of it, when my very days were vast seas of young children with no grown humans around to help.

The harder work is, of course, what you must do on the inside, the understanding that needs to happen in regard to your own childhood. I'm glad you're seeking counseling. I hope you'll enter into that process with a sense of strength rather than despair, because it is your strength and love that shines through your letter to me most of all. You have already come so far. That you have parented your daughters differently than the damaged way you were parented is perhaps the most meaningful achievement of your life, but there is more beyond the land of *I did better than them*. I have every belief that you'll find it; that you'll learn how to let your anger be only what it is and nothing more—a storm that passes harmlessly through you and peters out into the softest rain before it fades to sun.

I once gave my heart to ten angry boys. Though they seemingly have nothing to do with you or me or any of the basically good moms you and I know, my experience with them has informed my life in so many ways, and specifically my understanding of my obligations as a parent. I worked with the angry boys during the same time that I worked with teen girls in a middle school. My official work wasn't with these boys—I was employed to serve the girls—but because I had an office in the middle school and because I had the job title of *youth advocate* and because any program whose mission is to serve children living in poverty is invariably forced to scrounge for whatever it can get for free, I was enlisted to participate in an experiment of sorts.

The experiment was this: Convince the parents of these boys—who'd all done something bad enough that they'd been pulled out of regular classes and put into a special anger-management class—to come to the school to have dinner with their children as a family every Tuesday evening for ten weeks. The program would provide the food and the angry boys would serve it up. Each family would sit at its own table, separate from the others, in order to encourage family unity. After dinner, each angry boy would draw a card from a bowl and read what it said out loud to his family—it might be *my happiest memory* or *my dreams for the future*—and the families were meant to discuss this thing for fifteen minutes. After the discussions, the families would split up. The parents of the angry boys would go into a room where they'd meet with a team of social workers, group-therapy style, to discuss parenting challenges and joys; the youngest siblings of the angry boys would go into another room with a couple of interns, who were assigned to babysit; and the angry boys and their older and often even more angry siblings would go into a room with me. The youth advocate.

Hah.

The idea was that I'd lead the kids in games that would help them learn how to work cooperatively with each other without anyone trying to throttle anyone else. The first week was a disaster. One of the angry boys threatened someone's brother with a chair. Another punched someone very hard in the head when we played "duck, duck, gray duck." Bingo evolved into a melee. The hour felt like four.

I was actually trembling by the time we rejoined the parents and younger siblings in the school cafeteria, the rest of the building eerily dark and hushed around us. Once assembled, we stood in a wide circle—the ten angry boys and their families, four social workers, two interns, and me. It was time for our closing ritual, one of the social workers explained in a booming voice. We'd do this every week for the next nine, she said. First we'd sing a song. Next we'd do a thing called "rain."

I didn't know what "rain" was, but I didn't have time to inquire. I only followed along like the rest of the group, singing the song it seemed the social workers had made up themselves for this very occasion, catching the reluctant eyes of the parents of the angry boys as we all pushed our way haltingly through the inanely cheerful words. There were a few men

in the room—one real dad and a smattering of boyfriends—
but most of the parents were women about my age—late
twenties—though they didn't look like me or dress like me or
seem like me in any way. They seemed entirely like the moms of
the angry boys. Like they lived on the extremes. Either plainly
haggard or overly dolled up. Either very fat or very thin. Either
recently coked up or soon to be nodding off.

I felt like a fraud among them. How was I going to convince
their sons not to threaten one another with chairs?

When at last it was time to do "rain," the social worker led
us through it and I followed along again as the whole group of
us collectively reenacted a storm with our bodies. We began by
standing silently with our arms rounded into suns above us,
then we rubbed our hands together to create the softest hiss,
then we snapped our fingers to simulate the pitter-pat of rain-
drops, then we clapped our hands, first against each other, and
next against our thighs in loud watery smacks. At the height of
the storm, we were stomping our feet on the floor in a thun-
derous roar, until slowly, slowly we worked our way back up
again in reverse order—through the smacking and clapping
and rubbing ever more softly—until we were standing once
more like suns.

"That was really cool," said one of the angry boys in the
silence. "Can we please do it again?" he asked, and everyone
laughed.

He was the one who'd cracked the kid over the head too
hard when we were playing "duck, duck, gray duck." I was a
bit afraid of him that first night, and not just because he was
a big, intimidating brute of an eighth-grade boy. I'd kept him
particularly in my sights because I knew his story—the social

workers had briefed me about each of the boys—and his had stood out to me as sadder than most.

Two years before, when he'd been in sixth grade, he'd gone home from school one afternoon and found he was locked out. After he banged on the door and got no answer, he peered through the window and saw his father dead on the living room floor, overdosed on heroin. He believed he couldn't call the cops. The cops were not his friends. So he waited on the porch for his mother to come home, but she didn't come. She was a drug addict too, and a prostitute. The boy was her only child. He spent the night sleeping on the porch, huddled into his coat. In the morning, he walked back to school and told a teacher that his dad was dead.

He'd been an angry boy ever since.

I'm going to call him Brandon. After that first "rain" I stopped being afraid of him. He began stopping by my office in the quiet times when most of the other kids were in class. He'd worked out a deal with the teacher of his anger-management classroom that whenever he felt like he was going to act in an angry way, he could leave the room and walk up and down the school hallway taking deep breaths instead. It was a practice he'd been taught at school and it worked for him. Up and down he went, past my open office door, past my open office door, past my . . . until finally he'd back up and ask, "What you doing?" in a voice cloaked in such false nonchalance that it made my heart hurt.

"Nothing much," I'd say. "Come on in." And he'd sit down in the horrible story chair near my desk, where all the girls sat narrating their horrible stories, and he'd tell me his own stories, not all of which were horrible. His life was getting better, he told me. He was so happy his mother had agreed to participate in the Tuesday evening experiment. She was doing great, he said. She was getting clean and so was her boyfriend. When summer came they were going to get a dog.

The weeks passed. The Tuesday evenings came and went. A couple of the families dropped out. Others added new members: pregnant older sisters; new boyfriends and stepkids. Every week we did the same thing: dinner, discussion, group, song, "rain." *Kids need structure* is a phrase I heard a lot. *Kids like to be able to predict what's going to come next.*

More than anything they loved to do "rain." The ritual of it made them giddy. They smacked the shit out of their thighs to make a storm. Every week the silence in the wake of it rose off of us like a cure.

I never believed the boys were angry. I believed they were hurt and anger was the safest manifestation of their sorrow. It was the channel down which their impotent male rivers could rage.

Brandon was the angriest of them all, but he was also the sweetest. He took pride in calling himself my assistant. He didn't go home after school on Tuesdays and then return with his family for dinner like most of the angry boys. He came to my office and talked to me until it was time to help me set up the food in the cafeteria. He staked out the best table for him and his mom and her boyfriend, arranging the silverware just so, then waited for them to arrive.

On the last Tuesday of the program, Brandon and I taped streamers along the tables, a festive touch to honor the occasion. We had graduation certificates to hand out, and donated goodie bags for the families with things like toothbrushes and board games and sets of glassware inside. We had a giant sheet cake that said, *Congratulations Families! We're Stronger Together!*

It wasn't until the cafeteria was buzzing with people that I realized Brandon's mother and her boyfriend weren't there. He sat alone at his table. He went to stand at the school's front door as the sky darkened and the other angry boys drew their discussion cards from the bowl. We split up into groups, but still Brandon's mother wasn't there. A half hour later, there was a knock on my classroom door and one of the social workers asked me to step into the hall with Brandon. His mother had been arrested downtown—for prostitution or drugs or both, she didn't say. She wouldn't be released from jail until at least tomorrow, the social worker said in a steady voice. Her boyfriend would come as soon as he could. He'd stay with Brandon until his mom got back.

Brandon only nodded at the news, but when I put my hand on his arm, he jerked so violently away from it I thought he might punch me. "Brandon," I called as he stormed down the hall. "Please come back," I tried to say firmly, though my voice shook.

"You can't leave," the social worker added. "We're responsible for you."

He kept going as if we'd said nothing. I had nine angry boys and their siblings waiting for me inside the classroom. I could feel them simmering to a boil on the other side of the door. "Brandon!" I called more sharply, fearful he was going to run from the school.

"I'm not doing anything wrong," he yelled as he turned and walked back down the hallway toward me. And I realized he was right. He wasn't going anywhere and he'd never intended to. He was only doing what he'd learned to do, against all of his most visceral and reasonable impulses. He was taking deep breaths and walking. He was an angry boy controlling his rage.

Everything about that boy pacing the hallway tells me a story I need to know: that we do not have the right to feel helpless, Helpless Mom. That we must help ourselves. That after destiny has delivered what it delivers, we are responsible for our lives. We can choose to fling our kids into the grass or we can take deep breaths and walk up and down the hall. And everything about Brandon's mother tells me a story too. We are so far from her, aren't we? In so many ways, you and I and all the basically good moms we know are not even on the same planet as that woman. She failed and she failed and she failed.

But so have I. And so have you.

What compelled her to not show up that night? What force drove her to do whatever it took to get arrested when she should have been eating lasagna and cake in a school cafeteria with her sweet boy? What was she incapable of forgiving herself for? What did she believe she was helpless to?

I don't know, but I do know one thing. When it comes to our children, we do not have the luxury of despair. If we rise, they will rise with us every time, no matter how many times we've fallen before. I hope you will remember that the next time you fail. I hope I will too. Remembering that is the most important work as parents we can possibly do.

By the time youth group ended that last night of our Tuesday experiment, Brandon had stopped pacing. He alone accepted the graduation certificate and goodie bag on behalf of his family. He ate a piece of cake. He stood in the circle and sang the song the social workers made up and while we were singing, his mother's boyfriend arrived.

That night when we did "rain" it felt more significant than

it ever had before. Our suns were rounder; our hands rubbed together with more verve. We snapped and we clapped and we stomped so loudly it was like the clouds were dumping out their very hearts. We worked our way back from the storm, but instead of quieting it overtook us once more, none of us wanting to stop. It was too much fun. We went on and on and on, from snap to clap and back again, raging and raging, until finally there was nothing to do but raise our arms in surrender and admit that the rain was gone.

Yours,
Sugar

TINY BEAUTIFUL THINGS

Dear Sugar,

I read your column religiously. I'm twenty-two. From what I can tell by your writing, you're in your early forties. My question is short and sweet: What would you tell your twentysomething self if you could talk to her now?

Love,
Seeking Wisdom

Dear Seeking Wisdom,

Stop worrying about whether you're fat. You're not fat. Or rather, you're sometimes a little bit fat, but who gives a shit? There is nothing more boring and fruitless than a woman lamenting the fact that her stomach is round. Feed yourself. Literally. The sort of people worthy of your love will love you more for this, sweet pea.

In the middle of the night in the middle of your twenties when your best woman friend crawls naked into your bed, straddles you, and says, *You should run away from me before I devour you,* believe her.

You are not a terrible person for wanting to break up with someone you love. You don't need a reason to leave. Wanting to leave is enough. Leaving doesn't mean you're incapable of real love or that you'll never love anyone else again. It doesn't mean you're morally bankrupt or psychologically demented or a nymphomaniac. It means you wish to change the terms of one particular relationship. That's all. Be brave enough to break your own heart.

When that really sweet but fucked-up gay couple invites you over to their cool apartment to do Ecstasy with them, say no.

There are some things you can't understand yet. Your life will be a great and continuous unfolding. It's good you've worked hard to resolve childhood issues while in your twenties, but understand that what you resolve will need to be resolved again. And again. You will come to know things that can only be known with the wisdom of age and the grace of years. Most of those things will have to do with forgiveness.

One evening you will be rolling around on the wooden floor of your apartment with a man who will tell you he doesn't have a condom. You will smile in this spunky way that you think is hot and tell him to fuck you anyway. This will be a mistake for which you alone will pay.

Don't lament so much about how your career is going to turn out. You don't have a career. You have a life. Do the work. Keep the faith. Be true blue. You are a writer because you write. Keep writing and quit your bitching. Your book has a birthday. You don't know what it is yet.

You cannot convince people to love you. This is an absolute rule. No one will ever give you love because you want him or her to give it. Real love moves freely in both directions. Don't waste your time on anything else.

Most things will be okay eventually, but not everything will be. Sometimes you'll put up a good fight and lose. Sometimes you'll hold on really hard and realize there is no choice but to let go. Acceptance is a small, quiet room.

One hot afternoon during the era in which you've gotten yourself ridiculously tangled up with heroin, you will be riding the bus and thinking what a worthless piece of crap you are when a little girl will get on the bus holding the strings of two purple balloons. She'll offer you one of the balloons, but you won't take it because you believe you no longer have a right to such tiny beautiful things. You're wrong. You do.

Your assumptions about the lives of others are in direct relation to your naïve pomposity. Many people you believe to be rich are not rich. Many people you think have it easy worked hard for what they got. Many people who seem to be gliding right along have suffered and are suffering. Many people who appear to you to be old and stupidly saddled down with kids and cars and houses were once every bit as hip and pompous as you.

When you meet a man in the doorway of a Mexican restaurant who later kisses you while explaining that this kiss doesn't "mean anything" because, much as he likes you, he is not interested in having a relationship with you or anyone right now, just laugh and kiss him back. Your daughter will have his sense of humor. Your son will have his eyes.

The useless days will add up to something. The shitty waitressing jobs. The hours writing in your journal. The long meandering walks. The hours reading poetry and story collections and novels and dead people's diaries and wondering about sex and God and whether you should shave under your arms or not. These things are your becoming.

One Christmas at the very beginning of your twenties when your mother gives you a warm coat that she saved for months to buy, don't look at her skeptically after she tells you she thought the coat was perfect for you. Don't hold it up and say it's longer than you like your coats to be and too puffy and possibly even too warm. Your mother will be dead by spring. That coat will be the last gift she gave you. You will regret the small thing you didn't say for the rest of your life.

Say thank you.

Yours,
Sugar

ACKNOWLEDGMENTS

Thank you, Steve Almond, for your faith in me and for your friendship. I'll always be grateful to you for your many kindnesses.

Thank you to the thousands of people who wrote me letters and read the Dear Sugar column on TheRumpus.net. This book would not exist without you.

Thank you, Isaac Fitzgerald, Stephen Elliott, Julie Greicius, Antonia Crane, Elissa Bassist, Nancy Smith, Walter Green, and my many other colleagues at *The Rumpus* for your support, audacity, good work, and love.

Thank you, Kristen Forbes (aka Cupcake), for your assistance and all-around awesomeness.

Thank you, Robin Desser, Janet Silver, Russell Perreault, Angelina Venezia, Jennifer Kurdyla, and all the people at Knopf, Vintage, and the Zachary Shuster Harmsworth Agency who helped me bring *Tiny Beautiful Things* into the world.

Thank you to Playa for granting me the residency during which I completed this book.

Thank you, Brian Lindstrom (aka Mr. Sugar) and Bobbi and Carver Lindstrom (aka the baby Sugars), for so much, but mostly for loving me like the truest motherfuckers.

And lastly, thank you to my late mother, Bobbi Lambrecht, whom Steve Almond correctly called "the true original Sugar." She was right: that coat was perfect for me.

money. For me, it's a life calling. Someday, I want to build real haunted houses or work in movies. I take this seriously.

Which is why, when I see Patricia's mom's sports car rounding the corner, a sick acid roils in my gut. She and her team beat us last year. And they didn't win fair.

"Come on, Kevin," Tanesha says, noticing my stare. "We're going to win this year. Don't let her psych you out."

I nod glumly.

"Bloody Banshees forever," Julie says hopefully. Our little slogan.

"Bloody Banshees forever," Tanesha and I repeat.

I stare up at the house as we reach the wraparound patio. In the summer, this place is green and filled with birds and a gurgling fountain. But it's like the moment October hits, the house itself knows it's game time. The trees in the yard have already turned a deep red orange. The fountain no longer gurgles and instead sits heavy with fallen leaves and wary toads. And maybe it's my imagination, but the closer we get to the house, the colder it seems to become.

As if the house knows it's time to get scary.

As if it, too, is excited.

Our feet creak on the wooden front steps.

Behind us, a murder of crows startles from a tree, flying off in a flutter of angry caws and black wings and orange leaves.

Julie shivers.

"Do you think that's a good sign?" she asks quietly.

I smile.

"Definitely. I think it's a sign that this year is going to be the scariest yet."